Movement Training for the Modern Actor

Routledge Advances in Theatre and Performance Studies

1. Theatre and Postcolonial Desires
Awam Amkpa

2. Brecht and Critical Theory
Dialectics and Contemporary Aesthetics
Sean Carney

3. Science and the Stanislavsky Tradition of Acting
Jonathan Pitches

4. Performance and Cognition
Theatre Studies after the Cognitive Turn
Edited by Bruce McConachie and
F. Elizabeth Hart

5. Theatre and Performance in Digital Culture
From Simulation to Embeddedness
Matthew Causey

6. The Politics of New Media Theatre
Life®™
Gabriella Giannachi

7. Ritual and Event
Interdisciplinary Perspectives
Edited by Mark Franko

8. Memory, Allegory, and Testimony in South American Theater
Upstaging Dictatorship
Ana Elena Puga

9. Crossing Cultural Borders Through the Actor's Work
Foreign Bodies of Knowledge
Cláudia Tatinge Nascimento

10. Movement Training for the Modern Actor
Mark Evans

Movement Training for the Modern Actor

Mark Evans

Routledge
Taylor & Francis Group
New York   London

First published 2009
by Routledge
270 Madison Ave, New York, NY 10016

Simultaneously published in the UK
by Routledge
2 Park Square, Milton Park, Abingdon, Oxon OX14 4RN

Routledge is an imprint of the Taylor & Francis Group, an informa business

Transferred to Digital Printing 2010

© 2009 Taylor & Francis

Typeset in Sabon by IBT Global.

All rights reserved. No part of this book may be reprinted or reproduced or utilised in any form or by any electronic, mechanical, or other means, now known or hereafter invented, including photocopying and recording, or in any information storage or retrieval system, without permission in writing from the publishers.

Trademark Notice: Product or corporate names may be trademarks or registered trademarks, and are used only for identification and explanation without intent to infringe.

Library of Congress Cataloging in Publication Data
Evans, Mark.
  Movement training for the modern actor / by Mark Evans.
    p. cm.—(Routledge advances in theatre and performance studies ; 10)
  Includes bibliographical references and index.
  1. Movement (Acting)   I. Title.
  PN2071.M6E93 2009
  792.02'8—dc22
                                                2008047301

Extracts from Iris Young's "Throwing Like Girl" published in Donn Welton's edited collection, *Body and Flesh: A Philosophical Reader*, Blackwell 1998 printed by permission of Wiley-Blackwell.
Extracts from Jean Marie Pradier's "Towards a Biological Theory of the Body in Performance" from the *New Theatre Quarterly*, 1990, Volume VI, No. 2 reprinted by permission of Cambridge University Press.

ISBN10: 0–415–96367–2 (hbk)
ISBN10: 0–415–88395–4 (pbk)
ISBN10: 0–203–88354–3 (ebk)

ISBN13: 978–0–415–96367–1 (hbk)
ISBN13: 978–0–415–88395–5 (pbk)
ISBN13: 978–0–203–88354–9 (ebk)

For Vanessa Oakes

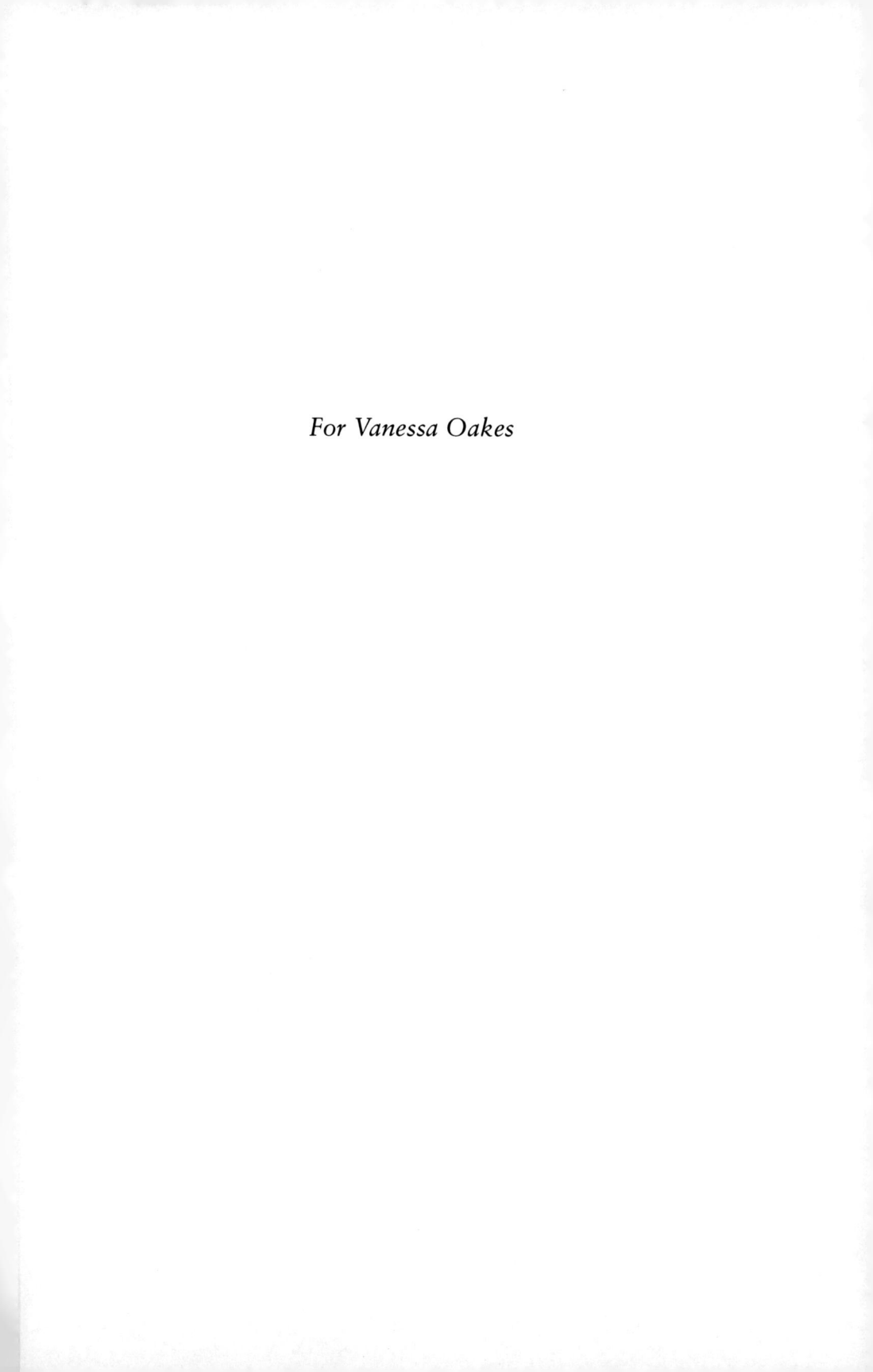

Contents

Acknowledgments		ix
	Introduction: Movement Training for Actors	1
1	Educating Efficient Labor for the Acting Profession	14
2	The 'Neutral' Body, the 'Natural' Body and Movement Training for Actors	69
3	Movement Training for Actors and the Docile Body	120
4	Movement Training and the Unruly Body	143
	Conclusion: Movement Training for Actors: Overview and Projection	176
Bibliography		187
Index		207

Acknowledgments

This book grew out of a doctoral research project which was itself the result of twenty five years of studying and teaching movement and theatre. It would not have been possible without the inspiration of my own teachers: Jacques Lecoq, Philippe Gaulier, Monika Pagneux and Desmond Jones, and the fascination with movement that they passed on to their students. The period of doctoral research was supervised by Bob Bennett, David French and the late Clive Barker, and I am deeply indebted to them for their patience, enthusiasm, support and advice. I would also like to acknowledge the generous support offered to this project by the movement tutors and students at the Drama Schools and training establishments surveyed. Their contribution to this project has been invaluable, and their passion and commitment to the field of movement training was a large part of what attracted me to this project in the first place. I am particularly indebted to Wendy Allnutt, Niamh Dowling, Vanessa Ewan, and Shona Morris for their time, their enthusiasm for the project, and the wealth of insight and experience that they gave me access to. I am very grateful to them, and to the Drama Schools who participated in this study (Central School of Speech and Drama, Guildhall School of Music and Drama, Manchester Metropolitan University School of Theatre, and Rose Bruford College), for their permission to use interview material in this book. My colleagues and students in the Performing Arts department at Coventry University have patiently endured my absences for research and writing, which have been generously supported at various stages through funding from the Coventry School of Art and Design.

Finally I would like to thank Vanessa Oakes for her endless patience and generous support over what must have seemed like an age of writing and a mountain of books. This book is dedicated to her, with love and admiration.

Introduction
Movement Training For Actors

> The stage is one place where the body is clearly on the line.
> (Dawson, 1996: 29)

> Every age has its characteristic body politics. Their historical study charts changes in the way that a multitude of bodies—from the 'natural' to the symbolic—have been perceived and interpreted.
> (Budd, 1997: xiv)

> At the end of the nineteenth century, the human body was rediscovered.
> (Jacques Lecoq in Lust, 2000: 105)

The twentieth century has witnessed a virtual resurrection of the body. Throughout the last one hundred and fifty years philosophers, artists and scientists have sought to grapple with the increasingly complex nature of our understanding of the bodies (colored, gendered, decorated, altered or shaped) through which we experience our various individual and shared worlds. The Western European sense of physicality and embodied presence has been progressively decentralized from a unitary male reference, and concepts of the body's passivity, plasticity and neutrality and its status as an object have been equally vigorously interrogated. The twentieth century has explored, and exploited, the body's cultural prominence with a rigor and enthusiasm particular to its time. Theatre embodies and concentrates complex cultural values with a fluidity and intensity that is particular to live performance (Roach, 1993: 11–12); the actor engages in an art which is distinctively body-based and which both creates and seeks its meanings in its psychophysical processes. A central driving force for theatre innovation throughout this century has been the realization that modern theatre can re-negotiate meaning in specific relation to the physical presence of the performer, in doing so re-constituting the relationship between action and intention, between mind and body. Modern movement training also offers to re-examine the physical presence of the actor and the relationship between the 'everyday' and the 'performing' body in a manner that speaks of the twentieth century fascination with the politics and economics of embodiment. Movement training for actors stands in interesting relation to other subjects such as sport, gymnastics, industry, education and medicine in so far as it represents a field of body practice which has been subject to very little in terms of either quantitative or qualitative research. Equally, whilst movement training for actors inevitably draws on discursive practices in other fields, no study has yet been undertaken to examine the nature and effect of that osmotic process—despite the fact that movement training for actors offers important points of intersection between many elements of these fields. As one Drama School movement tutor has opined: 'it's absolutely time for movement to be visible now' (Ewan, 1999a).

THE FIELD OF STUDY

Despite some variations, the majority of professional actors continue to enter their profession via some kind of formal training program. In the United Kingdom for instance, a report carried out in 2002 by the Institute of Manpower Studies on behalf of the Arts Council of England found that '86 per cent of actors working in the profession had received formal professional training' (NCDT, 2002). All British acting courses accredited by the National Council for Drama Training [NCDT] are required to offer a specified level, quality, content and amount of movement training within their programs (NCDT, 2008). Whilst the exact content and delivery differs from course to course, and from country to country, movement training (or the acquisition of specific movement skills and techniques) is central to most formal professional training regimes. The last ten years or so have seen the publication of several texts dealing with actor and movement training traditions in the United Kingdom, America, Asia and Australia, as well as an increasing interest in intercultural performance training and practice (e.g. Potter, 2002; Oida, 1992 & 1997; Meyer-Dinkgraffe, 2001; Watson, 2001; Martin, 2004; and, Zarrilli, 1995). Whilst there is much to be learnt from the comparative analysis of international approaches to movement training, this book sets out to do something different and to cover a subject previously ignored. Recognizing that all approaches to the training of the actor's body are embedded in a set of cultural assumptions around theatre and performance, as well as in a particular socio-economic context, this study seeks to analyze the nature and significance of these relationships within the specific context of the British theatre industry. The British theatre industry, and the professional training institutions associated with it, are internationally recognized as centers of excellence for Western Theatre practice; and, thus they offer a valuable and significant focus for an examination of professional actor training.

The relationship between traditional and alternative or non-western approaches has always been fluid. What for one generation was innovative and unusual, for the next may have become standard practice. In the United Kingdom, increasing internationalization and the erosion of cultural boundaries between the established and the alternative, as well as the impact of events such as the International Workshop Festival and the London International Festival of Theatre, have hastened and facilitated a process of assimilation (which has arguably taken less time in America and Australia). But, whilst a number of critical texts now interrogate the alternative practices associated with Jerzy Grotowski (Kumiega, 1985; Richards, 1995; Wolford & Schechner, 1997), Eugenio Barba (Watson, 1993), Tadashi Suzuki (Allain, 2002) and Gardzienice (Allain, 1997), the current mainstream principles and practices for the movement training of actors remain substantially under-researched. Several texts are available which outline practical exercises for traditional actor training, but they do not interrogate the cultural history and the ideological basis for such practice. For that reason, this study will focus not on specific exercises or specific practices, though examples will be referred to throughout, but on the wider context within which movement training for actors takes place and from which it (and the individual exercises of which it is composed) take their meaning.

This book focuses principally on the training of professional actors, and consequently takes as its starting point the principles and traditions which inform industry-accredited programs. This is not to invalidate the increasing range of opportunities for students in fields such as physical theatre and devised contemporary performance. Approaches to physical theatre training are covered in books such as Simon Murray and John Keefe's *Physical Theatres: A Critical Introduction* (2007). This study recognizes the historical significance of physical theatre training schemes, some of which have eventually become part of established conservatoire training systems. Over the last three decades there has also been a steady increase in the provision of mid-career training and continuing professional development. However the affect of such training has been limited by the relatively short duration of the courses and the limited number of spaces usually available. The lasting impact of alternative and innovative systems of movement training has tended to come historically from processes which developed over a significant period of time, which were driven by expert teachers, and which demanded prolonged and intensive mastery of skills and techniques. It is arguable whether workshop-based training can achieve this (cf. Murray & Keefe, 2007: 133–135). Drama schools represent an important area in which movement training is sustained, intensive and systematic; qualities which make it all the more interesting for a study such as this one.

Experience is written on everyone's body; the acting student learns to understand and master that process, then translate the relevant experiences of fictional others and write them on their own body. The general nature of professional movement training for actors is a trajectory from technique towards performance: the first year of the training is about the body and the self—'getting the body to work (. . .) naturally and easily' (Allnutt, 1999);

the second year is about transformation and character; and the third year is about public performance. This progression is reflected in the gradual reduction of timetabled movement sessions over the three years. The physical training at each school or institution is inevitably flavored by the training background of the respective movement tutors. The dominant influences on current professional teaching practice in British theatre schools are Rudolf Laban, Frederick Matthias Alexander and Jacques Lecoq. These three have attained the central status they currently have both in the United Kingdom and in America because they offer approaches which are compatible with the demands that western professional theatre conventionally makes on the actor. As the nature of theatre has changed, so have the physical challenges faced by the actor, and new training methods have found opportunities to contribute to the pool of expertise required by the professional theatre industry. The British drama schools that participated in the primary research for this book were chosen to reflect this range, each school offering a different emphasis within an approach that broadly embraces the core practices of Laban, Alexander and Lecoq. The British approach is a useful and successful (if perhaps predictable) balance–half way between the rigor of the predominantly traditional movement training at institutions such as the Moscow Arts Theatre School, and the relative eclecticism of American conservatoires and universities, which offer a wide range of movement skills and techniques and which are very open to new influences. For each of the tutors interviewed, and one senses for all movement tutors, the problem of movement training is the same—'how to communicate a whole human being on stage through the whole of your body' (Morris, 1999)—it's the solutions that are specific to their own culture, training and experience. Movement tutors generally feel that students have reached an understanding of how the training comes together for them by the end of the second year of full-time study. In this respect, and given that the intensive training has usually been completed by the end of the second year and only 'surgery sessions' and performances take place thereafter, this book focuses on the students' experiences in years one and two of their studies. Though social dance and period dance are taught in most schools, this aspect of the teaching is not what is distinctive or remarkable about movement training for actors. Over the twentieth century conventional dance classes have remained a consistent, largely functional, feature of actor training. Likewise Stage Combat (the skills and techniques involved in mock armed and un-armed combat) is a traditional vocational skill, a standard element of most drama school training, and an NCDT requirement. Acrobatics, martial arts, somatic therapies, circus skills, yoga, maskwork and Commedia dell'Arte are included in many training regimes, both in the United Kingdom and also in America and Australia, and offer the development of physical confidence and precision. For movement tutors, these skills are valuable but not essential to the training of actors; they are skills that an actor might easily acquire outside or after their drama school training. Though social dance and fencing were once the backbone of a nineteenth century actor's movement training, such skills are today less valued than the core practices and knowledges of movement training for actors (that which will later be identified as 'pure' or 'neutral' movement). The nature of movement for actors is not widely understood outside the drama schools; both drama school applicants and some industry professionals often assume that movement training will include a strong basic grounding in dance: 'I thought, when it said movement and we had to get tights and lycra and all that kind of stuff, that we'd be dancing' (Central School BA Acting for Stage and Screen second year student).

Movement tutors justify the focus on 'pure movement' through a specific perception of the professional actor's body as expressive, present, flexible and responsive rather than 'dancerly'. This distinction highlights a division within movement training for actors which will form an important theme through the chapters which follow: on the vocational side, movement training represents a method for translating a director's or writer's instructions into movements which actors feel they can inhabit and justify; on the personal side, the training can have profound effects on the student's whole life: 'it doesn't just affect you in college, it affects your whole life out of college' (Manchester Metropolitan second year student). Balancing the delivery of technical skills against the need to develop a core confidence in controlled physical expression is at the heart of the design of all movement training curricula. A seminar of movement tutors, choreographers and professional theatre practitioners, hosted by the National Council for Drama Training in 2001, discussed the question: 'what is it that the profession feels that it is not getting from the people who come out of the drama schools that it needs to get?' (Trevor Jackson in NCDT, 2001: 5). It also asked, 'what movement training for actors should consist of' (ibid). This study does not set out to answer these kinds of questions, but perhaps more importantly examines the ideological assumptions that underpin them. It aims therefore to provide a fuller understanding of principles that inform professional training practices, as well as examining the relationship of such training practices to the dominant theatre economy and the potential relevance of emergent alternative training methods.

THE STRUCTURE OF THE BOOK

Body techniques display three fundamental characteristics. First, as the name implies, they are *technical* in that they are constituted by a specific set of bodily movements or forms: 'The body is man's [*sic*] first and most natural instrument'. Second, they are *traditional* in the sense that they are learnt or acquired by means of training or education: 'There is no technique and no transmission in the absence of tradition'. Finally, they are *efficient* in the sense that they serve a definite purpose, function or goal (e.g. walking, running, dancing or digging) (Mauss 1973 [1934]: 75)

(Williams & Bendelow, 1998: 50)

Williams and Bendelow's summary of Mauss' ideas provides a convenient introduction to the structure of this book. The chapters that follow set out to identify the general sets of practices that constitute movement training for British actors; to undertake a critical analysis of the cultural traditions within which this training has developed and takes place; and, also, the extent to which they serve specific cultural, aesthetic, and socio-economic agendas. In examining the relevant cultural-historical conceptions of the body, and the general provenance of practices and approaches now used in movement training for actors, the intention has been to recognize, as one of the key perspectives, the culturally contingent nature of movement training. This is addressed through the identification, in Chapter 1: Part 1, of significant European developments in the understanding, conceptualization and study of movement, and in the application of these knowledges in the construction of general movement practices (physical education, postural therapies, self-improvement through movement, expressive movement). The second part of Chapter 1 sets out to identify the points of connection and intersection between general developments in movement training and the particular developments taking place within the field of British actor training. The social, economic, cultural and aesthetic importance of discourses around efficiency and the efficient body is identified within this chapter, which also provides the general context from which further themes are drawn out and theorized in more detail in the later chapters. The second chapter examines more precisely the concept of 'neutral body' movement training. This concept, central to the majority of the professional movement training regimes, is examined in relation to the parallel concept of the 'natural' body, and also to several paradigms of the 'natural' body. The 'neutral'/'natural' body marks the intersection of important conceptions of the body as integrated, organic, efficient and responsive. The third chapter analyses the impact of the movement training and related pedagogies (Michel Foucault's 'quiet coercions') on the construction of the student as 'actor'. As such, it addresses the docility that the training seems to imply, and teases out the features of the training which function to construct the student as a professional actor (in body and movement at least). The fourth chapter explores the extent to which the movement training encourages and allows actors to exceed their social construction as subjects, conjecturing that the professional actor's body actually requires slippage, leakage, wasteful excess and playful unruliness, as much as it does efficiency and docility; and that movement training provides significant models for the development and exploration of these qualities. This chapter engages theoretically with Judith Butler's work on performativity, but draws also on Elizabeth Grosz's writing on the 'volatile' body and Roland Barthes' concepts of 'grain', '*jouissance*', '*punctum*' and '*studium*' to interrogate some of the implications of Butler's social constructionism. It is these later chapters which draw the historical narratives of the early chapters into discursive interrogation. The structure of the book aims to reflect the complex nature of the field of study. The tension between historical narrative and discursive analysis, between examination of practice and interrogation of theory, indicates the need to deal with not one 'body', but many. To this extent it has been necessary to rework and re-examine certain key practices, the effects of certain historical periods, and the impact of certain practitioners from different, but overlapping, perspectives.

MOVEMENT TEACHING WITHIN THE INSTITUTION

> I think that movement is perceived as a female discipline, so if you're good at movement and you're a woman, then well then you would be wouldn't you.
>
> (Morris, 1999)

The study of movement training for actors is a challenging field whose history is composed as much of what Alexandra Carter calls 'gaps and silences' (Carter in Goodman, 1998: 248) as of the traditional stuff of research. We are a long way from 'those 'stages' in theatre history when women did not have bodies at all; when the male actor mimed the 'feminine'' (Aston, 1999: 8); nonetheless, over the last hundred years, a number of dominant patriarchies have operated on and through the discursive practices of actor training. The affect of these patriarchies, in general as well as within professional theatre itself, has been to marginalize the body and expressive movement such that its relative lack of historical visibility can now be seen as having gendered cultural significance. In many of the early British drama schools the whole ethos of the school revolved around the personality of the Principal—their aesthetic ideals, their theatrical contacts, their personal history within the profession, and often their personal ownership of or financial commitment to the institution. This can be seen as a reproduction of the structure and ideology of the Victorian/Edwardian home or small business. The Principal (whether male or female) became the embodiment and symbol of moral, physical and aesthetic standards. Within the professional educational 'family' of the early drama schools, movement training was almost exclusively taught by women. Movement classes were distinctive enough from the rest of the curriculum to allow tutors a level of autonomous power within their own areas of expertise. Movement teaching must have been an attractive career for women, offering as it did opportunities for independence, and for unrestrained, even expressive, physical activity. The predominance of women in movement training was possible because (as in the field of physical education) it occurred initially in a sphere separate from the activities of men, and did not therefore constitute a direct challenge to male activity and women's relationship to men. Judith Hanna, reflecting on the gendered origins of modern dance, describes how, at the start of the century, 'Women created new fields such as modern dance, social work, kindergarten teaching, and librarianship rather then compete in male professions' (Hanna, 1988: 131). Women's contribution to the history of movement training for actors has tended not to be acknowledged as fully as it should have been. Women tutors have been professionally categorized not simply in relation to their own contribution but also in relation to the key male theorist(s) from whom their own training can be traced. As in Dance, women tutors 'have rarely been accorded the historically defined conceptual status of (. . .) inventor' (Carter in Goodman, 1998: 248). Women's historical exclusion from the academic developments within the field, and the increasing emphasis women educators gave to expression over technical purity, helped to marginalize women's influence on policy. The dominant male experts (Laban, Lecoq, Alexander), in authoring their ideas, made these ideas 'theirs' and made themselves central to the location of authority and authenticity within movement training. Movement tutors could be categorized as followers of a particular 'master' teacher and might be perceived culturally as drawing their authority from this association.

> It's also to do with the power of the word, you know, that it hasn't been quantified, it hasn't been put down on the page, by a woman. So therefore it's going on, somewhere, quietly, ineluctably, non-verbally . . .
> (Morris, 1999)

Whilst the key international innovators in the history of movement training for actors were almost entirely male, those who created individual if more anonymous careers teaching these skills in drama schools were, and still are, mostly female.

Career structures in movement teaching are relatively informal. The recruitment of movement tutors is characterized by apprenticeship arrangements, deputizing and word-of-mouth—such that movement tutors often feel that they have fallen into the job. Movement tutors would typically train outside the system (at the Laban Centre, or the Lecoq School) or through apprenticeship, as few opportunities for formal training existed until fairly recently. Yat Malmgren ran a training course for movement instructors at the Drama Centre London, but since his death that option is no longer available. However the relocation of many conservatoire training institutions into the University and Higher Education sector has led to an expansion of postgraduate opportunities for those interested in pursuing a career in movement training or movement direction in theatre. Central School of Speech and Drama now offers a Masters program in Movement Studies, Manchester Metropolitan University offers a Masters program in Movement Practice for Theatre, and Guildhall School of Music and Drama offers a Masters program in Actor Training (Movement). Mime Action Group (now Total Theatre), following an earlier report (Kahn, 1990) organized a national conference and a seminar in 1993 to discuss the possible options for a nationally recognized movement/physical theatre training program; this initiative, though well supported, did not lead to further developments (Keefe, 1993a & 1993b), and although several schools of physical theatre emerged in the United Kingdom during the last two decades their impact on movement training for actors has so far been very limited. The general pattern, which matches the historical development of the subject, is that courses evolve around people. Without the driving force of a personal vision it seems difficult to reach agreement on what should be taught and how, or even to push through course validation. To compound the problem for those seeking work in the field, career routes are poorly defined and there is no formal forum as yet in which to negotiate what is, should, or might be involved. The post of Head of Movement is not always appointed as a full-time post and, with a few notable exceptions (e.g. Niamh Dowling at MMU), there is little opportunity for further promotion within the institution. The work is hard; long hours of preparation and planning can be required. Tutors may also be undertaking training themselves at the same time that they are teaching. The job requires a wide range of teaching skills: 'it's a physical, emotional and intellectually demanding job' (Morris, 1999). The result is that movement teaching can feel like a 'constant improvisation' (Morris, 1999).

The apprenticeship system is seen by some as offering a more rigorous approach than a teaching course; the trainee has direct contact with an 'expert' teacher almost every day for several years. It is also particularly appropriate for the nature of the subject: 'The transmission of [movement] knowledge is very much one-to-one (. . .) You have to be an expert in what you're practising' (Morris, 1999). But the economic factors involved in being an apprentice/assistant teacher mean that this route favors people with some level of financial support (partner, private income, flexible alternative employment). There is a danger that without a network and a training system that facilitates and encourages debate and the interrogation of practice, movement training could become closed to new theories and perspectives. The apprenticeship method may encourage continuity, but needs equally to guard against the erosion of vital and provocative difference.

MOVEMENT AND VOICE

> [M]y image was that there were layers, and there wasn't a hierarchy but there were layers. And definitely movement was the foundation layer, and then there was voice which included singing, and then there was the text and acting work (. . .) But now it's much more integrated.
> (Dowling, 2000)

Several movement teachers combine voice and speech in with their movement classes; nonetheless the division of voice and movement is generally maintained through the effects of tradition, employment and the text-based nature of a substantial amount of Western theatre. The close cultural association of voice, language and consciousness, privileged through their apparent transparency, has meant that voice and speech training has long been ideologically prioritized over movement training in drama schools. The breath connects the conscious rational spoken word with feeling and with the subconscious physical rhythms of life. In this sense voice is perceived as capable of transcending the actor's 'inner/outer' divisions, and of combining physical, emotional and rational meaning. Movement, on the other hand, is more commonly associated with bodily functions such as sweating, excreting, copulating, and ingesting; its materiality and abjection continually bringing it 'back to earth'. For Kant these were the very qualities which made dance and movement aesthetically impure (Rée, 1999: 358–359). Both critical theory and movement training practice have sought over the last twenty or so years to critique and challenge this divide between voice and movement, and between mind and body. When many movement teachers view the breath as a unifying and connecting factor rather than a source of division between voice and movement, clearly there is room to interrogate the validity of traditional distinctions at the level of pedagogic practice as well as theory. In the contemporary Drama School, voice and movement training are more closely associated. In some institutions voice and movement tutors work frequently together, and in general there is an acceptance of common themes which underpin the actor training process as a whole. This study seeks to address the cultural conditions that have created this ideological imbalance and that are operating to redress it.

MOVEMENT, WRITING AND AUTHENTICITY

Few books on acting tackle movement training in any real detail, and, in the current higher education climate, movement training will struggle to assert its credentials outside of the drama schools without the authority of academic texts. Books matter culturally. Many of the texts available on movement training itself [e.g. Barker (1977); Battye (1954); Callery (2001); Dennis (1995); Eldredge (1996); Lecoq (2000); McEvenue (2001); Marshall (2001); Mawer (1932); Newlove (1993); Pisk (1975)] focus on the technical aspects, describing the exercises and activities which a student might undertake in class. The accounts they give are often heavily reliant on metaphor—mainly because technical language cannot capture the complexity of the processes and of the subjective experience of movement in a language simple enough to communicate effectively in the classroom, or to the passive reader. Effective movement teaching demands the shared physical presence of tutor and student; the generality of a text cannot deal with the specificity of the individual body, and, perhaps more importantly, the theory becomes detached from the live teaching moment which gives it meaning and which contextualizes its practices. Movement teaching at drama school, despite the influence of key theorists, is focused not on practitioners but on practices—on educating the students' bodies, not teaching theory or history. As such, reading inevitably takes a back seat as the student's attention is first and foremost directed towards breaking the 'life mask' of conventional responses which close them off 'from the range of his (sic) potential presence to himself through his body' (Wilshire, 1982: 128). It is because this process necessarily takes place at the level of the lived body, and through an experiential process, that abstraction into the written word is so complex and inefficient. Plato's *Phaedrus* suggests that it is possible to go back to the origin of a thought—find its originator and thus get it at its 'freshest', as the pronouncements of an authoritative individual. In Plato's model of wisdom, writing things down effectively defers their meaning, and the 'original truth' no longer has an immediate 'presence'. Within the field of movement training, authority is similarly given to those who have studied 'directly' with the sources of expert knowledge (Laban, Lecoq, Alexander). The written word is, in this context, 'over-shadowed' by the immediacy and directness of the movement class. All writing about and of movement, however comprehensive, remains incomplete because, like a sex manual, it removes the very spontaneity it offers to organize (Roach, 1993: 220). We might further ask, what is being notated in the descriptions of exercises in movement texts—is it one particular student's experiences or the work of a 'perfect' student. Notation, however thoroughly conducted, will inevitably be selective, identifying some movements as worthy of attention and others as not. Photographs cannot capture more than the surface of the exercise and as such they tend to show the activity as a 'class' rather than as an experience.

Authorship raises one other problem for movement tutors—that of the ownership of exercises. Peter Brook tells of a conversation in London which reveals the futility of ownership claims in this context:

> One day (. . .) an American director said to me, 'My actors always do your "great exercise".' I was puzzled. 'What do you mean?' I asked. 'The special exercise you do every day.' I asked him what he was talking about, and then he described to me what we have just done. I had never heard of it and to this day I have no idea where it comes from. But I was happy to adopt it—since then we do it regularly and regard it as our own.
>
> (Brook, 1993: 67–68)

The question of ownership aptly illustrates the sense in which movement classes are different from the contents of a 'text' on movement. Attempts to 'own' exercises and movements are hopeless—how would teaching and workshops operate if such a form of copyright were to exist, how would such a restriction be policed, how would it function. Exercises are 'owned' socially (in being associated with the practices of a particular group of people) and individually only in so far as each group or individual (student, professional or teacher) makes them their own through their commitment to the exercise, through embedding it into their own and their students' body memory. The very process of the movement class and the tradition of direct transmission of knowledge functions to muddy the issue of ownership:

> Monika [Pagneux] said, "Well who's in my work?" She worked with Alexander, with Feldenkrais, she did Eutony work, she worked with Lecoq, she said, "Is it my work or is it theirs?" And you can see why. You don't want to write it down like it's hers but her work is what's special about her, that's what's unique, that's the difficulty. It's her *teaching* that's special.
>
> (Dowling, 2000)

For Dowling it is not content that matters, but the *process* of teaching:

> That's why movement teachers don't write. How do you write down that process? There is some part of you that feels possessive about (. . .) rocesses. And it's about a process of doing that is mine. I don't say it's my exercise, but that particular way of delivering it is mine.
>
> (Dowling, 2000)

The result is that movement tutors are both remarkably generous with their exercises and yet understandably protective of their processes (which are closely identified with the teacher's status and employability).

The labeling of exercises and practices seems to be a process which is always under negotiation, never completed, adding to the sense in which any written description can quickly become redundant as it needs constantly to realign itself to the changing context and language of practice. The implication is that labeling an exercise is irrelevant in terms of its efficient and effective execution. Writing on movement training struggles with the difficulty of communicating the lived experience of the exercise and the process of its integration into the student's nervous system, into their very way of learning. Joseph Roach (1993: 222) identifies Antonin Artaud as seminal in expressing the performer's frustration with language's effects in denaturing physical and emotional experience through its networks of existing categories and meanings. Movement texts may in this sense perpetuate the dichotomy between a discursive mind/text and a silent body. The movement textbook establishes the student as a passive reader, a perspective within which the body nearly disappears, visible only as an objective 'other' constructed within the discursive frame.

Relevant texts function then either to propose new technical metalanguages (for example Barba & Savarese, 1991), or to record and categorize exercises or suggest new ones (Dennis, 1995; Marshall, 2001; Newlove, 1993; Pisk, 1975). Looking at texts also highlights the need to recognize the differences between discourse registers used by practitioners and those used by some of the theoreticians. For Melrose this means that,

> somatic work should not be included within the writerly or scriptural economy of mainstream learning and transmission (. . .) but rather, that if it is in any way comparable with linguistic function, then we can only say of it that it begins its function as 'something like' the *anecdote*.
> (Melrose, 1994: 83)

For her, 'the anecdote (. . .) reveals the means by which an *expert knowledge* is appropriated, typified and personalised' (Melrose, 1994: 83). We can recognize the straightforwardly anecdotal in some of the texts on movement (the stark simplicity of Pisk is perhaps an exception) and register the value of its ability to 'draw the personal into the social' (Melrose, 1994: 84). But whilst the anecdote can offer multiple embodied perspectives; by the same token, it is easily marginalized as insubstantial and insufficiently stable, much like the movement practice it might seek to describe. The very nature of movement training means that the paths to knowledge are deeply personal and individually formed for each student. Writing for movement training (as opposed to about or around movement training) is thus faced with the challenge of writing about how the body can become sensitive to change, sensitized to its own learning process. Other models for writing the practices of the body have emerged through the feminist writing practices of Hélène Cixous, which attempt to remain open to the physical presence of the writer and to marginal 'other' experiences of the body, as well as through the writings of somatic body practitioners such as Miranda Tufnell, who together with the artist Chris Crickmay has explored how texts, images and different forms of reflective writing can move beyond documentation into a more interactive and physical relationship between movement and the word (Tufnell & Crickmay, 1990 & 2004).

1 Educating Efficient Labor for the Acting Profession

> Training, like the assembly of a machine, is the search for, the acquisition of, an efficiency.
>
> (Marcel Mauss in Carey & Kwinter, 1992: 464)

The primary aim of a drama school is to provide an effective training for professional actors. This was their original *raison d'être* and often today informs the criteria for the accreditation of their courses. Debate over how to fulfill this aim has informed the significant curricular and pedagogical changes in professional actor training over the last century. If there have been disagreements about the teaching of movement for actors, these can be placed within the wider context of the need to produce a professional actor able to respond efficiently to the needs of the industry. The chapters that follow will consider the manner in which specific knowledges of the body have historically operated (and continue to operate) to validate approaches to movement training for actors, against both societal and theatrical norms.

THE AESTHETICS OF EFFICIENCY

> In any field of endeavor, things may be done poorly or they may be done well.
>
> (Roach, 1993: 116)

A central hypothesis of this chapter is that systems of movement training for actors are discursively constructed around accepted knowledges of 'how movements are best done', and around particular forms of biomechanical and psychophysical efficiency. These knowledges have participated historically, and most notably, in the construction of regimes of physical training and physical education, as well as the development of time-motion studies. In early European history the feudal body was directly and actively productive; the body, its labors and the fruits of its labors belonged to the liege lord. The movement and gesture of the Commedia dell'Arte was related to this episteme of the body—the Commedia actor directly and actively produced gestures and movements which corresponded clearly to the master and servant/wife/lover economy of medieval and renaissance social relations. By the advent of Naturalism in the late nineteenth century, the actor's body was no longer productive itself, but mimicked and internalized productive action in a search for 'artless artifice'. Actors no longer wished to perceive their work as active and productive labor, but rather as an art and as a science. As a consequence more delicate and refined approaches to the use of gesture and movement were required; the excessive, 'grand' style of the nineteenth century gradually gave way to a style of movement which was marked by control, observation of everyday behavior, a middle-class reserve and a careful husbandry of effort. Increasingly actor training has sought to draw on knowledges of the integrated and organic body in order to facilitate the smooth internalization of dramatic action. In seeking to establish how the body was best to be used in naturalistic theatrical performance, movement training for actors then brought together the discourses of art and of science within the discursive frame of 'efficiency'. Efficient movement represented movement from which unnecessary addition had been removed, as well as movement that was 'fit for purpose' and which achieved the uninhibited expression of the internal impulse. We shall see how the different approaches to movement training variously offered the actor techniques which simplified their physical expression, which aligned movement with psychological intention, and which placed efficient enactment of the playwright's or director's vision at the heart of theatre's aesthetics.

Concepts of efficiency have marked strongly contested borders for the body during the twentieth century; borders which have attempted to demarcate complex ideological constructions such as race, gender, class and nationality, and which have been policed by the discursive processes of consumerism, mechanization, health and reproduction. Efficiency as a discourse arose through the operation of enlightenment science in the measurement of human physical and mechanical activity, particularly in relation to its purpose. The political function of this science of measurement—the maintenance of class power/control, the improvement of productivity and the consequent expansion of Western industrial capitalism—initially operated somewhat clumsily, in a manner likely to alienate those under scrutiny: 'In the end, the human being becomes just one more moving part in the industrial process' (Francis Sparshott in Souriau, 1983: xi). Efficient mechanistic movement was in this sense critiqued by some as potentially alienating for the human subject (McCarren, 2003: 151–157). However, the following analysis of the key concurrent developments within science, art and physical education over this period will reveal the extent to which the concept of efficiency has operated with increasing subtlety and influence. This chapter will therefore seek to examine key 'knowledges of the body' and their discursive function in shaping the movement training of actors. This will entail constructing a critical history of the relationship between, on the one hand, movement training and the traditional and modernist agendas driving its development, and, on the other hand, of the aesthetics of theatre movement. The chapter is consequently structured in two parts. Part One examines the development of knowledges of the body over the last one hundred and fifty years, alongside the role of those knowledges in producing physical training practices. In particular it seeks to unravel the effects of the discourse of efficiency on the physical training of the body. Part Two seeks to place the findings of Part One in the context of the theatre industry, the acting profession and the development of institutionalized training for professional actors. It will examine the processes through which and the extent to which discourses of efficiency have entered the movement training of actors. Other texts have looked at the psychophysical processes of the actor and the relationship between physical training and the actor's psychological processes of preparation. This study, whilst it acknowledges the significance of the actor's psycho-physical technique sets out to frame movement training in a wider cultural context, where the relationship between action and intention is not viewed as pure and acultural, but deeply immersed in the ideological structures which produce our minds and bodies.

PART ONE:
THE BODY—KNOWLEDGE AND PRACTICE

THE BODY, KNOWLEDGE AND NATIONHOOD—
PER HENRIK LING AND EUROPEAN GYMNASTICS

René Descartes effectively set the agenda for the Enlightenment period when, in addressing the question of how humans can know themselves, he proposed a reduction of truth to what can be apprehended by the mind. The result was 'an elevation of the mind, in contrast to the body, to what is most essential to us as persons' (Welton, 1999: 1). For Descartes, mathematics was the language of truth, and the body therefore could best be known in mechanical terms, through its extension in time and space. The growth of the natural sciences across Europe, from the Renaissance through to the Enlightenment, in this respect maps the spread of knowledge *of* the body (as opposed to knowledge *through* the body). A full understanding of the impact of this powerful episteme within the historical development of movement training for actors must take account of the manner in which the Cartesian approach to knowing the body has dominated not only the philosophy of the body, but also the body's treatment and status within our culture.

From the late Eighteenth century, developments in European physical education and training grew out of attempts to provide a system of physical training and education which was based on the scientific analysis of the body and on coherent principles of exercise. An important impetus to these developments was provided by the growth of nationalism in nineteenth century central Europe. This was reflected in an emphasis within male physical training on the military values of drill, fortitude, endurance, health and strength. Systems of physical education consequently placed an emphasis on the fulfillment of physical sequences to command, subordination of the body to discipline, and loyalty to the existing social order. The patriotism and brotherhood instilled within the German 'turnhalle' and 'turnverein', for instance, represent a sense in which not only the individual body but also the 'body politic' was being developed and strengthened. Though the gymnastics of Sweden, Denmark, Germany and Czechoslovakia were initially based on 'natural' activities such as running, jumping, lifting, they were eventually to become a series of prescribed body positions similar to military drill exercises. The European gymnastic tradition was primarily functional—its vision was the creation of a nation of fit and healthy patriots. The mechanical exercise of the body was enlivened and motivated by association with folk movements, national cultural heritage and the social identity of the community.

Without doubt the most influential gymnastic regime of the nineteenth century, both in Europe and later in England, was the Swedish System founded by Per Henrik Ling (1776–1839). Ling had studied at the Nachtegall gymnasium in Denmark and was a student of anatomy, physiology, philosophy and literature. He categorized exercises according to their function and effectively established kinesiology as a scientific foundation for body training. The aim of his work was broadly therapeutic, seeking to promote an 'harmonious development of the physical, mental, and moral qualities of the individual' (Brown & Sommer, 1969: 20). Ling's system was first brought to England by John Govart In De Betou in 1838 (McIntosh, 1968: 98); Betou practiced medical gymnastics and counted doctors in England among his early followers. It is probably from this initial connection with the medical profession that the conception that Ling's system was largely for the treatment of invalids grew. In England the medical profession took care to sustain its hegemony over the nation's health and fitness. In 1852, Mathias D. Roth, physician at the Hahneman Hospital, wrote *Movements or Exercises according to Ling's System for the Development and Strengthening of the Human Body in Childhood and Youth*, in which he stressed the importance of physical education being in the hands of those with a scientific knowledge of the human body. Foucault suggests in *The Birth of the Clinic* (1973) that the Enlightenment saw medicine transform the ways in which it analyzed, inscribed and read the body. For the early physical educators, the 'anatomical atlas' of the body was reserved for the 'clinical gaze' of the doctor. Though gradual changes meant that the medical establishment's grip on physical training was weakened, one residual effect was that the student's body was effectively 'pathologized' through the analytical gaze of the teacher and differences from authorized norms became 'abnormalities'. Early physical educators and doctors were effectively 'reading' from the same 'anatomical atlas' (Williams & Bendelow, 1998). The power struggle over the authorization of systems was to flavor much of the history of physical education and training.

English physical culture, from a slow start, drew increasingly vigorously on the developments in body training in France and Germany, primarily in response to political need. At the outset of the Boer War for instance, it was made shockingly clear the extent to which slum conditions and a lack of physical education had led to a weakened and physically unfit British work force. In Manchester, 8,000 out of 11,000 volunteers had to be rejected as physically unfit for military service (Searle, 1990: 60). Post Darwin, concerns about moral and physical degeneracy could be justified through reference to 'race evolution'. In this manner, the healthy body became associated with morality, Christianity and racial purity. Physical education could therefore also be seen as discursively linked to the repression of 'deviant' sexuality (that which was not concerned with 'breeding'), prostitution and eugenics (see Bland, 1995). Distinctions between 'health' and degeneracy marked the basis for justifications of class, gender and race differences which were foundational for nineteenth century patriarchy and imperialism. Sport and physical education in the early part of the nineteenth century had been largely the privilege of upper-middle class males. Peter McIntosh claims that, 'Socially, the cult of athleticism was closely bound up with the rise of a new middle class to educational privilege and political power' (1968: 16). Certainly little or no attention was paid to the needs of the population in general, and the working classes in particular, until it was politically necessary. Even then, the Government's initial response was largely based on the needs of the military. What was only beginning to be available was a comprehensive rationale, a theoretical basis which would enable physical training to work more effectively as discursive practice within society as a whole, and more productively in relation to the needs of specific industries and activities. The development of such a rationale would enable the student (in our case the student actor) not only to develop functional skills and techniques, but also to be placed more precisely within the cultural and commercial systems within which s/he had to operate.

ÉTIENNE JULES MAREY AND THE SCIENTIFIC OBSERVATION OF MOVEMENT

From the late nineteenth century, the 'impartial' logic of science was used again and again to reinforce the importance of efficiency (Taylor, 1964: 114) and of physical education and training. Its ability to do so was in part derived from the increased cultural status of the natural sciences, but it also derived from the invention of improved mechanical devices for the observation, recording and analysis of movement. In 1860 the French physiologist, Étienne Jules Marey (1830–1904), invented the Spygmograph to inscribe 'on a smoke blackened cylinder the form and frequency of the human pulse beat' (Giedion, 1948: 17). Not only was this an example of the ways in which technology was able to convert movement into a form of text, it also marked an important moment in the scientific analysis of movement—the ability to disassociate elements of movement and reconstitute them at will. In 1873 Marey published *La Machine Animale*, based on his studies of human and animal movement, and at around the same time, the American photographer Eadweard Muybridge (1830–1904) was exploring the use of rapid sequence photography to record human movement and reveal its constituent elements. Marey, aware of Muybridge's work, sought instead to capture movement on a single plate, from one point of view, and reveal its *shape, direction and flow*. The aspects of movement they were thus able to identify (see italics) represented features which were to inform almost all of the subsequent innovations in movement practice.

The very title of Marey's book is revealing, suggesting as it does that the body and its movement are both 'animal'—and thus part of the 'natural world'—and also mechanical—a Cartesian theme, central to the ideological formation of the 'efficient body'. The body is exposed as subject to the laws of natural science and mechanics, divisible into its separate elements and their functions, recordable, and, by implication, perfectible. The 'body-as-machine', and in particular the moving body as machine, became an increasingly common image during this period (McCarren, 2003), reflecting an epistemology of the body which has deep roots in the scientific knowledge of the enlightenment (Roach, 1993). The ambiguous status of the machine within early twentieth century culture is reflected in a number of cultural events, including Nikolai Foregger's *The Dance of the Machines* (1923), Fernand Léger's film *Ballet Mécanique* (1924), Reginald Berkeley's radio play *Machines: A Symphony of Modern Life* (1927), Fritz Lang's film *Metropolis* (1927) and Sophie Treadwell's play *Machinal* (1928). As a symbol both of scientific progress and of the hegemony of the industrial over the personal, the machine is a significant image in the development of physical training and education during the last century. Jacques Lecoq (1987) suggests for instance that the black costumes with white strips which Marey used to trace movement in his observations are consciously echoed by Etienne Decroux in the costumes for his performance of *L'Usine* (The Factory), a piece which deals with the human figure engaged in industrial action.

Marey's closest collaborator was his pupil, Georges Demeny (1850–1917). Demeny continued Marey's systematic study of movement, further developing the use of photographic techniques. Marey and Demeny had already begun to extend their studies into practice, developing approaches to physical education and even creating a 'station physiologique' at the Parc des Princes (Lecoq, 1987: 60). Demeny was to become Professor of Applied Physiology at Joinville and director of a course in higher gymnastic studies at the Sorbonne. His meticulous study of movement is not however entirely mechanistic.

Demeny believed that movement was a manifestation of life and that the stimulation to movement could be either external or internal, either mental or emotional. In particular his study of the motion of animals and birds convinced him that movement was not stiff or angular, but round; it was not jerky, but rather continuous, flowing out from the body in all directions and planes in conical or spiral or in figures of eight.

(Brown & Somner, 1969: 25)

Demeny's book *Mécanisme et Éducation des Mouvements* (1905) outlines the physiological functions of the muscles and the joints and the possible consequences for physical education. Whilst there is a clear focus on the body as human, as distinguished by its own functioning, there is also a sense of the importance and value of efficiency.

All methods of physical education must not only tend towards the improvement of the race, but must also teach each person in their work the way to obtain the best outcome with the minimum of effort and fatigue.

(Demeny, 1905: 517, author's translation)

As Demeny's words suggest, the quest for efficiency had nationalistic overtones. Scientific measurement of the functional efficiency of movement seems inevitably to have evoked discourses of race and nationhood.

FRANÇOIS DELSARTE (1811–1871)—GESTURE AND EMOTION

One of the first modern movement teachers to address the expressive potential of movement training as opposed to its purely therapeutic value was the French actor François Delsarte. Delsarte's method was based on careful and detailed personal observation. Whilst by no means as scientifically rigorous as Marey and Demeny, Delsarte's work was more significant in that it provided an approach which could be applied to movement in performance. Although Delsarte's greatest influence was arguably on the development of dance performance in late nineteenth and early twentieth century America (Ruyter, 1996a), he also had a profound influence on the teaching of movement for performance in Europe, and on several of the key practitioners examined in this study (e.g. Laban and Lecoq). Delsarte began his stage career as a singer, however as a result of inadequate teaching and over exploitation he ruined his voice. As a result of this experience he began a career as a singing teacher at the Paris Conservatoire and, in 1839, put together his own course in what he called, 'Applied Aesthetics', which included a codification of physical and vocal expression. Ted Shawn, an American dancer influenced by Delsarte's work, describes him as, a true scientist: setting out to discover how the human body moves under the stimuli of emotions, he collected a vast amount of data from first hand observation of the human being in every possible circumstance and condition and from those hundreds of examples, deduced basic laws.

(Shawn, 1974: 10)

Delsarte's system is in many ways an attempt to invigorate movement training by re-discovering a link between gesture and emotion, a link which will enable the expression of emotion, thought and imagination to take place with the greatest efficiency and the least inhibition. His aesthetics are predominantly the nineteenth century aesthetics of harmony, regularity and balance. For Delsarte, the entire physical world mirrors the trinary division of Father, Son and Holy Ghost in Christian religion, and this is also reflected in the division of 'man' into body, mind and soul: 'The Delsartian body is a universal signifying machine where nature's (God-in-nature and God-in-man) dictates hold eternally true' (Dasgupta, 1993: 97). The trinity extended to the following partitions: of the body into specific 'zones', each corresponding to areas of 'activity' (e.g. the arms and legs correspond to the 'vital' forces, the head to 'mental' activity and the torso to 'spiritual' activity); and of movement into groups of similar activity (concentric or inward, eccentric or outward, and neutral or normal). Alongside this trinary vision of the world, Delsarte proposed his Nine Laws of Movement: Motion, Velocity, Direction and Extension, Reaction, Form, Personality, Opposition, Sequence, and Rhythm. Each of these qualities of movement suggested to Delsarte an interpretation of the relationship between man's physical, mental and spiritual life, a significant change from the mechanical approach of early gymnastics. In contrast to the sustained tension of the traditional forms of movement such as gymnastics and classical ballet, Delsarte offered variety and a recognition of the importance of relaxation: 'a relaxation is necessary before a tension can be produced, and every tension is followed by a relaxation' (Shawn, 1974: 62). Delsarte recognized the torso as 'the source and main instrument of true emotional expression' (Shawn, 1974: 61) and saw that the removal of stiffness in the torso was a necessary step to provide clear and fluid succession of movement without obstruction.

Delsarte's failure to leave behind a written account of his work means that what survives are only the second (and sometimes third) hand memories and practices of his disciples, students and followers. His system eventually waned in popularity during the early part of the twentieth century. As a highly systematized account of practice, it was popular with teachers because it presented a coherent approach to analysis and explanation. But it was unwieldy, dauntingly detailed and restrictive for the vast majority of performers, who simply did not have the time or the patience to assimilate the ideas to the point where the practice became instinctual. With the advent of Naturalism, tastes in theatre began to change and Delsarte's codification of acting and gesture was increasingly associated with outmoded approaches to acting. As George Taylor suggests, 'his ideal of classical harmony (. . .) celebrated the stasis of being rather than the drama of becoming' (1999: 79). Within the context of Naturalism, the actor would no longer 'be judged by the intensity of a single moment, but by the unfolding of a consistent characterization' (Taylor, 1999: 79). Delsarte's system tends to fix the body within a category, a way of being; the system ultimately relies upon the impact of attitudes rather than changes.

Delsarte apparently believed that his principles were the key to all the arts, and this may explain why his disciples expanded their practices from 'movement education' to produce what we would understand as a 'life-style' approach—developing his theories into systems of gymnastics, dance, tableaux vivants, elocution, oratory, mental relaxation and self-presentation. Delsartism was to reach something like a 'cult' status in America during this period. Without doubt the appeal of his system to those involved in the training of actors must in large part have been due to the system's inclusiveness, and must also have been aided by its general popularity.

Delsarte's focus on specific areas of the body and their optimum expressive functioning, in conjunction with a conception for their integration as a totality, highlighted the necessity of dealing with parts in order to deal with the whole. Though his solution for bridging the inevitable divide between the body as parts and the body as a whole was to be discarded, the problem has remained for future practitioners and theorists. Delsarte was among the first to propose a study of 'pure' movement, where 'movement itself is the medium of the artist, and perfection and beauty (. . .) are the real goals' (Shawn, 1974: 46). In so doing he has, indirectly at least, influenced many movement teachers and theorists since; his work would almost certainly have been known to Dalcroze, Laban, Copeau and Lecoq. Without doubt Delsarte's desire to produce a physically literate adult population provided an important impetus for change, encouraging respect for and understanding of the exploration of physical expressivity and the physical education of children and young people.

Francis Sparshott sums up his significance as follows:

> Delsarte himself was not involved in the development of gymnastics and not interested in dance, and he had no dancers among his students: he was interested primarily in voice training and secondarily in the technique of stage acting. What made him especially suitable as an adoptive godparent for modern dance was a combination of three things: a wide-ranging empirical study of how people in different situations actually do move; an easily remembered and suggestive system of 'principles' for analyzing movements; and a line of inspirational patter suitable for filling dancers with convictions about the importance of their work.
>
> (Sparshott in Souriau, 1983: ix)

His work undoubtedly paved the way for the more sophisticated systems of movement analysis and movement psychology later proposed by Laban, and the free physical expression of Isadora Duncan and Dalcroze. Perhaps central to Delsarte's legacy is his conviction that, 'Nothing is more deplorable than a gesture without meaning' (Shawn, 1974: 24–25). He situates this meaning outside language and, according to his 'second generation' disciple Ted Shawn, gives it a primacy over speech that will later be echoed in the teaching of Copeau and Lecoq:

> Gesture is more than speech. It is not what we say that persuades, but the manner of saying it. Speech is inferior to gesture because it corresponds to the phenomena of mind. Gesture is the agent of the heart, the persuasive agent. That which demands a volume is uttered by a single gesture.
> (Shawn, 1974: 25)

PAUL SOURIAU (1852–1926)—AN AESTHETICS OF EFFICIENCY

> The finest performances are those where there appears to be no effort.
> (Dawson, 2002)

Paul Souriau was broadly contemporary with Marey, Muybridge and Demeny; however, he applied philosophy rather than photography to the analysis of movement, and as such he provides an interesting point of juncture between the scientific and the aesthetic analysis of movement. His work gives an important insight into the discursive framework for the practice of Copeau and Lecoq, and through them several generations of British movement tutors. In a manner not unlike Delsarte, whose work he must have known, Souriau distilled his ideas into a series of 'laws' regarding movement (Souriau, 1983: 14–26). These laws can be broadly outlined as follows: the law of average flexions, the law of stability, the law of asymmetry, the law of alternation, the law of compensation, the tendency to repetition, and the effects of habit. They are importantly different from Delsarte's laws in their emphasis on the inter-connectedness of the body. They also seek to address the expressiveness of the body, not through a complex Delsartean code of gestures, but through a more profound emphasis on what he describes as the 'Harmony of Body Rhythms'—an interdependency of body parts within which they exert an influence on one another (e.g. circulation, respiration, locomotion). This idea was to appeal to several movement training theorists during the twentieth century.

Souriau's major text, *The Aesthetics of Movement*, first published in France in 1889, follows in a direct line from the work of Marey and Demeny (Alter, 1994: 31). It develops their observation of the movement of animals and humans into an aesthetic, based on an attempt to differentiate the subjective from the objective in the delight we take in movement. Souriau was also influenced by Herbert Spencer (specifically his 1852 essay, 'Gracefulness' in Spencer [1901]), in his equation of 'the quality of gracefulness with visible economy of effort in human and animal motion' (Francis Sparshott in Souriau, 1983: vii).

Souriau identifies the three conditions for aesthetic value as: the mechanical beauty of movement, the quality of expression, and the perceptible pleasure it gives (Francis Sparshott in Souriau, 1983: xx). In focusing on both graceful economy and on the pleasure (and pain) of movement, Souriau brings together the industrial/mechanical discourse of efficiency and the Freudian discourse of pleasure and 'jouissance'. He prefigures Copeau, Hébert, Lecoq and the significant figures of French and British movement training in his focus on natural movement and its qualities of efficiency, expression and pleasure. In aestheticizing movement and drawing together efficiency and pleasure Souriau drew away from the simply mechanical and, using the earlier photographic analysis of movement as a foundation, attempted to provide a philosophical basis for viewing the natural as the source of aesthetic efficiency (a philosophical and cultural mission which will be examined in more detail in the next chapter). Francis Sparshott writes in his foreword to the English translation of *The Aesthetics of Movement*:

> Before judging and especially correcting nature, we must learn to know it. It follows, therefore, that our aesthetics must be based on the knowledge of those movements that are the most natural to us.
> (Francis Sparshott in Souriau, 1983: xx)

Souriau saw the 'effect' of movement as the primary concern; and thus the *pleasure* of a movement, he believed, also needed to be taken into account.

> If, in the final analysis, a movement brings us more pleasure than it costs in effort, we will find it, on the whole agreeable. The most agreeable movements are not, therefore, necessarily those that cost us the least effort but those that give us the most useful effect for the least effort.
> (Souriau, 1983: 10)

In conceiving of the body in this way, Souriau constructed a motivating desire for movement, a desire for the pleasure of perfection, of efficiency, or more precisely a desire for the pleasurable experience of effortless, graceful movement.

> [W]e instinctively attain perfection in movement. To move as much as possible with the least fatigue; to obtain the maximum result with the minimum effort; that is the fundamental law that regulates the development of all our activities, from the simplest locomotor movements to the most subtle manifestations of art.
> (Souriau, 1983: 13)

For Souriau, rhythm was one of the secrets to effortless beautiful movement. As rhythm is muscular, physical, spatial and temporal and therefore measurable, then physical artistry must be measurable too. If so, then by Souriau's reasoning the gymnast's or the performer's physical artistry is also quantifiable, principally in terms of 'the intelligent economy with which [s/he] performs complex bodily functions' (Francis Sparshott in Souriau, 1983: viii) and in terms of an adherence to the 'natural laws' of movement. Sparshott also suggests that efficiency, in Souriau's terms, should not be conceived of in purely mechanical terms, but that it should also be evaluated in relation to the intending will of the mover and to its ability to represent efficiency:

> the easiest movement is not, after all, the most graceful. We appreciate movement as expressive of the mover's will. The most beautiful movement is accordingly not the most efficient but that which is eloquent of efficiency: Movement clearly articulated by the mover to make its structure evident, to give it a perceptible purposiveness independent of any extraneous purpose it might have.
> (Francis Sparshott in the foreword to Souriau, 1983: viii)

Importantly Souriau is here suggesting that efficiency is not an absolute quality, but more a way of looking at things. This kind of analysis places action which is both economical and purposive as the basis for beautiful movement, and marks the efficiency of the body's response to the purposive intentions of the mover as a primary criterion for eloquence and grace. This means that for Souriau, and for others involved in the early development of movement techniques:

> The paradigm of beautiful movement, analyzed and reconstituted, is not that of the dancer but that of the gymnast . . . This should be shocking, but it is not surprising. Gymnastics was of immense social importance in Souriau's day, but artistic dance was not.
> (Francis Sparshott in Souriau, 1983: viii)

The early twentieth century interest in physical culture and the efficient body was clearly a product not only of this interest in gymnastics but also of a growing fascination with physical labor, sport and physical activity in general. Etienne Decroux's mime-plays based on sports and on factory work, Antonin Artaud's commitment to the 'athleticism' of acting, Eugene Sandow's performances of the 'perfect body' can all be seen as aspects of this same phenomenon. Sparshott suggests that the development of early modern dance and movement derived as much from the theoretical analysis of body movement of Souriau and Delsarte, and from subsequent developments in gymnastics and physical training, as from innovations within dance itself. It should be noted for instance that both Laban and Dalcroze were respected as much for their contribution to gymnastics and physical education as to dance, and that Jacques Lecoq was initially trained as a sports physiotherapist.

CLASSIFYING MOVEMENT: CAPITALISM AND THE EFFICIENT BODY

> At the beginning of the [twentieth] century, new regimentations of the relations between bodies and machines isolated the body's physical labor, giving it intrinsic interest while at the same time subjecting it to close analysis designed to yield the most efficient routinization of movement.
> (Foster, 1995: 12)

Physiological classification, measurement and analysis are, and have historically been, ways of controlling the body. Measurement as a science is static; it tends towards the preservation of the status quo, fixing and 'norming' the existing circumstances. In this respect it is similar to biological determinism, an enlightenment ideology which is, in essence, 'a theory of limits. It takes the current status of a group as a measure of where they should and must be' (Gould, 1981: 28–29). A vivid example of the use of measurement to normalize the body was provided at the World Fair in Chicago in 1893, where statues of a naked man and woman whose dimensions had been taken from averaged measurements of students at Harvard were displayed. This display provoked considerable debate with regard to the dimensions of the ideal female figure and how it could and/or should be attained. In one respect the World Fair statue was partial testimony that women were escaping the anatomical consequences of high fashion (stays and corsets), yet it was also evidence of a pre-dominantly patriarchal attempt to control the body and its image through measurement, evaluation and comparison.

The practice of measuring and recording the body, in its requirement for bodily stasis, both assisted and took impetus from the development of early photography. There is clearly a sense in which the movement analyses of Marey, Demeny and Souriau, and of many of those who followed shortly after, strive towards the technical purity of photographic observation. Souriau, for instance, sees movement observation as aspiring to a condition strongly suggestive of photography: 'It is easiest to study the laws of movement through the attitudes of our body, because motion is then arrested or sufficiently slowed down to permit accurate observation' (Souriau, 1983: 14). Photography was also associated with both the commercial development of physical culture and the growth of anthropological, anthropometric and labor studies both in Europe and further abroad; developments that, equally inevitably, invoke once again the complex interrelationship between mechanization, aesthetics, ethnicity and the efficiency of movement. Photography helped to categorize, fix and classify bodies—as measurable, as exotic, as objects of desire, as classed and/or gendered and/or ethnicized. The chapters which follow will examine the 'norms' against which the student actor's body has been measured and the possibilities for 'other bodies' to survive and thrive within the normalizing effects of the systems of movement training.

Any act of measurement evokes and validates the normative criteria against which the measurement is made. The work of Frederick Winslow Taylor (Taylor, 1911) and of Frank Gilbreth (Gilbreth, 1911) in formulating theories of physically efficient industrial labor measured physical activity against the capitalist imperative to maximize worker output and thereby increase profit. In doing so, their work acted culturally and socio-economically to validate efficiency as an important criterion for movement and physical activity. Though Taylor's and Gilbreth's work participated in a general social agenda which approved of and promoted physical efficiency within the wider context, it was grounded in an industrial and mercantile discourse of the body. Harlow Person, in his foreword to *Scientific Management*, a 1964 collection of essays by Taylor, describes the practice of scientific management as, 'a technique for conserving energy and increasing productivity by the use of scientific methods at the individual workplace' (Harlow Person in Taylor, 1964: xv). Taylorism entered the popular imagination through the time-motion studies and worker's exercise programs, through the mechanically precise routines of the Tiller girls (Burt, 1998: 84–100), and through the rhythmical and regimented mass gymnastic displays of the pre-Second World War period. However, whilst 'Taylorism' helped to promote general interest in both the perfectibility of the moving body (through increased physical efficiency in its use and labor), and in the economic value and importance of accurate and objective observation and recording of human movement, it did not impact directly on the development of movement training in this country. This was principally because it was not embodied in any coherent system of *preparation* for physical activity. As such Taylorism operated primarily on the organization of working class labor—the worker was observed, his/her movements analyzed, improvements made and (according to Taylor's mechanical logic) productivity increased. The body of the 'untrained' worker/laborer was normalized as inefficient, wasteful, in need of careful scrutiny and physical improvement. Physical training was, in this context, civilizing as well as industrially beneficial.

EMILE JAQUES-DALCROZE—EURHYTHMICS: RHYTHM, EXERCISE AND EXPRESSION

How was physical exercise to transform itself, to expand its possibilities beyond the simple construction of functional, obedient and patriotic bodies, and to make progress on the road towards the kind of class respectability enjoyed by the Public School sports? Aspiring actors and dancers, though they might aesthetically admire the 'nobility' of the working man, were unlikely to be attracted to schemes of exercise which were too clinical, mechanical and lacking in stimulation. One answer, as we have seen, lay in the work of Delsarte, which had reached England by the start of the new century; however, another came in the unlikely form of a portly and dapper Swiss composer and music teacher, Emile Jaques-Dalcroze (1865–1950). Dalcroze's initial innovation was in the field of music education, but his innate curiosity led him repeatedly to analyze and re-organize the elements of his work, expanding it into the field of movement. Whilst his approach to movement shares much with Delsarte's system, Dalcroze crucially focused on a heightened awareness of rhythm as an element that was essentially dynamic rather than static. The concept of rhythm marks a fundamental difference between Delsarte and Dalcroze, a difference that signifies a point of separation between the nineteenth and the twentieth centuries, a difference between stasis (with its focus on hierarchized measurements) and change.

Dalcroze's movement work began as an attempt to facilitate the teaching of musical rhythm. In seeking to understand the difficulty of one of his students to understand rhythm, he focused on the student's seemingly contradictory ability to copy naturally and unconsciously the rhythm of his teacher's walk. Dalcroze's subsequent investigations led him to believe that there would be value in the study of total body responses to the teaching of musical rhythms (Spector, 1990: 56). Though his initial objective was to develop musical awareness, the repercussions for the study of dance, theatre and physical education also soon became apparent. Equally apparent in the early years of Dalcroze's experiments are the tensions between nineteenth and twentieth century conceptions of the body. Dalcroze's work became an increasingly explicit criticism of the traditionally conservative academy, the Geneva Conservatoire, at which he was Professor of Harmony. His new ideas were not readily accepted by the Conservatoire authorities, which found the training too radical. Others criticized the students' dress as immoral, as, 'the active nature of Dalcroze's class soon led to the students' practice of wearing skimpy costumes, without shoes and stockings, (Rogers, 1969: 23). This combination of ideological and moral opposition grew to such a pitch that Dalcroze was dismissed from his post in 1904.

Not to be deterred, Dalcroze continued his teaching, founding his own school and continuing to develop his theories on rhythm, movement and physical expression. Central to his ideas was 'the position that the body or the mind could accomplish prodigious feats' (Spector, 1990: 56). Such a position drew on a vision of the 'purity' of the human mind and body, a purity which had become corrupted by the stifling impediments of everyday modern life. It also implicitly suggested a 'Golden Age', either in the past (conventionally seen as represented in the art of Ancient Greece) or the future, where graceful and efficient, effective movement was, or could

Educating Efficient Labor for the Acting Profession 29

become, the norm. The historical and cultural construction of the 'natural' and 'pure' body will be discussed in more detail in the next chapter, however this general phenomenon is a significant indication of the growing desire to find ways to disassociate movement and physical activity from the kind of functional, mechanical exercise which was associated with the modern, industrialized body. Exercise was to become a site of pleasurable, liberated, expressive movement—movement training was, in a manner which echoes Souriau, beginning to assume aesthetic values. To the modern sensibility, freedom on such a fundamental level as the body must have seemed very attractive. Irwin Spector gives a succinct and lucid description of the logic of Dalcroze's theories which reveals something of the unifying and educative intent of his work:

> Where a particular function could not be performed there was a reason for the lack of effectiveness; something blocked its success. It would be necessary to discover the impediment, to remove it, and thus to allow the body to operate in a normal manner. If the difficulty were a simple physical feat, its solution would be easy. The required physical act need only be practiced (*sic*) until it became manageable. If there were some other inhibition, something, for example, that the mind did not readily understand, then the solution had to be approached from a mental standpoint. Should the difficulty lie in the relationship between the mental concept of the problem and its physical accomplishment, something had to be developed to connect these two stages. The problem centred on the physical means for stimulating the mind, of activating the nervous system to the point where it could respond to the mental stimuli, of developing physical reflexes so that the muscles would do the will of the mind easily and quickly.
> (Spector, 1990: 56–57)

Reading this description, it is easy to see the attraction of Dalcroze's approach to those involved in making theatre and training actors. The ground for so much of what was to come was being prepared in Dalcroze's sensitive approach to teaching and his search to liberate the body's expressive potential.

'KEEP FIT'—A NATION EXERCISES: EFFICIENCY AND THE FASCIST BODY

In the 1930s, only a few decades later, the recreational potential of physical education led to the popularizing of less formal approaches to exercise: 'While girls at Bedford and the other [Physical Education] colleges were still constructing tables in the Ling tradition, the nation's womanhood was swept off its feet by "Keep Fit" and the Women's League of Health and

Beauty' (Fletcher, 1984: 90). 'Keep Fit' played on the growing consumerist interest in 'sex-appeal' and beauty. It represented a popular movement away from functional rationalism and the joylessness of the Ling system towards exercise regimes which were more 'natural', easier to integrate into modern life-styles, and more personally satisfying; but its aim was still to promote physical exercise for everybody. The roots of its success lie in the spread of the middle class desire to de-urbanize (already evident in the growth of suburban living—see Worpole [2000]). While cities retained their hegemonic status as sites of economic, social and cultural power, they also became the locus for the working out of powerful tensions—between the city as a dynamic and cosmopolitan meeting place for people and the city as a site of moral and physical decadence. Outdoor exercise was given increasing importance, and 'naturalness' was valued—good food, early hours, open windows at night, walks in the country, even naturism and nudism.

The naked body is an ambiguous icon for movement training in the early twentieth century. It was used variously to symbolize the 'naturalness' of the body, the purity and honesty of the moving body, also the liberation of the erotic body and the 'perfectibility' of the human physique. During the early twentieth century, experiments in 'natural living' took place in several parts of Europe; at Ascona in Switzerland for example, in 1913, the dancer/choreographer Rudolf Laban (1879–1958), together with his family and collaborators, lived a lifestyle of vegetarianism and nudism. This kind of 'natural' living was conceived as 'an antidote to the bourgeois intellectual society of *fin-de-siecle* Europe' (Preston-Dunlop, 1998: 28). In Germany, the Youth Movement of the early twentieth Century also developed as 'a protest, against the materialization of life' (Mueller, 1929: 202). Dr Ludwig Mueller, a German delegate at a 1929 conference on Education and Leisure, announced that, 'In 1900 every fifth German lived in a big city, and in the same year each Berlin building housed an average of seventy-seven inhabitants' (Mueller, 1929: 202). Exercise is seen in this context as providing access to a renewed simple moral purity. Developments such as the German Youth Movement drew enthusiastically on rural folk traditions and communal outdoor activities. Clearly this was in part a reaction against the modern, urban, mechanized environment of the city; however the same agenda also readily opens itself to nationalistic notions of cultural identity through movement, dance and physical education:

> one year ago in the big Berlin Stadium, I saw 10,000 students of Berlin schools, strong ones and weak, all doing the same gymnastic exercises and all in unison. It was a wonderful sight, and showed me the life of our schools from our point of view. It was a wonderful sight.
> (Mueller, 1929: 205)

It is difficult to read this statement without hearing echoes of the National Socialist ideology that was to surface so violently only a few years later. However the ideals of community, common physical humanity and vitality also come through in Mueller's text and the misappropriation of such ideals by the fascists should alert us to the dangers of viewing such activities as politically neutral, rather than the dangers of the activities themselves. Ramsey Burt points out that 1920s and 1930s body culture was 'neither exclusively German nor confined to those sympathetic to right-wing nationalist ideologies' (Burt, 1998: 110). Indeed left-wing German nudists proclaimed that, 'Proletarian nudity was intended as a purgative of deep-seated anti-sensual prejudice and a rational method of discarding the chains of bourgeois ideas around proletarian minds' (van der Will, 1990: 31). The resulting ideological contest over the body was to ensnare several movement practitioners, including Laban. These conflicts and contradictions are most evident in Laban's work as the choreographer for large-scale amateur events for the 1936 Olympics. Valerie Preston-Dunlop describes how Laban directed vast movement choirs as part of the celebratory week for amateurs at the Olympics. The first section had as its theme

> the struggle for space and for a territory. What better theme for a Nazi dance? But Laban treated it as a battle for each person to find relief from the daily regimentation of space by searching out a place in which to be an individual in a self-constructed small community (. . .) The fourth *Reigen* [section], 'Weilhe', was a dedication, again a Nazi theme. But Laban did not have it as a dedication of the self to the State but to harmony between people and between people and nature.
> (Preston-Dunlop, 1998: 195)

Laban's attempt to subvert the National Socialist ideology of the dancing body was bound to lead eventually to his removal from posts of authority and his exile. German National Socialist ideology sought to reassert national boundaries not only through military and geographical intervention, but also through embodied boundaries where the Aryan physical ideal and the aesthetics of the dance were intended to police the exclusion of the racially impure. Imagery from the 1930s (for instance the films of Leni Riefenstahl) shows how the naked or semi-naked body could be used as a part of fascist iconography, where the individual becomes merged with the image of a perfect, pure and racially contained community of bodies. In this manner physical culture, physical education and movement training all increasingly participated in important ways as expressions of a wide range of conflicting, and sometimes contradictory, discourses of race and nationhood. The body could then be liberated through unrestricted and expressive movement and a return to the sensuality of movement, or it could be disciplined into a celebration of its service to the nation and the race. The 'Keep Fit' movement marked the popularization of physical education, but it was, nonetheless, politically ambiguous in its emphasis on national health, mass exercise and the domestic role of exercise for women. Perhaps its most significant effect was to provide a supportive cultural environment for the work of those such as Margaret Morris and Rudolf Laban who sought to bridge the divides between physical education and exercise, and theatre, dance, and self-expression. It should also remind us that the body can never be entirely personal, but is always in some important respects political.

THE ART OF MOVEMENT—THE RISE OF LABAN AND THE FALL OF LING

During the mid-century, as a result of the increasing interest in 'natural' movement, the strict Swedish gymnastic regime popular in the early decades gave way to a more expressive approach to movement, based largely on the teachings of Rudolf Laban. Even before Laban's arrival in England in 1938, as a refugee from the German National Socialists, his work had reached this country through the activities of several dance and physical education students who had trained with him in Europe (Fletcher 1987: 153). Students, such as Joan Goodrich and Diana Jordan, who had studied with Laban in Germany, returned to teach what they understood as 'positive' or 'absolute' dance; absolute,

> because it dispenses with any kind of external aid, seeking neither to be pantomime nor illustration of an idea or an event, but an independent art, possessing its own laws, which cannot be given in so many words, any more than the 'absolute' music of an orchestra or . . . instrument can be given.
> (From *Journal of School Hygiene and Physical Education* Vol. XVI (1924), quoted in Fletcher, 1984: 95.)

Laban would have known of the work of Delsarte and Dalcroze, though he disagreed with them. He was always careful to ensure that he did not openly acknowledge any influence (Preston-Dunlop, 1998: 14–15). However he did acknowledge the importance of several English movement teachers (Madge Atkinson, Ruby Ginner, and Margaret Morris) within his own genealogy of Modern Dance (Foster, 1977: 80). Their work indicates not simply the strength of Laban's influence but also the general public interest in all physical training that stressed a 'natural' and expressive approach to movement. By the late 1940s Laban's approach was pre-eminent, effectively blurring the lines of distinction between gymnastics and dance. In 1945 Laban opened the Art of Movement Studio in Manchester; and in 1948 his book, *Modern Educational Dance*, was published.

The expansion of Laban's influence from dance performance into physical education and other areas of movement training (in part the result of Laban's financial need to generate multiple sources of income) was a development not entirely welcome to male physical trainers, who saw it as moving the subject away from its traditionally positivist base (a position aligned with traditional male strengths and historically related to constructions of physical activity which emphasized female weakness). After the Second World War, male gymnasts and physical trainers had returned to civilian life with an interest in extending the functional physiological approach which had informed their military training—strength, stamina, testing and measuring (e.g. circuit training)—to gymnastics and physical education. However Laban's systematized but expressive approach to physical training had already attained a degree of official credibility and general recognition, and was proving particularly popular at the intersection between physical education and dance/theatre performance training.

Laban's approach to movement was holistic. Whilst it might seem that his work emphasized the expressive over the mechanically efficient, this would be to misrepresent the breadth of his vision He was, for instance, closely connected with the development of industrially efficient labor during the 1940s through his collaboration with the management consultant Frederick Lawrence. The results of this project, published in their book *Effort* (Laban & Lawrence, 1947), formed the basis for a comprehensive vision of the relevance of movement study to the improvement of everyday life. But for Laban, efficiency did not just mean observation and measurement; it involved the bringing into play of a theory of movement analysis and the vital importance of rhythm and 'swing'. Laban, significantly, saw his work as dealing with 'the basis of movement rather than consisting of a series of technical movements' (Preston-Dunlop, 1998: 219).

FROM 'POSTURE' TO 'SELF-IMPROVEMENT'

The journey from Ling to Laban can best be illustrated through the changing perception of 'posture'. Posture was understandably valued in the first half of the twentieth century as a way in which the health of the body could be objectively monitored and measured. Until the 1950s, posture was regularly used as an indicator for the general health of school children, who had their posture recorded and evaluated. So ingrained was the association between good posture and the healthy and attentive child that even until relatively recently pupils were expected to 'sit up straight' when a head teacher entered the class. Posture deals with the presentation of the body on a clearly superficial level, and as such required nothing more than a passing acquaintance with anatomy and physiology. Changes were to come from two fronts. On the one hand, the materialist ideas of William James, Carl Lange and G. H. Lewes prepared the way for a conception of the self which brought the mind and the body far closer together. On the other hand, the early twentieth century revival of interest in the classical Greek body saw a renewed commitment to the body as an important element of the subject's sense of self. These changes can also be mapped through the rise of interest in naturism, spiritualism and the East, in changes in fashion and in sport. The body was no longer to be viewed as simply an instrument or machine which needed a purely physiological approach to its proper maintenance.

These changes meant that good posture was redefined from the inflexible ideal of the military parade ground or army gymnasium. Instead the body became the site for an increased fascination with the 'how' and the 'why'—as opposed to the 'what'. Taylorism and Fordism had 'sought efficiency by means of economy of scale in production' (Martin, 1997: 544) and encouraged a mercantile economy of the body, an economy geared to productivity and standardization. Their influence had operated through the construction of ideologies of gender, home life, health, and morality which functioned to coerce the worker into hygienic and domestic habits which would preserve the worker's value as labor capital. The 'new efficiency', in starting with the idea of efficient movement as a more complete expression of the 'self', allowed for the gradual dissolution of conventional historical gender stereotypes and generated a sense of the body as intimately connected to the individual's creative development. The twentieth century actor would still find themselves required to warm-up, to practice and to exercise, perhaps even to 'work out', both during training and as a professional actor, but the emphasis would change from the mechanical acquisition of technical skills, to the preparation of the body as a source of creative energies. Though Laban perceived the value of an integrated and holistic approach to posture and movement, he preferred to focus his energies and attentions on the expressive functions of movement rather than on developing a vision of the interaction between mind and body which might allow for the successful re-education of inefficient body use. For an approach to posture and movement based on a sound physiological (as opposed to purely kinesthetic) understanding of the body we need to look to elsewhere.

THE ALEXANDER TECHNIQUE

Frederick Matthias Alexander (1869–1955) invented a technique for the re-education of the body through the inhibition of badly conditioned physical responses. His starting point was the identification of key physiological features of efficient and effective movement. Through study and observations Alexander identified the importance of what he called 'Primary Control', the (re)alignment of the head-neck reflex and consequent improvement of the general use of the body. Like Laban, Alexander proposed not so much a series of exercises as a journey, through movement, towards a more profound understanding of the body and its use.

Alexander was an actor, and remained interested in theatre throughout his life. In reaction to voice problems early in his career, he undertook a detailed analysis of posture and its effect upon the efficient functioning of the body. Like Laban, his technique sought to encourage an efficient response to stimuli, an aim self-evidently attractive to creative artists. Alexander moved to London from Australia in 1904 (Huxley, Leach, & Stevens, 1995: 156), and taught in London and America for several years. Michael Gelb draws most probably on Edward Maisel (Alexander, 1986 [1969]: xvii) when he suggests that among Alexander's early pupils were several celebrated actors, including Sir Henry Irving and Viola and Beerbohm Tree (Gelb, 1981: 15). Alexander's interests covered a wide field of activity and this diversity, together with the high charge for classes (Edward Maisel in Alexander, 1986: xvii) and his desire to ensure that any teachers he trained were themselves thoroughly versed in his work, meant that his teaching, though popular, was not as rapidly disseminated as that of Laban. It was to take almost another twenty-five years before a formal training program was instigated for Alexander Technique Teachers (Gelb, 1981: 17). Alexander also published several books outlining his theories (1910, 1923, 1932, and 1941); however, he does not write with any particular eloquence and despite the success of his books among his followers, his theories and work did not become well known until the 1960s. From the 1960s onwards a number of his former pupils, and others whom he had influenced, succeeded in further disseminating his work through their own teaching and publications (e.g. Todd (1937) [reprinted in 1968], Maisel (1969), and Barlow [1973]). Hardly any mention is made of theatre and acting in Alexander's own books, and it has been largely up to those who came after him to promote its relevance for actors and dancers.

Like Laban and other movement theorists of this time, Alexander saw the body as a key site for the struggle for freedom from the debilitating effects of modern urban life. He felt that the body was naturally capable of expressive and efficient movement; but, he also believed that 'civilization' and the anxieties of urban, technological life operated to disfigure the body and to impair individuals' abilities to express themselves fully and freely. These issues will be revisited in Chapter 2. The second part of this chapter will seek to position the general history outlined above in respect to its impact on actor training.

FROM PHYSICAL EDUCATION TOWARDS MOVEMENT TRAINING FOR ACTORS

The first part of this chapter has provided a sense of the general ideological, educational and cultural context within which movement training for actors has developed, and has identified the leading theorists and practitioners in the field of physical education and training. The aim has been to locate movement training within the context of the general discursive transformation of the body during the twentieth century and within the context of changing practices of the body-in-action throughout the century.

The development of movement training for actors can be understood as negotiating its cultural status, its social acceptability, and its key practices within the space shared between the contexts outlined above and the historical traditions and demands of the theatre industry. It is this space which the second part of this chapter seeks to examine.

PART TWO:
MAKING THE BODY OF THE MODERN ACTOR

> The search for a physical system of actor training, a process, a technique, a discipline whereby the body may be reliably mastered, characterizes the best thinking about the art of acting in the twentieth century.
> (Roach, 1985: 194)

The concept of efficiency is directly linked to the notion that mastery of technique is not a mysterious achievement or chance genetic ability, but that it comes from 'professional skills knowingly applied' (Roach, 1993: 116). Roach identifies Diderot's vision of the potential power of science to illuminate art as a crucial turning point for the study of acting, a point from which the training of actors acquired systematic rigor and consequent social, economic and cultural momentum. This second part of the chapter examines the manner and extent to which theatre training draws on the discourses of science, exercise, efficiency and technique.

THE SOCIAL STATUS OF THE ACTOR'S BODY

Throughout its history the acting profession has been popularly associated with moral laxity, perhaps reflecting a perception of the physical processes of acting as degenerate—the actor's body seen for instance as infinitely bendable to the whim of its owner (or whoever was paying for the actor's labor), and the actor's art as the perversion of the 'genuine' sincerity of everyday expression into the 'false' sincerity of performance. The actor was perceived as part of a migrant work force, a person 'for hire', and in this sense as someone who would always be an outsider. Such factors conspired to enable theatre managers to force actors to work long and hard hours, for little or no pay or job security. Though the acting profession was eventually to turn its back on the poorer booth actors, street performers and variety acts in the search for social respectability and professional credibility, it is clear that a wealth of popular physical skills and orally transmitted knowledge and history was lost to the theatre with their silent demise; a wealth which only partially survived in music hall and variety (the eccentric dancing of Max Wall and Nat Jackley for instance had its roots in the acts of the

Penny Gaff Clowns, the Silly Billies and the Ballet Clowns [Mayhew, 1968]). The booth actors were often possessed of a wide range of self-taught or apprenticed physical skills, including: acrobatics, dancing, juggling and clowning. These skills were passed on through informal systems of apprenticeship; no books or training academies existed, and the artists themselves did not have the financial security to undertake a formal institutional training (if such a thing had existed). Once again we see a conception of the body as the artisan-actor's instrument, something to be hired for its productivity in the same way as the conventional artisan's materials and tools.

From about 1860 onwards the social standing of the acting profession began to improve. Well-educated newcomers started to join the profession and we see the emergence of the 'gentleman actor'. This trend reflects the general improvement in financial return for the successful metropolitan companies and actor managers, together with an increased recognition within the profession that the best way to attract the money of the middle and upper-middle classes was to 'tidy up their act' and provide more decorous and culturally acceptable fare. The old system had meant that theatre tended to be a 'family business', with many actors following in their parents' footsteps. By the start of the twentieth century, the profession was attracting many more middle class actors. Whilst this represented a rise in the social status of the actor, it implied that pretty much anyone could become an actor depending on their luck, talent and popular appeal. Several measures were consequently deemed necessary to control the influx and to assure professional quality. Training had previously been by apprenticeship or by private tuition, neither of which offered any structured body of learning and neither of which demanded anything other than a willingness to pay. This haphazard approach to ensuring quality meant that efforts to establish a base-line standard for actors were doomed to fail. As a result attempts were finally made to create a more rigorous and coherent system of training, through the establishment of schools and academies for the training of actors.

NINETEENTH CENTURY ACTOR TRAINING AND THE INDUSTRIAL PROCESS

Up until the start of the twentieth century, it was accepted that much of the training of the professional actor took place 'on-the-job'. Trainee actors sought places as apprentices and received handed down advice from the more experienced members of the company (Barker, 1995: 99; Cairns, 1996: 13; Taylor, 1999: 73). This introduction was seldom an easy one, as the work of the apprentice also included menial tasks, often for little or no financial reward. The unstructured, craft-based nature of the training contributed to perceptions of the actor as of low social esteem in comparison to the 'learned' professions. The training that was available had developed in response to the nature, structure and organization of the theatre industry at this time. The popular conception of the theatre of the nineteenth century is of well-established actor managers touring the country or performing in large London theatres. This is, of course, only a partial picture. At the base of this structure were large numbers of performers struggling to make ends meet in an industry where poverty was rife and injury common. The Victorian social historian, Henry Mayhew, in his compendium of London workers, *London Labour and the London Poor* (Mayhew, 1968), lists a wide range of acts who existed on the fringes of the theatre and entertainment industry. Many of the itinerant entertainers recorded by Mayhew tell of skills being self-taught, passed on through families or acquired through hard (and sometimes cruel) apprenticeships. One performer tells how,

> When father first trained me, it hurt my back awfully. He used to take my legs and stretch them, and work them round in their sockets, and put them straight by my side. That is what they called being "cricked".
> (Mayhew, 1968: 90)

Women artists often suffered similarly, one of Mayhew's interviewees recalls a woman who continued her act as a contortionist well into pregnancy and experienced problems giving birth as a result. Broken limbs and dislocations were frequent and performers could only rely on the support of fellow artists or benevolent funds to help them through the periods of unemployment. Such disregard for the body, viewed simply as an instrument of production, echoes the physical rigors of much labor in industrial Victorian England. The Victorian body was often physiologically distorted in response to its socio-economic context, and the reconstitution of the body into new shapes within popular variety acts of the period is a possible reflection of this. Interest in the acrobat, the contortionist, the strong man and the balancing act can be seen as a response to the physically intensive labor many people had to endure in their working lives (industrial, agricultural and domestic). The contortionist renegotiates the body and its possibilities and representations, whilst at the same time showing it to be no more than a flexible and malleable medium to be controlled and abused at will, as if naturalizing the unnatural.

The training of the street performers generated a profligate waste of talent and ability. The body of the performer was controlled by hard financial imperatives and by the fierce discipline of the apprenticeship rather than by any concern for the physiological limits and expressive range of the body. Within this tradition, the 'legitimate' actor's knowledge of various basic skills—dancing, basic acrobatics, effective gesture and confident stage movement—was simply assumed, and viewed as 'artisanal' in that the aesthetics underpinning them are based on functionality and graceful presentation rather than inherent artistry or the creative development of the artist or art form. The model of training at this end of the theatre industry is in this sense a model with distinctly functional and laboring connotations, a model we can see as indirectly related to the drill-based physical education regimes of the period.

SUCCESS AND RESPECTABILITY

There is a misconception that English acting has historically eschewed the physical. Such a perception represents a limited and class-based view of theatre history. The physical skills of some of the popular nineteenth century actors and performers were considerable; a few achieved notable success. By the 1880s a troupe calling itself the Hanlon-Lees achieved such success and popularity with their trap door and acrobatics spectaculars that they toured as far as Paris, where Emile Zola remarked that they 'laid bare, with a wink, a gesture, the entire human breast' (Southern, 1970: 105–8). However, from the Theatres Act of 1843 through to the early twentieth century, such specialty acts as the Hanlon-Lees existed in a separate world from the 'serious drama'. Though the actor Edmund Kean (1789–1833) is supposed to have learnt his trade touring the country with a company of strolling players, and is reputed to have been a capable and accomplished acrobat, by the end of the century such a career cross-over as his was far less likely and much harder to achieve. Already divided by the duopoly established through Charles II's letters patent in 1660, the worlds of the serious or 'legitimate' actor and of the strolling player or variety act further diverged as a result of the Theatres Act into an estrangement, which, whilst never total, has proved over the last 150 years to be effectively irreversible (despite the amalgamation of the respective unions in the 1960s).

To maintain this socially valuable distinction, actors who considered themselves as professionals rather than artisans realized that they would need to distance their work from that of the popular variety artistes (Sanderson, 1984: 118). The move towards professionalization took place through changes in the social background of many actors, the improved possibilities for financial success, and the creation of controlling organizations (the Actors' Association and the Actors' Union), and perhaps most significantly through the development of 'professional' training and education. As the acting profession became increasingly popular with the middle classes, the functional physical skills of the artisan actor or performer were shunned by aspiring professionals. Accomplishments such as tumbling were undesirable for the education and apprenticeship of the socially aspirational actor. Professional status was going to mean undertaking a training that was systematic, scientific, industry-relevant, suitably genteel, and based on respectable aesthetic principles. The formal training available at the end of the nineteenth century in this sense reflects the tastes of the time. The emphasis on elocution and deportment indicated an aesthetic of physical expression that drew extensively on the existing aesthetics of social dance, theatre dance and oratory. These conventions appear to have drawn their cultural provenance from classical texts and statuary, their social provenance from the leisure practices of the upper and middle classes, and their medical provenance, as has already been shown, from scientific advances in the understanding of anatomy, physiology and psychology. The gains from a systematized approach to actor training were to be social, professional and technical—actors better trained in skills and techniques valued both by the theatre industry and by society at large would be able to lay claim to higher social status.

THE EARLY DEVELOPMENT OF THE ENGLISH DRAMA SCHOOLS

The first institution which might justifiably be described as an acting academy was the Musical and Dramatic Academy founded in Soho Square in 1848. This family business was however small and short-lived. Next a Royal Dramatic College was established in 1859. The foundation stone was laid by the Prince of Wales in 1876, further establishing its respectability, and the college opened in 1882. However three years later financial difficulties forced it to close. The London Academy of Music was founded in 1861, offering among other things, classes in elocution and voice production, followed in 1880 by the Guildhall School of Music. Gustave Garcia, author of *The Actor's Art* (1882), who taught at the London Academy of Music from 1882 to 1904, developed courses which incorporated the system of gestures and expression proposed by Delsarte (Sanderson, 1984: 37). At the same time the older system of apprenticeship training became more formalized in the training companies of Frank Benson and Sarah Thorne. In 1904 Sir Herbert Beerbohm Tree founded an academy specifically for actors and offered lessons above his theatre in the Haymarket. This was eventually to move to Gower Street and become the Royal Academy of Dramatic Art [RADA], receiving its royal charter in 1920. In 1906 Elsie Fogerty founded a competitor institution, the Central School of Speech and Drama, and moved into rooms in the Royal Albert Hall. Though initially derided by the acting profession, it soon became clear that there was to be no shortage of willing applicants to these schools. Kenneth Rea points out that the academies' almost total reliance on fees for their financial survival meant that the student's ability to pay was a primary concern (Rea, 1981: 48). The schools drew together this mix of influences to create systems of training which: prioritized the teaching of voice production; recognized the value of the professionally experienced specialist tutor; and was closely related to the most respectable figures of the acting and theatre professions.

The training, in the early days of these institutions, focused largely on meeting the demands of the established theatre of the time. So it is not surprising that little attempt to formalize a systematic approach to training is evident in the school curricula of the time. The 1905 syllabus at [R]ADA included: elocution, acting (classical and modern comedy), dancing, deportment, mime and fencing. Theatre in this country was still broadly unconcerned with, if not downright suspicious of, theories of acting, and the persistent belief in acting as an innate ability meant that academies were seen as offering little more than polish, technique and practice. As a result, some of the teaching may have resembled nothing so much as drill. In her autobiography, *The Story of My Life*, Ellen Terry recalls her early instruction in appreciative terms:

> One of the most wearisome, yet essential details of my education is connected with my first long dress. It introduces, too, Mr. Oscar Byrn, the dancing master and director of crowds at the Princess's. One of his lessons was in the art of walking with a flannel blanket pinned on in front and trailing six inches on the floor. My success in carrying out this manoeuvre with dignity won high praise from Mr. Byrn (. . .) who had a theory that "an actress was no actress unless she learned to dance early." Whenever he was not actually putting me through my paces, I was busy watching him teach the others. There was the minuet, to which he used to attach great importance, and there was "walking the plank." Up and down one of the long planks, extending the length of the stage, we had to walk first slowly and then quicker and quicker until we were able at a considerable pace to walk the whole length of it without deviating an inch from the straight line. This exercise, Mr. Byrn used to say, and quite truly, I think, taught us uprightness of carriage and certainty of step.
> "Eyes right! Chest out! Chin tucked in!" I can hear the dear old man shouting at us as if it were yesterday; and I have learned to see of what value his drilling was, not only to deportment, but to clear utterances.
> (Terry, 1908: 20–21)

Despite her evident enthusiasm for this instruction it is impossible not to recognize within this account echoes of the relentless drilling of the poor street performers and the mechanical bark of the drill sergeant. These exercises represent traditional knowledge and expertise that seem to have become fossilized into rigid dogmas. Such dogmas, for the most part no longer in vital and healthy contact with the theatre forms which gave them meaning, survived as part of a subculture of theatre life and education constructed upon the personality of the teacher, the rigidity of tradition and the need for discipline and some form of technique and control, however acquired.

MOVEMENT TRAINING IN THE EARLY ACADEMIES

The regular presence of social dance and fencing on the curricula of the early drama schools indicates the respectable status such activities had already acquired. These were movement practices associated with grace, finesse and gentility—qualities appropriate for the social class to which many actors aspired, from which increasing numbers were drawn and whose behavior was the subject of many of the plays they performed. As long as theatrical tastes did not demand a 'natural' style, the old artificiality hardly seems to have mattered. Problems arose as the conventional relationship between emotion and gesture became fractured, obsolete and unconvincing. In response to the growing popularity of naturalistic drama, the actor increasingly aimed to use gesture not to codify the character for the audience, but to express what the character might actually have *felt:*. Basic skills of co-ordination were not going to be adequate to help achieve the convincing expression of emotion. It is within this context that we can understand the influence and importance of innovations in movement training, such as François Delsarte's work in Paris, which despite its limitations, did seek to establish, 'a direct, causal link between outward appearance and internal feeling' (Taylor, 1999: 75).

DELSARTE'S INFLUENCE ON MOVEMENT TRAINING IN THE EARLY DRAMA SCHOOLS

The journey of Delsarte's ideas from Paris to the drama schools of London is not an easy one to trace. The transmission of physical practices requires the kind of personal contact over a sustained period of time that commonly goes unrecorded. We must rely on the traces left by practice and pedagogy. The French stage and the Paris Conservatoire were very much admired in England during the late Victorian and the Edwardian era, the latter appreciated as an important model for effective theatrical training (Sanderson, 1984: 39). Nonetheless, when Tree announced, in 1904, the principle subjects to be studied at his newly founded Academy of Dramatic Art, he made no direct mention of Delsarte's system, proposing only: dancing, fencing, acrobatics, mime and period gesture. Two years later, in 1906, the syllabus had been expanded to include calisthenics and a subject called, 'The Art of Expression'. The actor Robert Atkins, who became a student at Tree's new Academy in April 1905, recalls in his autobiography that the curriculum included 'body control under the Delsarte system' (Atkins, 1994: 19). Michael Sanderson describes the relevance of the Delsarte system to the actor training as:

> a system of physical exercises especially valuable for relaxing the body, giving it flexibility of movement and loosening up the stiffness of everyday carriage. It was particularly important for girls of the day, who were brought up to cultivate a rather rigid reserve as part of their modesty. Their elaborate clothing and relative lack of participation in sports reinforced this. The academy realized that it had to break down these inhibitions and the physical limitations that were their consequence if it was to turn its rather well-bred students into actors capable of expressing emotion.
> (Sanderson, 1984: 43)

This suggests that the teaching of functional skills (dance, fencing, mime, and period gesture) was, even at this early stage, giving place to the importance of general fitness and physical expression.

Sanderson records that Delsartean expression and gesture was being taught at [R]ADA as late as the 1930s (Sanderson, 1984: 190). Both in England and in America, Delsarte's ideas held theatrical and pedagogical sway well into the first half of the twentieth century. Trish Arnold recalls for instance that Katherine Hepburn was a fan of Delsarte's work and suggests that this influence can be detected in Hepburn's early films (Arnold, 1999). Alongside their lessons in physical expression, students at [R]ADA at the start of the century also had classes in mime with Madam Cavalazzi and dancing led by Louis d'Egville (Atkins, 1994: 22), a teacher of dancing, deportment and carriage. Madam Cavalazzi appears to have been a charismatic teacher— Atkins describes her as, 'Mistress of the Mime, a one-time ballerina, a fiery Italian. Under her we lived, loved and died in every possible posture' (1994: 21). The d'Egville family ran classes for the finishing education of young ladies in bowing, social graces and deportment at their own private school. Louis d'Egville's input into the instruction at the Academy reflects the need for young actors to be well schooled in the simulation of upper class gestures, deportment and carriage. Such simulation was very necessary; it both flattered the social aspirations of student actors and their parents, and provided the young middle class actor with the ability to act convincingly in plays which reflected an upper-middle class social and cultural hegemony.

DRAMA SCHOOLS AND MOVEMENT TRAINING AS THERAPY

Central School, founded shortly after [R]ADA, was established and run by Elsie Fogerty, who had studied at the Paris Conservatoire in the 1880s (and would therefore almost certainly have been exposed to the ideas of Delsarte). The initial focus of the school was on the teaching of speech technique and elocution. From 1908 to 1914 this expanded to include dancing (including classical ballet), fencing and physical training. One of the teachers at Central School during the early decades of the century was Dr. Henry Hulbert. Initially a teacher of physical training, Hulbert later devised a system to teach voice and physical training in conjunction. He saw great value in:

> physical training and dancing for relaxing the body and helping the breathing necessary for vocal culture. He also emphasised the value of the physical perception of rhythmic movement as an aid to the development of coherent speech.
>
> (Sanderson, 1984: 48)

Much of Hulbert's theory and many of his practical exercises are described in his book, *Eurhythm: Thought in Action—The Principles and*

Practice of Vocal and Physical Therapy (Hulbert, 1921), both the title and content of which may indicate the influence of Emile Jacques-Dalcroze and his system of Eurhythmic exercise. Though Hulbert makes no direct reference to Dalcroze in his book, the tone and nature of his ideas and exercises indicate that he was at the very least aware of Dalcroze's work. Dr. Hulbert outlines his 'Principles of Eurhythmics' as: 'rhythm, purpose, control, co-ordination, correlation, progression, and correction in action' (1921: 13), and follows this with a list of seven 'laws of movement'. Though these do not bear an exact relation to Delsarte's laws and principles, they at least admit of the possibility of influence and echo the assumption of a need for such categorization and analysis. The rationalist approach to acting which Hulbert's and Delsarte's systems implied were also evident in the popularity of the acting approach proposed by the French tutor Constant Coquelin. Coquelin's book *The Art of the Actor* was first published in France in 1894, but was certainly available in an English translation by Elsie Fogerty in 1932. Coquelin stressed the double nature of the performer, his work was used as a source of ideas for 'a new modern emphasis on the body, its physical actions, and the control of the intelligence' (Risum, 1996: 68).

Whereas [R]ADA maintained its status through strong links with the commercial theatre, Central School developed a reputation for close links with the medical profession. Fogerty was presumably keen to draw on, make use of and in effect publicize developments in the scientific understanding of voice production and the physiology of speech. The frontispiece of Hulbert's book proudly describes the author's medical pedigree, including a post as 'House Surgeon and Clinical Assistant in Throat Department at St. Thomas' Hospital London'. This point of distinction between the two drama schools illustrates the complex tensions between, on the one hand, a growing commitment to the development of the actor's body as an expressive instrument, and, on the other, the flourishing of various scientific understandings of the workings of the human body and its 'correct' physical functioning. In some respects the 'expressive' body justified the place of movement training in the drama school curriculum and the broad content of the training; whereas the 'healthy' body affected the detailed content, the pedagogical approach and the principles and exercises used in delivery.

CLASSICAL BODIES—REDISCOVERING THE IDEAL

Etymology reveals the cultural histories to key concepts in physical education and movement training. The word 'gymnasium', for instance, comes from Ancient Greek words for 'to train naked'. Late Victorian moral prurience dictated that whilst naked exercise was generally acceptable for men, such liberated activity would be quite unsuitable for women. By contrast, Calisthenics (from the Greek for strength and beauty) was, at least until the late twentieth century, defined by the Oxford English Dictionary as 'gymnastic exercises suitable for girls; training calculated to develop the figure and to promote graceful movement' (Onions, 1973: 270).

The nineteenth century revival of interest in the physical standards of Ancient Greece seemed to find a natural association with the ideas and practices suggested by Delsarte, Marey, Demeny and Souriau. Many of those exploring the potential of Delsartism and Greek Dance within expressive performance tended in their creative work to follow common practices: wearing the same style of ancient Greek gown; dealing with classical themes and stories; and drawing on physical poses and imagery from classical statuary and sculpture. Both the dancer Isadora Duncan, and the influential American Delsartean Genevieve Stebbins, found within this new classicism a physicality that could be specifically feminine; both in the sense that as women they could create their own careers and their own creative agendas, and in the sense that they could explore their own physicality with greater freedom of expression than that allowed within the traditional dance forms. The aesthetics of the near-naked classical female body relate to a conception of the female body with its own cultural history. The use of Greek tunics as a dance costume may seem insignificant to us today, but at the time Victorian puritan morals were still so strong that exposing anything other than feet, hands and face in public was considered improper. The female body was conventionally constrained within a corset, corset cover, chemise, shirtwaist, petticoats and frocks (Summers, 2001). The wearing of loose tunics and bare feet was, within this context, seen as virtual nudity. It is possible in this respect to see movement training at this time as playing an important role in helping to establish a conception of a natural body, with its own organic laws and its own beauty, which did not need to be shaped and re-formed, but rather needed to be understood and allowed its own free expression. In this sense, it is the need for an efficiency of free and flowing movement that helped to justify the eventual rejection of unnecessarily restrictive clothing.

The classical body was also an attractive and acceptable model of the healthy integration of mind, body and soul. A balance of exercise and aesthetics was recognized by classical scholars as a key aspect of Athenian civilization. The classical body also offered a model deeply sourced in organic, ritual movement and in a mythologized humanity—a model culturally promoted by the intellectual impact of the Cambridge 'Ritualists'. The late nineteenth century revival of interest in Ancient Greece and the artistic and physical standards of antiquity seemed to find a natural association with Delsarte's ideas and with those of some of his followers. Nancy Lee Chalfa Ruyter argues that the ardent Delsartean Genevieve Stebbins was possessed of 'a belief both in the existence of absolute and eternal principles of 'true art' and in classical Greek art as the most perfect embodiment of those principles' (Ruyter, 1996a: 76)—a position we can see repeated in many other early twentieth century movement practitioners.

ISADORA DUNCAN (1878–1927) AND THE GREEK REVIVAL

There is some suggestion that Isadora Duncan, as a young girl, studied the Delsarte method (Craig, 1977: 251; and, Duncan, Pratl & Splatt, 1993: 29–30) and later the art of Ancient Greece (Duncan, Pratl & Splatt, 1993: 36) before developing her own approach to dance. Certainly Duncan's own costume choices cannot be separated from the trend among American Delsarteans to wear the same type of ancient Greek-style gown, to deal with classical themes and stories, and to draw on physical poses and imagery from classical statuary and sculpture. Duncan did much to make acceptable the notion that dance could have a social purpose, not merely an aesthetic one (Daly, 1995: 36), a notion subsequently to be picked up and developed by Dalcroze and Laban. The cultural acceptability given to her work through its association with Ancient Greek art helped her to establish her dance as 'natural' in terms which seemed to bridge the nineteenth century Art/Nature divide. Such a practice also appealed to Stanislavski who knew Duncan and included some of her teachings in his own actor training regimes (Rene, 1963).

For Duncan, the efficiency of movement lay in the degree to which it could be purified of the social codifications which had taken place over the ages (Eynat-Confino, 1987: 66). Movement would be pure when it followed its own dynamics. Laban wrote of Duncan that she had the courage, 'to demonstrate successfully that there exists in the flow of man's movement some ordering principle which cannot be explained in the usual rationalistic manner' (Laban, 1948: 6). It did not seem to occur to her that the Greek dance she so admired as 'pure' movement might also have been codified. Whilst she did bring simplicity and a new kind of 'naturalness' to movement—she encouraged leaping, walking, skipping and running as training exercises—her movement was not simply the expression of 'pure' emotion but a revised and 'modern' stylization of individual responses to music.

Duncan's influence on movement training for actors stems in no small part from her passionate efforts to rediscover 'the natural cadences of human movement' (Eynat-Confino, 1987: 68), a mission which resonated with the efforts of Stanislavski and Jacques Copeau. In locating the art of dance as something which 'must be based upon and flow from life' (Isadora Duncan quoted in Daly, 1995: 209), Duncan was recognizing its relationship with the theatre. Her nomadic life and her untimely death, coupled with the failure to construct and preserve any coherent system of training, have meant however that her influence has been indirect, consequently perhaps hard to quantify, and therefore underestimated.

RUBY GINNER, IRENE MAWER, MADGE ATKINSON AND THE ENGLISH GREEK DANCE REVIVAL

We can best identify the relationship of the Greek Dance Revival to movement training in England through examining the work of some of the key figures. Though none of them achieved Duncan's fame and notoriety, all contributed to a greater or lesser degree to the rapid changes in body training which took place during the first four decades of the twentieth century. Madge Atkinson was a pioneer of 'natural movement' within physical training, working extensively in Manchester in the 1920s. She was influenced by Aimie Spong, a Duncan pupil, and by the educationalist Rudolf Steiner. Echoing Dalcroze, her work focused on the unity of music and movement, and emphasized the qualities of timing, speed and flow (Foster, 1977: 78) and the use of bare feet and natural human movements. Margaret Morris was a pupil of Raymond Duncan, brother of Isadora. She opened her own school of movement training in 1910, and strove to promote her own form of natural movement through courses, performances and her own form of dance notation (subsequently eclipsed by that of Rudolf Laban). Though the work of both was well-known and achieved relative success ('Natural Movement' is still listed as a dance style by the International Society for Teachers of Dance [ISTD] and the International Margaret Morris Movement continues to run courses to promote her work), their work is not as historically significant for theatrical movement training as that of the Greek Revivalist Ruby Ginner (1886–1978).

For Ginner, movement offered a place from which to resist what she saw as the pernicious effects of modern industrial life, forces she perceived as crushing the vitality out of life. After early success as a professional dancer, Ruby Ginner pioneered the revival of Greek Dance in England, founding a school for Greek Dance and Movement with the mime teacher Irene Mawer (the Ginner-Mawer School) and later the Association of Teachers of the Revived Greek Dance in 1923. The 'technique' of Ginner's Revived Greek Dance was based on lines and angles of the arms and body which, in a manner reminiscent of Delsarte, were seen as signifying specific moods (e.g. 'spiritual ecstasy'). Greek dance was associated with the dramatic (hence the association, through Mawer, with mime) and in the early part of the century was conceived of as principally signifying feeling—'Every kind of step, gesture, and pose can be used to express all shades of dramatic feeling' (Ginner, 1933: 64). Ginner was an advocate of a return to classical physical virtue. She saw in the high period of classical Greek culture a model of physical perfection, with the body and the soul integrated in movement. She viewed art as a process of civilization, a struggle to escape from the decadence caused by moral or political weakness. Her view of modern life betrays her nostalgia for a 'golden age' of physical perfection.

> The natural physical rhythms of mankind are being slowly crushed out of existence. In many of the arts and crafts, in the daily necessities of life, in labour, and in travel, the free, glorious, and rhythmic movement of the body has given place to the action of the machine.
>
> (Ginner, 1933: 18)

The twentieth century is here perceived as disruptive, unsettled, a period of upheaval and uncertainty, and movement is proposed as a potential site for resistance. 'In the midst of this struggle the arts are wrestling, somewhat blindly, for a new life; and it is interesting to note that the art of the dance in particular is now of universal appeal' (Ginner, 1933: 11–12). Ginner's approach was deeply moral, and in this sense less 'modern' than that of her contemporaries. She was opposed to the expressive work of Duncan, Dalcroze and others. For Ginner,

> The present fetish for the free expression of personal sensation has, in many of the arts, led to a sentimentality, a lack of restraint and even morality, which is nowhere more obvious than in the art of movement in some of its present forms.
> (Ginner, 1933: 41)

Ginner, like Dalcroze, was participating in a search for body practices which would enable the dancer to discover a unity of body and mind reminiscent of the classical ideal and strongly associated with a concept of an idealized 'natural' state of being.

> A study of the rhythms of Nature is invaluable to the student of the dance.
> In Nature the student will find stability, poise, rhythm, every degree of force and speed. The effort to imitate them will develop these qualities in the human body.
> A sincere study of the movements of Nature will, in both child and adult, exercise the powers of observation, broaden the sympathies and understanding, develop an appreciation of beauty, produce simplicity and directness of thought and action, lift the spirit to joy and the body to exhilaration. The initiation of the rhythms of Nature must always come from personal observation.
> (Ginner, 1933: 140)

Ginner's idealization of the Greek ideal, indicative of the cultural tastes of the period, represents a paradigm of the 'natural/neutral' body which will be an important consideration in the next chapter. Her work is also important in its own right; Ginner's students included many who were to become influential figures in the history of English dance and movement training and performance. Though largely ignored by historians of English dance, she is an important connection between the influences of Duncan and Laban in this country, and vital in placing their influences in a larger cultural context. Echoes of both can be found in her writings, specifically in her attempts to analyze the processes leading to expressive movement:

The movement must pass from the centre outwards, that is, the dancer must have a clear conception in her mind, which will arouse the emotion in her heart, and thus the action will pass from the centre of her physical being outwards to the extremities.

(Ginner, 1933: 144)

Through her work with Irene Mawer, and her commitment to the cultural value of dance and movement, Ginner represents an important English presence in a field dominated by continental practitioners. In supporting the recognition of movement's cultural heritage she contributed significantly to the developing profile of movement training and to its status as part of a professional and sophisticated training for performance. Along with Duncan, Atkinson, Morris and the female principals and teachers at the burgeoning physical education colleges, Ginner provides a strong-minded, passionately committed role model for women in the early decades of the century—promoting a body no longer simply mechanically efficient, but graceful, expressive, flexible and unrestrained.

CRAIG, THEATRE AND MOVEMENT

It has been argued already that Greek Revivalism can be seen as representative of a specifically middle class point of resistance and unease towards the machine. The move towards increased mechanization throughout England, and across Europe, was driven by largely commercial pressures for the application of new technologies. In the late nineteenth century theatre, mechanical and scientific advances led to rapid improvements in stage machinery and stage lighting, improvements naturally welcomed and promoted by the theatre managements of the time and by many of the artists with the vision to perceive the new possibilities for design. The extent to which this mechanization of scenic design provoked consideration of the role of the actor on stage is strikingly evident in the work of Edward Gordon Craig.

Edward Gordon Craig (1872–1966) believed that theatre should not be open to the unpredictability of personal affectation and random trivial impulses, but that it required the performer to become an 'über-marionette', offering an ideal of technical precision. Craig introduced the importance of design as an overall concept in the theatre. The mechanical precision and reliability of the puppet was a potent image for the level of control and awareness Craig suggested should be required of the actor. Craig seems to have felt that movement could form one of the foundations of a new stylized art of the theatre. In the same way that Isadora Duncan sought inspiration in the past for a dance that could be re-born as an art, as an independent medium for expression which did not necessarily rely on music, so Craig also looked to ancient culture, to the Renaissance theatre, and to the Far

East for a theatre suitable for artists rather than 'stars'. In part, Craig's preference for the 'über-marionette' sprang from the problem of finding actors capable of producing the kind of movement effects he desired—his ideas and ambitions for the theatre ran ahead of the training available. The new efficiency Craig sought was not efficiency of imitation, but of revelation; he did not want actors who evaluated their movements in terms of naturalness (superficial similarity to the movements of everyday life), but rather in terms of necessity:

> we have to put the idea of natural or unnatural action out of our heads altogether, and in place of it we have to consider *necessary or unnecessary action*. The necessary action at a certain moment may be said to be the natural action for that moment.
> (Craig, 1911: 35–36)

It is in this sense that we can align Craig's ideas with those of Stanislavski—both searching for a psychophysical efficiency through which the actor's impulses can find their most appropriate expression.

Craig refused to formulate a coherent system of movement training. He had a passionate distrust of all systems—'they threaten genius and stifle expression' (Craig, 1983: 89). This meant that many of his insights and innovations remained page-bound and consequently had little impact on professional practice during his lifetime. His ambitious, positivist mission was to identify the 'rules of movement': 'Craig assumed that there must be logical, *universal* patterns of expressive non-mimetic movement, which had yet to be discovered' (Eynat-Confino, 1987: 79). In this respect he is drawing on the legacy of Delsarte, but also reached forward to the work of others such as Peter Brook and his projects in Iran and Africa in the 1970s (Smith, 1973 and Heilpern, 1977). Craig's influence can be better understood with the perspective of time. His emphasis on the importance of movement, of masks, and of intention and design over chance can now be recognized as a valuable contribution to the efforts to establish acting as a modern art. He was appreciative of the work of Mawer (Craig, 1977: 246–247), and a passionate advocate for Duncan's work. His influence on movement training for actors was constrained by the relatively short life of his own school, and his difficulties in moving beyond theoretical formulations for effective stage movement. He may even, through his insistence on the malleability of the actor and the dominance of the director, have fostered the idea that training should produce an actor who is docile and uncritical. It was to be left to others to find a way of training actors in the movement skills appropriate for a modern artist.

DALCROZE AND THE THEATRE

Dalcroze had from an early stage in his movement-teaching career recognized the value of his work for dancers and performers, but his initial priority was the teaching of music through movement. It was not until 1906 that he was to begin a collaboration that was to bring his ideas and practices the kind of attention that would promote their influence across Europe. The Swiss theatre designer Adolphe Appia (1862–1928) had already been inspired by the work of the composer Richard Wagner, in whose compositions he perceived a liberation of music which enabled it to function as a central driving force within the dramatic action. However, he could not conceive of a way in which the actor, the human body, could also take its place as the carrier of action without breaking the rhythmic spell of the music. Then, in 1906, he attended a demonstration of 'gymnastic rhythmique' by Dalcroze and his pupils in Geneva. He was spurred immediately to write to Dalcroze and to enthuse that,

> Your instruction makes music a thing which concerns the entire body, and thus resolves the problem in the most practical way. No more do you consider the body and its posture: you seek out unity.
> (Spector, 1990: 83)

The collaboration with Appia was fortunate. Appia had the vision to perceive the full implications of Dalcroze's work and to place in his way the challenges which would provoke further innovation and development. Both Appia and Dalcroze seem also to have been aware of the extent to which their aims aspired to a new level of physical virtue.

> In *gymnastique rhythmique* [beauty] is an educative virtue which predisposes the individual to a wise economy of forces. The realisation of beauty is always the natural consequence of it . . . As one communicates to the body a musical problem, it [the body] is transfigured.
> (Appia & Odier, 1990: 88)

His overarching vision was thus built on an understanding of rhythm as the universal element. Rhythm, for Dalcroze, functions to embody and conjoin discourses of beauty and economy in movement. Just as for Marey, Demeny, and Souriau, so for Dalcroze too, these qualities seem related not to some external artificial criteria, but to a perception of the nature of the body in motion. Dalcroze,

> did not conceive of separate forms of rhythm for music, movement, gesture, and speech. There was only one rhythm, and, while it was best developed through music, its "impression" on the body through musical sources would inevitably lead to "expression" in movement and speech.
> (Rogers, 1969: 25)

Appia and Dalcroze's close communication was to last from 1906, through various projects and productions, until Appia's death in 1928. The single most significant and influential collaboration between the two centered around Dalcroze's school of 'Eurhythmics' at Hellerau, near

Dresden in Germany, where Appia was for a decade a member of the staff (see Beacham, 1985 and 1994). In 1909 Dalcroze had given a demonstration in Dresden which so impressed a local businessman that he invited Dalcroze to move his school to Hellerau, a small town constructed around the idea of an harmonious and liberal community. The neo-classical influences in the architecture of the School building also indicate that Hellerau can be seen as participating in the general revival of interest in ancient Greek culture as a model for a vibrant, pre-industrial and 'healthy' approach to physical education.

The success of the Hellerau experiment was bound to draw attention. The appeal of Appia and Dalcroze's unified vision of theatre, music and movement would clearly not be lost on others seeking to revitalize theatre and theatrical expression. At one point it appears that Dalcroze and Appia themselves hoped that 'the outcome of their endeavours will be a new style of acting' (unknown journalist, 1914, in Rogers, 1969: 27). Hellerau was deeply influential as a model for movement and theatre training, its influence undoubtedly assisted by the many great names of the theatre of the period who beat a path to its door, including: Jacques Copeau, Max Reinhardt, Leopold Jeßner, Rudolf Laban, and, importantly for English theatre, Bernard Shaw and Granville Barker (Beacham, 1994: 104). One of the visitors to Hellerau in 1911 was a Russian aristocrat with a passion for theatre and dance, Prince Sergei Wolkonsky. Wolkonsky was Superintendent of Russia's Imperial Theatre, and invited Dalcroze to undertake a demonstration tour of Russia in January 1912 (Nathan, 1997). This tour brought Dalcroze into contact with the actors of Stanislavski's Moscow Arts Theatre, and he also gave a presentation at the state theatre in St. Petersburg, which was under the direction of Vsevolod Meyerhold. Eurhythmics was subsequently to become part of the training at the Moscow Arts Theatre's First Studio in 1912, and to influence both Stanislavski's and Meyerhold's ideas on movement (see Stanislavski, 1979: 48–71; and, Meyerhold, 1969: 149).

Foster (1977) suggests that Eurhythmics were practiced in England from about 1912, and that by 1920, 'over 2,800 pupils had undertaken courses in Eurhythmics in this country and [that] most of these went to run courses for others' (Foster, 1977: 78). Certainly by the 1920s Eurhythmics was being taught in schools and promoted by significant figures in Physical Education (Foster, 1977: 78), and was eventually to impact on the popular imagination through *Music and Movement*, a BBC Radio program for adults and children presented by a trained Dalcroze teacher, Ann Driver. Even as late as the mid-twentieth century, Joan Littlewood was using Eurhythmics as a method to develop her actors' sense of self-awareness and economy of movement (Murray & Keefe, 2007: 153; Leach, 2008: 82). The significance of Dalcroze as a dynamic meeting point for the theories and practice of several teachers both before and after him must not be underestimated. In the introduction to his text on the complete method, *Méthode*

Jaques-Dalcroze: *Pour le développement de l'instinct rythmiques, du sens auditif et du sentiment tonal, en 5 parties* (1906), Dalcroze quotes Delsarte, "To each spiritual function there responds a function of the body; to each big function of the body corresponds a spiritual act." This quotation ties together so much of the development in training for physical expression during this period, resonating for the philosopher (William James), the actor/teacher (Constantin Stanislavski) and the dancer (Isadora Duncan).

A DIFFERENT KIND OF DRAMA SCHOOL

The teaching experiments and theatre innovations of Edward Gordon Craig in Rome, Adolphe Appia and Emile Jaques-Dalcroze at Hellerau, Constantin Stanislavski in Moscow and later Jacques Copeau in Paris, naturally took time to impact on training in England and the rest of Europe. The idea of a drama school as a seedbed for training a 'new breed' of actors, able to cope with the demands of a 'new' theatre, appears to have been a distinctly European concept. Certainly it was an idea which more readily took root in the cultural melting pot of Europe between the Wars. As teachers attempting to apply the rigors of 'modern' scientific inquiry to the nature and practice of theatre, the leading practitioners were required to show a particular faith in the value of research. Their creative passion, and often their own financial commitment, enabled a new vision of theatre and its needs to generate and promote new approaches to training. These innovators were training the actor to become a 'modern' artist—'modern' in the sense that the actor's process was to become more central to the idea of the theatre event. The conventional measure of success for the actor had been their ability to use their 'instrument' effectively within pre-defined, socially constructed parameters and traditional, socially and culturally constructed, 'knowledges' of the body. The new systems and processes suggested however that the actor's success could be measured by the extent to which they were able to explore, to be 'true' to, the potential of their instrument. Implicitly that exploration meant drawing on new 'knowledges' of the body. The 'new' actor would be able to liberate their expressive and creative potential as an actor, through an objective re-discovery of their body, their 'instrument'. The rules for doing things poorly or doing things well, once enshrined in catalogues of gestures and attitudes, were now inscribed on the actor's sense of self. Movement training could be analyzed in respect of its purpose, and improved. Changes in how the body was understood helped provide a receptive cultural environment for the 'improvement' of movement training regimes for actors. In the new training systems we find the implicit assumption that being a better artist/actor meant being a better human being, and conversely that learning how better to function as a person would lead to improvements in the actor's art and in their life. The modern actor has come to embody the performance of self-improvement.

JACQUES COPEAU, MICHEL ST. DENIS AND THE ENGLISH DRAMA SCHOOLS

In 1915, the French theatre director and actor trainer, Jacques Copeau, also visited Dalcroze and was so impressed with eurhythmics as a system of movement training that he invited a Dalcroze pupil, Jessmin Howarth to work as a movement teacher with his company. Miss Howarth reportedly 'not only drilled the troupe regularly each day in rhythmic gymnastics but also observed each rehearsal' (Rogers, 1966: 178–179). Copeau attempted to use eurhythmics as an element in his actor training, but with limited success. He later came to view eurhythmics as too inextricably linked with music and too self-consciously movement orientated to be of use in the training of actors. Copeau turned instead to the physical education methods of Lt. George Hébert (1875–1957), a French physical training instructor, whose 'natural gymnastics' seemed more appropriate for the acquisition of a flexible and responsive body (Felner, 1985: 40–41; Leabhart, 1989: 9–10; Ruffini, 1995: 62). Hébert's method included everyday movements such as 'pulling, pushing, climbing, walking, running, jumping, lifting, carrying, attacking, defending, swimming' (Lecoq, 2000: 71) and he was less obsessively concerned with repetitive exercise than many other instructors of the time. Copeau also devised exercises for his students which focused on detailed and imaginative observation and recreation of the movement of animals, perhaps drawing on the analysis provided by Marey's work on animal movement.

Michel St. Denis was Copeau's nephew, a student at his uncle's École Vieux Colombier in Paris in the 1920s, and his principle disciple. St. Denis first visited England in 1931, on tour with the Compagnie des Quinze, an offshoot of Copeau's Burgundian troupe Les Copiaux. His work attracted much favorable attention in England, and as the Compagnie des Quinze found it increasingly hard to survive financially in France, St. Denis was attracted to the idea of transferring his work to England. In 1935, in collaboration with George Devine, St. Denis founded the first of his schools for actors, The London Theatre Studio. Through his involvement in the London Theatre Studio, and later in the Old Vic School, London, and the Drama Division of the Juilliard School in New York, St. Denis was to become a major influence on the development of English-language drama school training. St. Denis' program was innovative in at least two of its key themes: that the training of the actor should be 'organic', blending the skills and creative training of the actor into work where the elements were 'sympathetically inter-related' (Wardle, 1978: 56); and, that the training, though tailored to the needs of a flexible, modern and creative professional actor, should happen in an environment which set itself outside and apart from the commercial demands of the theatre at large. Though critics (and some students) at the time complained that this was training for work which did not exist (Yvonne Mitchell in McCall, 1978: 81), the pioneering influence of these schools in the post-War period was to be significant.

Ex-pupils of St. Denis were to end up in senior positions in many of the major English drama schools. After the Second World War, drama school principals (both those who had trained with St. Denis and increasingly also those who had not) sought out movement teachers who could provide the same sort of physical training that St. Denis had proposed, including European movement training. Trish Arnold tells how the Principal of LAMDA employed her because he specifically wanted someone to teach movement in the same sort of way as it was taught at the Old Vic School (Arnold, 1999). The interest in what was known at the time as Central European Dance came principally from the influence of Rudolf Laban, Kurt Jooss and Sigurd Leeder (all of whom arrived in England as refugees at the start of the War). Arnold suggests that St. Denis was important both in placing expressive movement at the heart of the new training regimes and in drawing together several continental threads.

St. Denis' vision of a simple ensemble theatre, based on the creative skills of the actor, had no time for the commercial and social niceties of the conventional theatre of the early and mid twentieth century. Irving Wardle writes of St. Denis' teaching at the Old Vic School in the late 1940s:

> Embarrassment was seen as irrelevant because the training took no account of ugliness or beauty. All bodies were instruments, each with its proper range. And whether the student was in possession of a flute or a double-bass, what had to be done was to correct its faults and put it in tune. Hence the initial stripping down process in which the personality was dismantled and the physique returned to the cradle.
> (Wardle, 1978: 111)

Such a statement marks a new 'professionalisation' of the actor's body whereby scientific knowledge of the body and its physical capabilities, its 'nature', is transformed into expert professional knowledge and practice. In this manner the student actor's body is brought within 'the orbit of professional power' (Vertinsky, 1994: 3) and constructed within a network of new knowledges around professionalism and theatricality.

LABAN AND THE ENGLISH DRAMA SCHOOLS

Joan Littlewood refers to 'Central European Movement' classes led by Annie Fligg during her time at RADA in the 1930s as being 'a first taste of Rudolf Laban's work' (Littlewood, 1994: 69). Laban's influence was to develop gradually over the next few decades as pupils from his various teaching establishments went on to perform, teach and research in their own right. His impact was reinforced through the success of a number of publications (including Laban, 1948 & Laban, 1950) which sought to relate his ideas to the teaching of movement and to its potential use in dramatic contexts.

Much of his work was focused on the education of dance teachers in schools and the use of dance as part of a physical education curriculum (Willson, 1997: 38), however his work with Frederick Lawrence (Laban & Lawrence, 1947) on 'Efforts' and the analysis of physical labor was to prove also applicable to the physical characteristics and dynamics of dramatic roles. A number of leading theatre movement teachers (Yat Malmgren, Jean Newlove, and Litz Pisk) trained with Laban or studied his methods. Indeed, Laban was himself interested in setting up courses for mime and theatre movement (Preston-Dunlop, 1998: 257), but none of his plans were to come to fruition. His only direct involvement in actor training appears to have been through Joan Littlewood's Theatre Workshop and Esmé Church's Northern Theatre School in Bradford (Preston-Dunlop, 1998: 240–241).

His work was attractive to those teaching acting on a number of counts. He combined an analysis of movement in 'scientific' terms (observation and deduction) with a conception of the human being as a whole and integrated organism. His analysis of the body and its functioning was rigorous, but not mechanistic, linked as it was both to an understanding of the body's ability to express personality and emotion and to a rejection of Cartesian dualism (Preston-Dunlop, 1998: 32). Laban's psychophysical conception of movement, and the logical coherence of his approach (a condition for one kind of efficiency), have made his work attractive to those seeking a movement approach which is compatible with the logic and structure of Stanislavski's acting theories: 'they are both totally, utterly logical. They have a logic base, and a simple logical language, that is basically about action, drive and motivation and impulse' (Ewan, 1999a). The assimilation of Laban's work into the English drama schools marks the period during which movement began to become a fully rationalized system of training. Laban's methods and ideas, fulfilling the potential suggested by the work of Delsarte and Souriau, brought together the idea of purposeful movement with a vision for its psychological signification. In many respects movement training must have become both more exciting but also more daunting; for those who felt self-conscious in movement there was no longer to be the possibility of hiding behind routine and orderly obedience. For the post-war drama school student, movement training increasingly came to involve disciplined and efficient physical self-expression. Laban's ideas and practices, introduced through the work of his ex-students (for example Jean Newlove and Geraldine Stephenson) and promoted by the success of Littlewood's work with the Theatre Workshop, didn't take long to 'become a staple part of the teaching program of most acting academies' (Barker & McCaw, 2001: 157).

Laban believed that the key to enriching life lay in the exploration of elements common to all human movement.

> It is not artistic perfection or the creation and performance of sensational dances which is aimed at, but the beneficial effect of the creative activity of dancing upon the personality of the pupil.
>
> (Laban, 1948: 11)

Several of Laban's students were to be important in disseminating his practice and ideas. Both Kurt Jooss and Sigurd Leeder, who also found themselves exiled from Germany at the outbreak of the Second World War, incorporated many of Laban's ideas in their performances and in their own teaching. Leeder's teaching approach, which is described in Jane Winearls' book, *Modern Dance: The Jooss-Leeder Method* (1968), was to influence Trish Arnold and her teaching at LAMDA and Guildhall School of Music and Drama. Joan Kemp, a former movement tutor at RADA, was also trained by Leeder. Jane Winearls (1908–2001) was herself a student of Greek Dance with Ruby Ginner in the 1930s, and later trained with Sigurd Leeder. In the 1960s she became the first full-time university lecturer in Dance at Birmingham University.

One ex-student of Laban who has had a profound influence on the application of his ideas to the teaching of movement for actors was Yat Malmgren (1916–2002).

> Central to Malmgren's approach was the body of work entrusted to him by Laban—a precise, detailed analysis of the non-discursive symbolism of dance, expressing import without specific meaning, and of gesture and the role it plays in underlying the act of speech, which forms the basic abstraction of all drama.
>
> (Fettes, 2002)

Malmgren taught for Laban at the Art of Movement Studio between 1954 and 1955. Following the death of Bill Carpenter, with whom Laban had been collaborating on movement and character analysis, Laban was to entrust Malmgren with his unfinished text (Preston-Dunlop, 1998: 263–264). Malmgren combined Laban's system of movement analysis with Jungian typological analysis. Laban had already begun to relate movement to psychological intention. His collaboration with Carpenter, and the later work of Malmgren, related the Jungian psychological functions of Thinking, Sensing, Intuiting and Feeling to Laban's factors of Space, Weight, Time and Flow (O'Connor in Watson, 2001: 51). The basis of his method is that all behavior is reduced to six 'Inner Attitudes'—'Near', 'Mobile', 'Adream', 'Stable', 'Awake' and 'Remote' (O'Connor in Watson, 2001: 51; see also 'The Work of Yat Malmgren' [Video, 1997]). Malmgren resisted invitations to formulate the approach into a published text, preferring instead to insist on the importance of *experiencing* the work. As with any system, it can seem formulaic at first and requires complex combinations of character paradigms to be learnt and employed.

> The physicalisation of motivation, with a corresponding emphasis on the sensate body, is at the heart of [Yat's system] as might be expected from a Laban influenced process. The actor analyzes character in terms of physical, movement-based images, which become icons of action (movement images) that the actor can back-reference in order to inform performance. [Yat's system] negates Cartesian mind-body dualism: the

body is the mind; the mind is the body. Motivation travels from the mind to the body, just as it can journey from the body to the mind. Therefore motivation can begin with an idea or a gesture; a reciprocity exists that means the one will necessarily stimulate the other.

(O'Connor, 2001: 51–52).

In 1954, Malmgren was invited by George Devine to work at the Royal Court and by Laban to work at his Art of Movement Studio in Addlestone, Surrey. He assisted Peter Brook and John Gielgud on their production of *The Tempest*. In 1960 he was invited to join the staff at the Central School of Speech and Drama by John Blatchley (an ex-pupil of Michel St. Denis), and then later joined in the establishment of the Drama Centre London. He remained as a core member of the teaching staff at the Drama Centre until his retirement in 2001. A thorough and detailed analysis of Malmgren's system can be found in Vladimir Mirodan's unpublished PhD thesis (Mirodan, 1997).

Just as influential as Malmgren for many current movement tutors was the Austrian-born movement teacher, Litz Pisk (1909–1997). As a young girl, Pisk had been sent to study with Isadora Duncan's sister, Elizabeth. She later trained as a designer (working with Bertolt Brecht among others), leaving Austria for England in 1933 where she taught at RADA before being asked to join the staff of the Old Vic Theatre School. Her teaching has clear links to that of Laban (Preston-Dunlop, 1998: 257), but, like Malmgren, she developed an approach that was distinctively her own. Pisk provides a link between the central European dance traditions of Duncan, Laban and Dalcroze and the new drama training within St. Denis' schools and their offshoots. In terms obviously attractive to the actor, she refers for example to movement as something which, 'starts from an impulse and is joined to the centre of the mover' and which springs from the actor's 'physical, emotional and mental sources' (Pisk, 1975: 9). A charismatic personality and an influential teacher, Pisk provided a powerful role model for women movement teachers in the latter half of the twentieth century.

ALEXANDER TECHNIQUE FOR ACTORS

At the end of the nineteenth century 'deportment' was a common part of the theatrical education of the aspiring actor. The influence of Ling and Delsarte, though valuable in other respects, did little to change this kind of approach, dealing as they did with mechanical efficiency and the symbolic significance of movement. The learning of correct body use was still associated with drill and discipline rather than with therapeutic self-improvement. By the early twentieth century, posture and deportment must increasingly have seemed unnecessarily blunt as educational and therapeutic tools for the training of actors. For the student actor, the Alexander Technique provides a model of the body as more subtly perfectible, despite the disfiguring effects of modern life. Economy and efficiency of movement are, within the Alexander Technique, re-categorized so that movement can be assessed against process rather than 'end-gaining'. The Technique is thus able to combine physiological alignment with individual intention, psychophysical process and personal body use. The resultant movement aesthetic is based on economy, personal expression, and freedom from inhibition. Though the Alexander Technique has become a feature of the movement training at several drama schools, its influence has been limited by two factors. On the one hand the costs for the ideal arrangement of one-to-one tuition can often be prohibitive or restrictive without adequate funding; and on the other, Laban-based approaches have tended, through their more rapid dissemination, to dominate the field. Niamh Dowling's position at Manchester Metropolitan University [MMU] as Head of Theatre, as well as Alexander-trained Movement tutor, is therefore worthy of note. Within the training at MMU, the Alexander Technique is central not only to Movement, but also to Voice and Acting—'the whole course now tends to have a very strong physical foundation' (Dowling, 2000). For Dowling, 'the Alexander Technique is (. . .) fundamentally about releasing the imagination' (Dowling, 2000). Just as with Laban's work, the psychophysical nature of the Alexander Technique is valued for its alignment with conventional acting methods: 'it's a psychophysical activity, for that reason it feeds really well into Stanislavski work which talks about a psychophysical activity' (Dowling, 2000).

It has taken Alexander's work several decades to get to the point where it now has a significant influence on movement training for many actors. But its influence has also paved the way for the impact of similar approaches such as the work of Moshe Feldenkrais (Movement Awareness and Functional Integration) and Gerda Alexander (Eutony) and their synthesis in the work of Monika Pagneux, with whom Niamh Dowling studied. Much of this work, which flourished with the growth in interest in somatic therapies during the 1960s, is only just beginning to impact on actor training in the United Kingdom and has been subject to only limited critical examination. These somatic practices represent a desire to 'work on' the body, coupled with a recognition of the mechanistic and soulless nature of traditional gymnastics. Gymnastics saw the body as the problem—prone as it was to disease, error, irrationality and desire; somatic practices suggest the body as the solution—possibly too much so. Whilst both Alexander (and later Feldenkrais) sought heightened awareness and conscious control of the body, this was not to happen simply through reason, but through the muscles re-educating the mind (Shusterman, 2000). The Feldenkrais approach does not restrict its intervention to the function of the 'primary control' (the head/neck/shoulder relationship) which is so central to Alexander Technique, and may have much to offer actor training in helping to move the emphasis of movement training away from the head and towards a more grounded physicality. However the relatively small number of qualified Feldenkrais teachers means that it is not likely seriously to challenge the Alexander Technique for some time.

JACQUES LECOQ, THE FERRYMAN AND THE ATHLETE—RESEARCHING THE ECONOMY OF PHYSICAL ACTION

Jacques Lecoq (1921–1999) in many ways draws together a number of the threads of this chapter. Lecoq trained initially as a movement therapist and 'came from a background in sport and kinesiology, in which he was trained to analyse movement' (Leabhart, 1989: 100). He began to teach physical education at the age of nineteen and approached the teaching of movement to theatre people in the same way as he had taught athletes to swim (Leabhart, 1989: 88). He was introduced into theatre work through the co-operative society, 'Education par le jeu dramatique' (EPJD), which was founded in 1946 by leading figures of the French theatre of the time. After the war, Jean Dasté (Copeau's son-in-law) saw Lecoq perform with a young student group and asked him to join his company in Grenoble. Under Dasté, Lecoq continued to study Copeau's particular mix of maskwork, acrobatics and theatre movement. From 1948 to 1956 Lecoq lived, worked and taught in Italy, an experience which enabled him to explore the popular roots of the Italian tradition of Commedia dell'Arte, and of tragedy. This combination of dramatic movement analysis and his wide ranging knowledge of physical education, and the application of both in the practice of accessible theatre, has been important in the sustained success of his teaching career until his death in 1999. As a teacher, Lecoq has directly influenced a significant number of English drama school movement tutors (including: Trish Arnold, Shona Morris, Sue Lefton, and Jane Gibson) and indirectly influenced many more.

The ideas of Delsarte and Souriau would have been part of Lecoq's cultural heritage, but he was also aware of the 'natural gymnastics' of Georges Hébert. John Rudlin traces a direct line from Georges Hébert, to M. Moine (a Hébert trained teacher at Copeau's École de Vieux Colombier), to Jean Dorcy and Jean Dasté, and finally to Jacques Lecoq (Rudlin in Hodge, 2000: 68). Lecoq admits his own debt to Hébert's natural method in his book, *The Moving Body* (2000: 71). Lecoq's Paris school was to find its final home in a disused gymnasium, a symbolic return he himself noted with approval (Lecoq, 2001: 12). Lecoq's meticulous approach to the analysis of movement owes much to the French tradition of scientific, anthropological and philosophical movement analysis represented by the work of Marey, Souriau, Paul Bellugue (Professor of Anatomy at the École des Beaux Arts in Paris from 1936 to 1955) and Marcel Jousse (anthropologist and author of *Anthropologie du Geste* [1974]). The teachers at his school, whilst all ex-pupils, have also brought a range of other influences to bear within the pedagogy of the school (e.g. Monika Pagneux, who trained with Mary Wigman and with Moshe Feldenkrais). His teaching also owes much to his study of Commedia dell'Arte and other stylized forms of physically expressive theatre (Tragedy, Melodrama, Pantomime Blanche, Clowns).

There is a passage in the video film of Lecoq's work and teaching, *Les Deux Voyages de Jacques Lecoq* (1999), where we see Lecoq teaching a movement sequence based around the action of the *passeur* (water boatman). Lecoq demonstrates the relaxed and easy action of the *passeur* in a short and cyclical mime sequence, pointing out to the students the moments of push and pull, the dynamics of the action, the correlation between action and breath. In his book *The Moving Body* (2001), Lecoq mentions this exercise in the context of a section entitled 'Researching the Economy of Physical Action', where he describes the place within his teaching which he gives to the close reproduction of 'everyday' physical actions:

> For this I make use of labouring trades: the boatman, the man working with a shovel or a pick, the wood-cutter, or I use sports exercises, such as pull-ups or weight lifting (. . .) Avoiding psychological explanations, we research the most economical form of a physical action, so that it can serve as a reference point.
>
> (Lecoq, 2001: 77–79)

Watching the video it is possible to see the relaxed ease and grace with which Lecoq, at this point in his late seventies, manages the imaginary pole. His delight and fascination in the rhythms and dynamics of the action is clear, he seems to 'taste' the movement as he performs it. Perhaps this can be understood as one way in which the physical action is embodied as a reference point. 'Tasting' the movement enables its actions, its sensations and its impulses to be compared to the psychophysical memory of past performances of this and other actions. Soon he has the group of students he is teaching exploring the movements, 'tasting' the actions, and developing a sense of the dramatic potential each action contains.

Lecoq's interest in this and in similar 'labouring' actions may well have some of its origins in his early training as a sports physiotherapist, but may also come from his time working with Jean Dasté's company Les Comediens de Grenoble in Grenoble. As an ex-pupil of Jacques Copeau, Dasté would no doubt have introduced the young Lecoq to Hébert's system of gymnastics (which Dasté had learnt as a student and used in his own teaching). The work of Dasté's troupe must also have drawn on his experiences with Les Copiaux, Copeau's rural experiment in taking a theatre of simple means to unsophisticated audiences in rural France, surely also an influence on Lecoq's fascination with simple physical labor. The *passeur* exercise, and the experiences that influenced its adoption within his pedagogy, reflect Lecoq's deep respect for the actions of the laboring man or woman. Lecoq's attention to detail is a form of testament to these invisible actors/teachers. A fascination with labor is also an attitude with a certain cultural history, evidenced for example in Etienne Decroux's mime performances of manual labor (*Le Menuisier* and *La Lessive*, 1945) and factory labor (*L'Usine*, 1946), in Dario Fo's interest in the relationship between Italian song and the actions of Venetian boatmen (Fo, 1991: 31–33) and in Laban's work on 'efforts' with Frederick Lawrence (Laban & Lawrence, 1947). In each case, the actions of laborers are examined as the sources for sets of movements and gestures, which become abstracted within specific cultural economies of the body. In this way the actions and regulations of physical labor are placed centrally among the ways of knowing the body proposed by the teaching. The practices of Lecoq and other mime practitioners (Decroux, Marceau, Barrault and Fo) are often concerned with the aestheticisation of the actions of labor. However, though reminiscent of the time and motion studies of laborers' movements by Taylor (1911) and Gilbreth (1911), Lecoq's analysis is closer to that of Laban in that it aims not simply to improve functional efficiency through abstraction, but also to explore the relationship of specific actions to dramatic impulses, evocative of emotional and dramatic states. Significantly, where Laban analyses movement through the abstraction of his eight movement Efforts, Lecoq uses the movement of the elements, of materials, of animals, never allowing abstraction to draw the student out of the world with which they must dramatically engage.

In late eighteenth and the early nineteenth century England the annual competitions between professional water boatmen began to attract attention from amateur rowers, an interest which was eventually to lead to the development of rowing as an amateur sport by Oxbridge colleges (Holt, 1990: 108–109). By the twentieth century, punting had become strongly associated with the leisure activities of a privileged few. Its evolution into a sport is described in detail in R. T. Rivington's book *Punting: Its History and Techniques* (1983). Rivington values efficiency of movement: 'The fault of the novice (. . .) is to use too much effort' (Rivington, 1983: 173). His detailed description of 'correct' punting techniques and styles neatly illustrates the abstraction of the ferryman's skills through the construction of punting techniques based on scientific knowledge of the body and its physical capabilities. The ferryman's labor activity is thus transformed into expert knowledge and practice. Looking over Rivington's step-by-step illustrations of punting technique or the efforts of Lecoq School students to mime the action of '*le passeur*', it is possible to read the production of a 'body-which-performs' and of a body which through that performance is culturally re-positioned within a specific and controlled sphere of knowledge. The performance of the activity of punting is however a representation, an imitation, a discursive re-writing of the act of labor. The physical actor and the sportsperson do not 'ferry' anyone anywhere; their 'journey' is symbolic. This abstraction of the form of an action marks an attempted erasure of the discursive inscriptions of class and labor around punting. It marks a desire on the part of the actor and the athlete to ennoble their practice; an action's quality can now be judged on its efficient performance and not in relation to its historico-cultural context. Yet this aestheticized action is nonetheless a haunted action, left largely unfilled with the life-blood of functional intention, awaiting purpose, seeking justification. It is into this void that Lecoq places the possibility of dramatic significance.

The Lecoq school students seek to perform the action of punting with clarity and efficiency. Going (literally) nowhere, they must search inwards for purpose and direction; in the void opened up by the absence of functional intention arises the students' own need to make sense of the actions. We see the students repeat sections of the exercise, 'tasting' the action and exploring possible dramatic intentions for their movements. Presumably, for Lecoq, it is this desire to 'make sense' of their actions which draws the students' psychic energies through the dramatic space and into the environment in which they are performing. Likewise, the outer space of the physical actions is mapped onto the inner psychic space of the student performer. The efficiency of the body is thus repositioned from the purely functional performance of actions with the minimum expenditure of energy, to include the production of a dramatic interior space within which the actions and movements generate meaning. Psychology is avoided, in the sense that it is not the starting point for the student, yet its effect is produced through the exercise—a relationship between the actions of the body and the inner space of the performer is generated through their enactment.

Field notes from the observation of classes show that the use of exercises to evoke 'inner' dynamics is a teaching method also used in drama school training

> Tutor suggests that it is like testing the language of efforts to see how well it works within the task, does it 'hold water'. They should look for 'inner' and 'outer' movement—the effort may be visible, maybe not. They need to experience the movement sequence to explore the thought or feeling that is motivating it, creating the 'inner' movement effort.
> (Field notes—observation of class at Central School, 13 March 2001)

Lorna Marshall (movement researcher and former movement tutor at RADA), in her book *The Body Speaks*, likewise advises her readers:

> As you make an action, try to 'listen' to what is happening inside your consciousness. What does this movement evoke in you? A feeling? A memory? A mood? An atmosphere? (. . .) All are aspects of your inner landscape.
> (Marshall, 2001: 26)

The significance of the student's construction of an interior self in this manner will be examined in further detail in Chapter 3.

DRAMA SCHOOLS, HIGHER EDUCATION AND TRAINING FOR WORK

The educational environment in which vocational drama training now takes place has changed almost beyond recognition from its condition at the start of the twentieth century. Two reports (HEFCE, 1999 & Marchant, 2001) have highlighted the extent to which actor training has increasingly become part of the much wider Higher Education economy. The institutional developments which have led to the assimilation of the drama schools' courses into the HE sector have been driven by a mix of economics and educational politics. The ability of the major drama schools to offer places to the most talented students was initially compromised at the start of the twentieth century by the lack of any system of organized student funding. This situation was only partially rectified after the Second World War by the implementation of a discretionary student grant system; a system which was subject to gradual erosion during the 1980s and 1990s as pressure on the funding of Higher Education increased nationally. Attempts were made to address this situation in 1997 through the Arts Council's Interim Funding Scheme, which led to a subsequent government-funded scholarship award system in 1999. This scheme, the Dance and Drama Awards (DaDA), is currently funded by the Learning and Skills Council, and assists with fees and maintenance for up to 58% of students at independent vocational training institutions. During the second half of the century the number of drama schools rose slowly, as did the number of University and College courses offering training in theatre performance skills (until 1998 degree courses attracted mandatory student grants). The intensive training offered by the drama schools necessitates a relatively low staff-student ratio and high contact hours, which also means that the drama schools, most of which are without significant financial resources or assets, are forced to charge fees at a level high enough to pay directly for that level of tuition. The annual tuition fees for drama school degree courses in acting are currently around just over £3,000, with the rest of the costs being covered by the 'parent' Higher Education institution. The average annual tuition fees for an acting course at an independent drama school can be as much as £10,000, making the total cost of training at an independent London drama school as much as £50,000 (NCDT 2004). As of 2008, NCDT figures indicate that 56% of drama school students are on degree courses, 39% are on DaDA courses (with only three fifths in receipt of a scholarship), and 5% are paying full costs at an independent accredited school. The financial realities for students have influenced drama school governance such that the majority of courses are now degree programs in Higher Education and are state funded. There are suggestions that universities may in the future be allowed to charge what they consider to be the market worth of their courses. Such a move might eventually narrow the financial distinction between a university degree and a drama school training, or it may offer 'parent' universities the opportunity to charge what they perceive as the higher market value of the conservatoire-style actor training in their course portfolios. The latter scenario may even encourage an increase in the number of conservatoire-style courses.

The influence of NCDT accreditation processes and the validation processes for Higher Education bodies has without a doubt had its positive aspects. The nature and purpose of the training has been rigorously examined and clear statements have been produced regarding the aims and objectives of the courses. The relationship between the training offered and the demands of the industry has also been more closely scrutinized. The transition into the Higher Education sector has not, however, been without problems, many of which arise from deep-rooted divisions over educational aims and the principles informing them. The relationship with the theatre industry has always been a necessary consideration in the design of actor training. The drama schools have, for instance, traditionally measured their status and success by the number of their graduates who gain employment on stage or screen, as much as by the artistic excellence of their student productions or the innovative practice of their teachers. Historically several of the major drama schools have institutionalized their relationship with the industry through the development and/or maintenance of close liaisons with theatre companies. NCDT course accreditation has operated to strengthen the connection; graduates of NCDT accredited courses now qualify for full membership of the actor's union, Equity, on completion of their course. However from the mid-twentieth century onwards a significant contradiction is revealed at the heart of this relationship, a contradiction deepened in some respects by the gradual assimilation of vocational drama training into the publicly funded education sector. Two potentially conflicting agendas are at work within the current organization of training provision. On the one hand, the industry demands new performers who are able to demonstrate specific skills and abilities (such as those specified in the NCDT *Accreditation Guide* [2008]). On the other hand, there is a strong sense of the need to try and look ahead to the needs of the industry in the next ten or twenty years. Similarly the students themselves, whilst they recognize the importance of industry level competence, feel that the learning of skills and techniques is not, for them, distinguishable from a broader and more profound personal journey. Actors are 'driven artists', that is to say that alongside the desire to be competent at their craft there is an equally pressing sense in which they undertake their work as part of a personal, and personally satisfying, mission (Throsby, 1994).

In the end we are faced with the contradiction that the system as currently constituted trains efficient bodies for an inefficient industry. Although, '[it] has been estimated that there are just under one million people in Britain looking for work in and around the acting industry' (NCDT, 2002), nonetheless (or as a consequence) the 'working' life of the actor revolves around long periods of unemployment and underemployment. The inefficiency of the system creates an economy of poverty, where the industry can in effect 'cherry-pick' from a vast pool of aspiring, well-trained potential employees.

> Except for those at the top of the profession actors earn comparatively low salaries and most have to undertake temporary periods of alternative employment between engagements.
>
> (NCDT, 2002)

Flexibility, endurance and efficiency as an actor are the cost of getting a job. An actor's career and status is relentlessly defined by their current ability, not their past achievement. In many respects acting has always required flexible responses, but as the traditional forms of theatre dissolve under the gradual effect of the digital and new media revolution, that need for flexibility is likely to be intensified.

> In the nineteenth century, fatigue "provided the key to the efficient utilization of the body's energies by determining its internal limit" (. . .); in our day [and for the actor], flexibility may play a similar role.
> (Martin, 1997: 552)

Despite the fact that the theatre industry is increasingly awake to the value of movement training for actors, the multiple psychophysical efficiencies of the actor are tested to the limit (as they always have been) by the inefficient nature of the industry. The student actor, constantly encouraged to interrogate their body's expressive potential, cannot be prepared for the inertia and waste of unemployment.

CONCLUSION

> [T]he right gesture never does more than is necessary.
> (Harrop, 1992: 46)

Science placed physiology at the heart of the search for an objective understanding of good body use. As a result we have seen how engineering, anatomy and sport came to provide important paradigms for correct and efficient movement. Theatre (and dance) accommodated these paradigms within their training systems not simply because of their scientific probity, but also because they have become part of the aesthetics of the time—a modernist aesthetic of simplicity, purposefulness, logic, and health. A system of actor training may thus be conceived of as 'efficient' on several levels; but it can never detach itself from the general discourses of efficiency. On one level the aim of actor training might be conceived of as providing the industry with a competent and well-skilled work force—that is to say that student actors are well trained in all the skills which are necessary to enable them to fulfill contractual obligations with regard to the parts they are hired to perform. However on another level efficiency might also be taken to relate to the ease with which the trained actor can achieve self-expression or the creative interpretation of the work of others—that is to say that the psychophysical processes of expression operating within the actor should work with as little interruption, inhibition or distortion as possible. There is of course some overlap here—the two aspects both complement and conflict with each other. The tension between training for work and learning for living is central to the history of movement training of actors and in some respects marks the intersection between themes to be developed in two later chapters. It also marks an important point of divergence between the professional actor and the performer who may seek deliberately to work outside the culture and economy of the conventional theatre industry. Alternative theatre/training practice has tended to develop outside the drama schools within the supportive framework of a small community (Odin Teatret, Gardzienice), within higher education institutions (universities or art colleges), or from within the expanding network of workshop and short course opportunities (International Workshop Festival, Centre for Performance Research). Significantly, all of these offer opportunities for what might easily be conceived of as wasteful, excessive activity in that it is typically non-linear, selective and shares much with the development of alternative lifestyles and holistic body practice.

If training for actors focuses too strictly on the efficient body it will become restrictively functional and vocational and will cease to be able to provide a force for change and development within the industry. Likewise, if drama schools become less and less independent and increasingly rely on their connections with the industry and the Higher Education sector, it is likely that the opportunities to experiment will become fewer. Drama schools are repositories for significant knowledge and experience, but could they do more to provide, encourage and draw on experiment and research? Research and experiment may not be 'efficient' (a hotly contested issue in early twenty-first century higher education policy) but surely they are necessary to ensure that training is not only industry relevant, but also able to respond to the changes beginning to impact on the traditional industry. The production of physically or psychophysically efficient actors is a complex process that requires the delivery and acquisition of sophisticated body-knowledge. The demands of the industry and the marginal position of movement training within the institution (until fairly recently) may mean that concepts of physical efficiency will be largely determined and judged by industry norms. Efficiency would thus become ideologically linked to access to the profession. If only trained actors can fulfill their professional requirements efficiently then the role of the expert movement tutor is assured and may even be maintained without reference to the activity of acting itself (might teachers no longer need to practice as performers?). Recent criticisms of the conventional training of actors (Mamet, 1998) focus on the manner in which dominant approaches to acting operate through a power/knowledge modality, but this does not completely eclipse the obvious reality that some level of physical competence and co-ordination is a necessary element of effective stage communication. In fact actor training may be an important example of the ways in which training and education can work to create a place for potential resistances to docility. Training that simply aims to meet the needs of the theatre industry can, as a result, become inherently conservative. Nonetheless, the competitive drive to find better ways for student actors to learn can draw in new ideas, new ways of working, and new conceptions of the body. The power dynamics of the industry are such that most training innovations will struggle to impact significantly on conventional theatre practice. Such changes, just as at the start of the twentieth century, require financial support, individual dedication, powerful advocates and the commitment of students to a vision that has not yet come to fruition if they are to become established.

There can be no doubt that it is in the actor's interest, both as a potential employee and as a creative artist, to develop efficient, uninhibited body use and economical management of their physical and psychophysical resources. The movement training of actors offers a complex but resonant paradigm for the late capitalist human condition. Actors find themselves on an intersection where the docile body of the hired laborer meets the unruly body of the creative artist; where training inscribes the body as at once 'natural' and 'universal', and as individual and rebellious. The theatre industry requires student actors to learn to manage their bodies and their emotions in the service of a director and a playwright, creating a situation where it is inherently difficult for the actor to reconcile what may be consciously shown and what may be somatically felt. Yet at the same time, the same industry demands spontaneity, charisma and unpredictability to maintain key aspects of its offer to its consumers. In fact this very schism is, in some views of the acting process, basic to the actor's ability to function as an actor. The movement training of the actor is an important part of a process which (usually) aims to *empower* the student, enabling them to understand the nature of this schism between efficiency and inhibition, to make creative use of the social construction of feelings, and to reconnect to an 'unconsciously knowing body' (Williams & Bendelow, 1998: 143). Such 'body-knowledge' could be of real benefit to a society struggling to deal with the emotional division of labor, class, gender and ethnicity. These issues will inform the content of the chapters that follow.

2 The 'Neutral' Body, the 'Natural' Body and Movement Training for Actors

The human body is the ground zero of our being.
(Polhemus, 1998: 102)

Historically, dominant knowledges of the body have sought to prioritize and universalize certain functions of the actor's body, typically functions that are considered to participate in producing effects (arousal, intrigue, desire, amazement or terror) upon the spectator. Such knowledges validate, and are in turn validated by, the socio-economic structures of the theatre industry, which prioritize such effects as productive and profitable. Actors' bodies have then been trained (and hired) in direct relation to their ability to fulfill these functions. Nobility, grace, beauty, sensuousness, agility, vitality, athleticism, and poise have all been valued for certain roles; likewise robustness, coarseness, plainness, ugliness, fatness, aggression, hesitancy and clumsiness have been (more selectively) valued for others. The former set of attributes has generally been dominant in setting the norm of the actor's body in twentieth century theatre. Against this norm, all actors' physical attributes are subsequently positioned in a clear socio-cultural and economic hierarchy. Actors, for example, are generally expected to be able-bodied in order to perform in the major companies and play the major parts. Thus the actor understandably desires a body ready for work, able to generate varied, multiple and fluid meanings, in effect a body which within the parameters of theatrical taste at any particular time, can perform as 'natural' and able to engage in an uninhibited manner with their environment so as to create the illusion of 'naturalness'. In this sense, the Occidental actor desires a body that is understood in theatrical terms as 'neutral'. For the actor then, the 'neutral' body is a body 'ready to work' (Morris, 1999) and also a body shaped by the cultural history and the cultural economics of the 'natural' body.

This chapter is therefore concerned with the notions of the 'natural' and the 'neutral' body within the historical formulation of movement training, and the significance of these concepts for an appreciation of contemporary professional actor training. It will examine the genealogy of these concepts and analyze the manner in which they are applied in practice. After Foucault and Butler, the 'natural' body and the 'neutral' body can no longer be treated as simple material entities, but should also be recognized as ideological constructs and as pointers to complex and specialist discursive practices and processes. Broadly speaking, this chapter will map the progression from training regimes based on the acquisition of specific skills and a 'naturalness' which was socially recognizable, towards regimes which increasingly recognize the diversity of bodies and their needs. We can recognize in Shona Morris' assertion that,

> [T]he neutral body isn't the perfect body. The neutral body is *your* neutral body, is your body without tension, with alignment that is physiologically possible for your body'
>
> (Morris, 1999)

that this is a pedagogy that is based on process not just product, on the acceptance of difference. It is a pedagogy that is responsive to the personal and professional needs of individual students. It is also a pedagogy with its own cultural history.

The previous chapter has examined the manner in which concepts of physical and psychophysical efficiency were and are constructed in relation to what is 'natural'. The 'neutral' body draws inevitably on the same discourses, whilst remaining situated within the actor training economy. The development of the 'neutral' body of the actor can, for instance, be historically situated in relation to changes in aesthetic tastes and in the employment structures within the theatre industry at the start of the twentieth century. The 'stock' company (where certain 'types' of actor played certain 'types' of roles) was a system which, despite its failings, survived from its early Tudor origins until well into the twentieth century. As late as the start of the twentieth century, plays were still being written with the structure of the 'stock' company in mind, and actors were being employed with regard to their ability to fill a particular type of part. However significant changes were under way, patterns of employment in the theatre had started to change from as early as the mid-nineteenth century, when the advent of the railways had led to changes in the touring patterns of theatre companies and in the nature and length of contracts. At the start of the twentieth century the number of middle class actors entering the profession increased markedly (Sanderson, 1984: 12–23 & 293) reflecting a change in the social status of the profession which was also accompanied by changes in the nature of plays written for the theatre and in the social presentation of the theatre event itself as a sophisticated and civilized activity. Over the first half of the new century, this was to mean the slow demise of the 'stock' system. At the same time, as we have seen in the previous chapter, significant changes were taking place in the training of bodies for industry, military service, medical experiment, and sports, and of course

The 'Neutral' Body, the 'Natural' Body and Movement Training 71

for artistic, creative, popular or erotic performance. If the actor's body were to be rigorously and purposefully trained (and increasing demands on the versatility and skill of the actor clearly meant that it was), then that training would inevitably come under pressure to be measurable against some approved standards. Such benchmarks needed to be flexible, effective and physiologically sound, to appear politically uncontroversial, and to provide a solid base for the development of theatrical technique. The drama schools, as a result, faced the difficult task of providing a training which was efficient and also relevant to the industry it supplied; which increasingly had to enable actors to expand beyond the restrictions of the 'stock' system to the multiple challenges of the repertory company; and yet, which was nonetheless acceptable to the tastes of the largely middle class constituency from which it drew most of its students. Thus the twentieth century actor gradually ceased to require a body which was narrowly and conventionally efficient within the terms of the nineteenth century theatre and started to recognize a need instead for a body which was organically efficient, flexible and expressive—in effect more 'natural'. The concept of the 'natural' body was to provide an acceptable foundation on which architecturally to design, measure, support and construct the 'neutral' body of the new student actor. Understanding the historical and cultural construction of the 'natural' body is thus an important element in understanding the embodied operation of historical ideologies of power, knowledge and efficiency within movement training of the actor's body.

'NATURAL' BODIES AND EARLY TWENTIETH CENTURY ACTORS

In the late nineteenth and early twentieth century several discourses operated, sometimes explicitly sometimes tacitly, to identify and establish the cultural identity of the 'natural' body. Such a body was to be variously perceived as unfettered, undivided, uncorrupted, unurbanized and even undressed (Toepper, 1997). In this respect the 'natural' body was also a (contested) site for the negotiation of ethnic, gender, and class identity and of notions of health and disability. Such negotiations were, and indeed still are, intensely political and in this respect are representative of the struggles for power over the multiple bodies of modern society. We must therefore regard the idea of the 'natural' body with suspicion; twentieth century history has certainly taught us to be wary of attempts to prioritize particular bodies as more or less 'natural' than others (see previous chapter; also Burt (1998) and Taylor & van der Will [1990]). Throughout the twentieth century, the association of movement training of various kinds (e.g. sport, dance and exercise) with the concept of the 'natural' body aimed to 'elevate' such activities, and operated to give them social, aesthetic and ethical respectability. This relationship also worked in the opposite direction, so that the 'natural' body rapidly came to be seen as a 'body-which-moved'. In so far as acting sought to become more 'natural', it had of necessity then to encourage the body of the actor to move, to move expressively, and to do so 'naturally'.

During the late nineteenth and the early twentieth centuries, the idea of the 'natural' body evoked specific discursive practices operating within the modernist project: the application of knowledges developed within the 'natural sciences' to the analysis of the body; 'naturalness' as efficient, purposeful and economical body-use; the isolation of the body as a site of aesthetic pleasures; and public reaction to urban expansion and rural revival. We have seen earlier how the tensions that these practices produced are revealed in the dilemmas faced by the early German 'ausdrucktanz' movement, which by the 1930s found itself caught between the 'natural' (liberated, often naked) dancing body and the 'natural' (regimented and regulated) national body. The 'natural' body inherently raises the possibility of an embodied subjectivity which is somehow more healthy, integrated, organic and expressive and less restricted, inhibited, alienated and awkward than an 'unnatural' body. Institutions of social, economic or political power might of course seek to manipulate such an ideal towards achieving a healthy, strong, pliant and content workforce/militia/breeding-stock. Nonetheless such a contested site as the 'natural' body might also (perhaps even by virtue of its instability) provide a point from which disciplines and coercions around the body could be identified, located and even resisted.

The complexity of the cultural construction of the 'natural' body is clearly evident with respect to bodies of gender and of class. Many of the drama schools, at the start of the century, were financially compelled to accept students on their ability to pay the fees, and as a result tended to find themselves used as finishing schools despite their aspirations to be rigorous training providers for the profession. Typically women outnumbered men by a significant ratio, and many attended simply 'to learn deportment and similar graces' (Norman MacDermott in Sanderson, 1984: 49). To the extent that the student actor's body was 'naturalized' within this training, it was educated to appear 'natural' in a set of very specific social circumstances or their theatrical representation. The new training offered at institutions such as [R]ADA and Central School of Speech and Drama sought to elevate the status of the acting profession and as such the trained actor's body was to be a body which could dance, fence and use mime and gesture eloquently. The training implicitly characterized working class physicality as clumsy, coarse, awkward and thus 'unnatural'. The performance of working class physicality was only acceptable in a 'character' role, elsewhere it was restricted to working class entertainments such as the Music Halls, Variety, and the Circus, where robust and vernacular physical expression had long established traditions of its own. Those performers whose bodies did not conform to the norm would find their opportunities for work restricted to sensationalist drama, fairgrounds or the circus. An actor with a disability could only succeed if she or he was able to conceal it through skill, costume or force of reputation, or if they were to trade on the Victorian fascination with the 'unnatural'.

Whereas for men the 'natural' body acted historically as a discourse that permitted them to negotiate a revitalized and newly expressive masculinity through the practice of 'physical culture', women were generally still expected to accept that their body was 'naturally' conditioned for social and domestic roles. The predominance of middle class women students within the early drama schools may therefore in part explain the focus on gentler forms of exercise such as calisthenics, dance, gesture and deportment. Grace, control and expression were prioritized over strength and vigor. Such an emphasis, whilst attractive or acceptable to middle class students, also had its critics. Joan Littlewood, for instance, during her time as a student at RADA between the wars, found little to stimulate or interest her in much of the training—with the important exception of Annie Fligg's classes in Central European Movement. The nature of the training also contributed to the creation of the stereotypical image of the physically effeminate male acting student. Certainly some successful male actors of the time made a point of emphasizing a robust heterosexual physicality as part of their approach to acting. Sir Frank Benson, for example, notoriously insisted on rigorous sports practice for his company, such as: 'soccer, rugby, water polo, hockey, cricket, etc.' (Benson, 1931: 41). For Benson, the young actor should learn 'to fence with both hands, single stick, foils, sword and buckler, sword and dagger and bayonet exercise, riding, running, rowing, swimming, walking, dancing, jumping, etc.' (Benson, 1931: 55), a daunting array of physically demanding activities, perhaps more honored in the breach than the observance. Despite the acting profession's history as a generally tolerant and supportive environment with respect to sexuality and gender, it is also clear that the body and movement training of the actor could still mark important boundaries. At the same time, the increased access to and interest in movement, health and fitness, initiated in part by male physical culture, was also to create a social environment in which women could negotiate a body which could be active, un-corseted, expressive, at ease—in effect more physically 'present', and in which men were increasingly permitted to move expressively and with grace and finesse.

PARADIGMS OF THE 'NATURAL' BODY

We can more clearly understand how these changes came to pass by examining the key cultural paradigms of the 'natural' body in operation during this period. Jen Tarr (2002) argues that the early twentieth century concept of the 'natural' body arose out of dissatisfaction with the physical degeneration created by industrial society. As such, the 'natural' body rapidly came to be associated with models of the body drawn from the natural sciences, from the study of and nostalgia for childhood, from anthropology and from classical history. Concerns around racial purity were equally important in forming the parameters for the 'natural' body within what was at the time a strongly imperialist culture. These paradigms represented potent images of a pre-lapsarian body, a body placed at a distance from the debilitating influences of modern industrial society and which is in or has returned to a pure state of existence, unsullied by modern life; a body reconnected to its organic physical possibilities (although uncritical of its cultural preferences). For the student actor, these and other paradigms have operated historically to conjure up particular knowledges operating to construct the actor's body.

THE 'NATURAL' BODY, THE NATURAL SCIENCES AND GYMNASTIC EDUCATION

The previous chapter has already established the importance of modern gymnastics in creating bodies that were physically efficient and healthy. 'Modern' gymnastics originated in Germany, deriving in part from the educational theories of Jean-Jacques Rousseau. Rousseau stressed the importance of games and play for children in the development of a sound body, of natural expression, and also of the discovery of self. Though these ideas were largely rejected in Rousseau's native France, they found support in the naturalistic and philanthropic schools of Germany where gymnastics was increasingly linked to wider educational and social reform and to a vision of the ideal citizen. The Swiss educational reformer Johan Pestalozzi (1746–1827) developed 'natural' gymnastics as distinct from 'art' gymnastics and prefigured the work of his pupil, Friedrich Froebel (1782–1852), who stressed the importance of an harmonious concept of human development, one which acknowledged the importance of physical development through play. Within this educational tradition, the child was privileged as untainted by the degenerative influence of modern, urban society, and thus needed nurturing through an education that respected the 'purity' and 'naturalness' of childhood. In their holistic and humanist approach to the training of the body, these gymnastic systems can be seen as precursors to the movement therapy work of Frederick M. Alexander (and later Moshe Feldenkrais). Far from expecting a degree of rigorous, repetitive exertion from those learning his system, Alexander developed approaches to movement which involved very simple and subtle physical exercises; his work had, after all, developed out of his own reaction to pain and injury. In his movement work, pain and injury are aligned with over exertion and the dominance of the conscious mind over the body. For Alexander, the 'social' body is something that is learnt, a collection of particular habits of movement that limit the variety available to the well co-ordinated person, leading to discomfort and inefficiency.

The 'Neutral' Body, the 'Natural' Body and Movement Training

For the movement tutor this meant that an appropriately trained body would, as a matter of course, be a body which was trained in accordance with the principles of anatomy, mechanics and physiology. The 'natural' body would then be a body that was mechanically efficient; and, as we have seen in the previous chapter, significant effort was put in to ensuring that movement training enabled the actor to perform with the optimum economical use of their physical energies. Such a body could also be identified as a body which was either 'pre-social' or 'extra-daily' in that it distinguished the work of the student actor as specialized, idealized, universalized and exceptional. Such qualities of economy and distinctiveness also marked a class-based area of difference, functioning to discriminate against the 'excess' which was seen as typifying working class entertainment at this time.

THE 'NATURAL' BODY AND THE GREEK IDEAL

The rediscovery of the culture, art and athletic sports of Ancient Greece from the nineteenth century onwards contributed to the creation of another important paradigm. As has been previously noted, the Ancient Greeks' holistic approach to the development of body and mind satisfied nineteenth and early twentieth century nostalgia for a lost athleticism that could represent and develop similar qualities of mind. Ancient Greek culture provided a model of acceptably 'noble' (and, in the conventional and highly selective constructions of Hellenic culture and history of the time, reassuringly male-dominated, white European) physicality for those wishing to escape from the rampant industrialism of the early twentieth century. In this manner the 'natural' body could remain 'civilized' and white, as opposed to 'primitive' and black (Daly, 1995: 90), just as it could remain 'noble' and educated as opposed to 'degenerate' and uneducated. Writing and practice around the 'natural' 'Greek' body thus operated as instruments of social control, producing body norms that were socially and politically acceptable. Construction of such 'norms' of course ignores the cultural appropriation of Ancient Greece by Western Europe, denies Greece's historical connections with North Africa and the Middle East, and obscures the history of homosexuality in Ancient Greek culture.

The Ancient Greeks, so it seemed to nineteenth and early twentieth century sensibilities, rendered nature into art, collapsing the two so that human movement becomes part of an aesthetic, and even cosmic, unity (a distinctive element of some of the influential writings and practices of Nietzsche, Gurdjieff, Duncan and Laban). An association with Greek culture meant that the 'natural' dancing body could be allowed to perform naked or nearly naked; the nude in Greek Art gave nudity in modern arts practice cultural legitimacy. European interest in nudism at the start of the twentieth century (Dutton, 1995: 108) suggests that the influence of the

Greek nude extended beyond art and into life-style choices. The Greek nude represented a sanitized ideal body. By the early twentieth century, reference to Greek culture had become an indication of education, culture and refinement (Daly, 1995: 112), and could be read by educated wealthy audiences as such. In this manner, innovative movement practices such as the work of Duncan, Ginner, Laban, Dalcroze and Delsarte were able to operate strategically within normally restrictive cultural contexts, transgressing the norms of fashion in the name of higher artistic ideals. For them, as for the Government committees examining the physical welfare of the workforce, physical education was an important way to a population of 'taste' and greater understanding. By 1931, Sir Frank Benson was to praise the Greek ideal of the panathlete, 'combining swiftness and agility with strength and endurance' (Benson, 1931: 56) as a model for the physically trained actor, and not much later Ruby Ginner's colleague Irene Mawer was to become a movement teacher at a London drama school, both effectively marking the cultural value accorded to Classical practice.

Significantly, whilst Ancient Greek culture had become fashionable, acceptable and influential, and was embraced whole-heartedly by a number of theatre artists, the movement practices of 'other' cultures (specifically black African, Southern Asian and also Eastern Asian) were far more selectively used and appropriated. Perhaps the best known form of movement practice from the East is Yoga; while it is difficult to place an exact date on the arrival of Yoga in the West, it is clear that it was well known to Stanislavski and much valued by him in the construction of his System (Carnicke, 1998: 140–145). However the relevance of Yoga to Stanislavski's work has been obscured and marginalized as his System has spread beyond Russia and into other theatre cultures. In this respect Yoga, as with other forms of Indian dance theatre, has remained more of an exotic spectacle within Western theatre practice. Only within the twentieth century development of European alternative theatre practice has Asian dance theatre been able to exert influence (for example Artaud and the Balinese dancers (Hayman, 1977: 77), Brecht and the Peking Opera (Brecht, 1961: 130–136), and Barba and oriental dance theatre [Barba & Savarese, 1991]). Greek Culture had the benefit of being not only uncontested as 'white', but also a 'dead' culture and, as such, it could be manipulated and re-appropriated with greater ease.

THE 'NATURAL' BODY AND THE NOBLE SAVAGE

The concept of the 'natural' body suggested access to the kind of special relationship with nature associated with Rousseau's 'noble savage'. While the idea of the 'noble savage' was a potent myth—from the essays of Montaigne through to the Enlightenment (Hall & Gieben, 1992: 310–311)—it was from its beginnings tainted by its western colonialist connotations and its implicit assumptions around the achievements of western civilization. Ann Daly (1995: 114) draws attention to Duncan's preference for Ancient Greek culture, specifically in relation to her scornful dismissal of black Afro-American culture and movement practices as primitive. For Duncan, Greek culture enabled her to construct an elision of the heroic and the eternal with the liberated and the pure, and such associations must also have contributed positively to her efforts to establish her work as socially acceptable and culturally valuable. After reading Nietzsche in 1903, Duncan began to appreciate more fully the 'Dionysian' in the world around her and her work began to express more confidently the sensuality, irrationality and cruelty of Nature. The influence of Nietzsche's writings and Duncan's dance in promoting the 'spirit' of dance, the possibility of 'dancing the thing itself' (Daly, 1995: 95), should not be underestimated. The work of artists such as Auguste Rodin, and the evolutionary ideas of Charles Darwin, also encouraged expansion of concepts of the 'natural' to include qualities of sensuality, rawness, ugliness and weight. The social impact of such ideas must ultimately have been liberating for white men and women, even whilst (and perhaps because) they challenged and disturbed traditional conventions of ethnic behavior, beauty and grace. The unrestrained 'natural' body was in this respect not welcomed unequivocally, but trivialized, derided and scorned by some critics as an exotic 'fashionable' novelty or as an affront to civilized society, if only in order to make the work of women and black artists seem less 'threatening'.

F. M. Alexander also privileged the 'primitive' (the 'under-evolved' savage, the physically 'innocent' child) as an example of the human body untainted by the effects of modern urban and industrial society. Alexander, for instance, writes of the 'primitive savage' that his

> physical co-ordination and development (. . .), like that of the animal which he encountered daily, had reached (. . .) a fine state of excellence.
> (Alexander, 1986: 67)

In this manner, he associates the 'savage' (in this case he is presumably meaning the Aboriginal Australian) with the animal, implicitly establishing both an evolutionary hierarchy and his place on it. His admiration for the 'savage' is also tempered by a suspicion of 'free expression' as potentially intoxicating and dangerous for 'underdeveloped' sensibilities:

> music and dancing are, as every one knows, excitements which make a stronger appeal to the primitive than to the more highly evolved races. No drunken man in our civilization ever reaches the stages of anaesthesia and complete loss of self-control attained by the savage under the influence of these two stimuli.
> (Alexander, 1986: 100)

78 *Movement Training for the Modern Actor*

In aligning self-control with evolutionary progress, Alexander seems to imply that the 'savage' is in a Darwinian sense inferior. For Alexander, the route to 'natural' physical expression is not through 'free expression' but through training, thus confirming a social order predicated on education and a 'civilizing' process. The 'natural' body is achieved through a form of *via negativa*, whereby the student comes to unlearn that which is habitual and restrictive and has to rediscover the 'mechanical and other laws, deduced from untold centuries of human experience' (Alexander, 1986: 105). Through this rediscovery, and the practice of inhibition, conscious control is re-exerted over the body in a manner that is in line with efficient and effective body use. This is an important development which can be taken as representative of the trend over the twentieth century to shift the emphasis from the production of a specific 'natural' body towards a 'natural' process of body use and body learning. It can thus be perceived as configuring the trained 'natural' body, and subsequently the process of training the 'natural' body, as cultured and culturing rather than 'primitive' or 'savage', thus again privileging the white western (and implicitly male) body.

Within the English drama schools of the early twentieth century, movement training can be seen as developing along lines compatible with the paradigmatic practices examined above. Construction of the training in line with these paradigms enabled the drama schools to do several things: to meet the industry requirement for actors comfortably able to represent a specific social class; to meet the commercial needs of the industry for actors of increasing physical versatility; to respond to the broader social developments in education and fitness; and, to be seen to align their training with contemporary understandings of human nature. The 'natural' body of the pre-Second World War actor represented the theatrical embodiment of these requirements.

FROM 'NATURAL' TO 'NEUTRAL': COPEAU AND THE NEUTRAL MASK

From the mid-1930s onwards, changes were afoot that would represent probably the most significant development in movement training for actors during the twentieth century. The previous chapter examined the impact on English actor training of the arrival in England of Jacques Copeau's nephew, Michel St. Denis. One of the most important elements that St. Denis was to bring from his experiences with Copeau into the drama schools that he helped to found was the 'noble' or 'neutral' mask (Rudlin, 2000: 72–74). For Copeau, and thus also for St. Denis and for those with whom he was to work, the 'neutral' mask was a tool to release the body's expressive potential. In doing so it also functioned to draw together many of the elements which had previously existed as disparate parts of what were adhoc physical training regimes, creating a rationale for their integration and a discursive framework within which they could cohere and 'make sense'.

Jacques Copeau first explored the training potential of a 'blank' expressionless mask in 1921. Initially he used just a stocking or handkerchief over a student's face to reduce facial expression to a minimum. Later this was developed into a more solid and formal mask with the help of the sculptor Albert Marque, who also used more durable materials. Marque insisted on the maxim that 'A good mask must be neutral; its expression depends on your movements' (Dorcy, 1961: 13). Copeau's students,

> at once reported a new sense of confidence and authority, "a power and unknown security—a sort of balance and consciousness of each gesture and oneself." (. . .) the ego subsumed in the id, ready, if required, to then select a new ego for portrayal without the interpolation of self-interest and cacoethes [bad habits] from the original.
> (Rudlin, 1986: 48)

The mask also introduces an element of ritual and transformation into the students' work, removing the student actor from the 'everyday' world through the design of the mask, the rituals involved in putting on the mask, and its effect on the wearer's physical awareness. Jean Dorcy, a student of Copeau's, describes in detail a semi-ritualized process for preparing to work in the mask (Dorcy, 1961: 108–109), which is clearly intended to remove the student actor from the everyday and induce something like a trance state in relation to the mask.

The 'neutral' mask and the rituals involved in its use are, for Copeau, crucial in enabling the actor to experience, and then manipulate, the performative socialization of the body. For Copeau, 'The actor would have to be stripped as bare as the stage; only then could he express himself clearly and simply' (Eldredge & Huston, 1995: 121). Echoing the avant-gardists' rejection of the social disciplining of the subject, Copeau considered that, 'The actor always starts from an artificial *attitude*, a bodily, mental, or vocal *grimace*' (Copeau in Cole & Chinoy, 1970: 220), and that it was only by eradicating this attitude that the actor could,

> know how to be silent, to listen, to answer, to remain motionless, to start a gesture, to follow through with it, come back to motionlessness and silence, with all the shadings and half-tones that these actions imply.
> (Copeau in Cole & Chinoy, 1970: 222)

Copeau's rigorous attempt to 'detach the act of performance from the prison of self' (Wardle, 1978: 60), drove him away from a theatre of stars and towards actors who could do anything, but without being anything in themselves. For some critics however, this 'neutral' actor was seen as an actor of 'the second rank', docile and malleable (Wardle, 1978: 60). Nonetheless, unlike Craig, Copeau was able to sustain this experiment for long enough to see it bear some fruit. The survival of his work owes much to the later successes of several of his former pupils in taking his practices back into the commercial and state subsidized theatre; a process which inevitably diluted some of its early Puritanism.

THE FRENCH CONNECTION—MICHEL ST. DENIS, JACQUES LECOQ AND THE NEUTRAL MASK

The use of the mask demanded a disciplined body and in this manner drew students into a more profound engagement with their own physicality, proving a catalyst for a newly invigorated approach to movement. As a pupil and colleague of Copeau, St. Denis was well-versed in 'neutral' mask training by the time he arrived in England, and it was to form an important part of the teaching at the London Theatre Studio and, after the War, at the Old Vic Theatre School (Wardle, 1978: 62–63). The mask techniques used by St. Denis exerted a slow but steady influence on the development of movement training from the mid-century onwards. Throughout the twenty years following the Second World War these techniques were promoted throughout the English drama schools, both through St. Denis' own influence and through that of his colleagues and students. 'Neutral' mask and body training was to be further vitalized by the foundation in 1956 of the École Jacques Lecoq in Paris. From the 1960s onwards, a steady flow of English students at the École Lecoq returned to teach at Drama Schools, including Sue Lefton and Jane Gibson, and later Shona Morris and Lorna Marshall. The success of the 'neutral' actor training, its ability to draw together other theatre teaching practices and to provide actors able to respond to the post-war ensemble style of acting, meant that, by the last quarter of the twentieth century, most movement tutors found a knowledge of 'neutral' mask and body work was a professional necessity.

It is revealing that those in the English theatre searching for a more rigorous, integrated and innovative approach to actor training turned towards the European mainland. The lure of the bohemian avant-garde of France and Germany in the early decades of the century meant that a steady flow of actors and students traveled abroad for their inspiration. Equally, the political instability in Europe and the growing enthusiasm for innovation in England meant that key practitioners such as Laban and St. Denis were attracted to these shores and were able to establish successful teaching careers. At a time when one might expect nationalism to be at its height, it seems that some parts of the English theatre were quite willing to open their doors to influence from abroad. This interest can be seen as part of a wider internationalism, one associated with political democracy and a consequent theatrical move from the star to the ensemble, from the inhibited theatre of the drawing room drama to the physically expressive performance of popular drama and dance (see Carter, 1925).

THE NEUTRAL MASK AND MOVEMENT TRAINING

From its beginnings in Copeau's school in Paris, the Neutral Mask has been used primarily as an instrument for the students' training, not for performance:

> The neutral mask is a way of understanding performance, not a way of performing. The mask is a tool for analysing the quality of the body's action. The mask hides the face, but reveals the attitudes and intentions, the nuances, the feeling tones, that are otherwise only dimly sensed in a person's motion or stillness. When he carries it, the actor must communicate through his whole person; and the spectator must perceive the expression of the whole person.
> (Eldredge & Huston, 1995: 127)

The effect of the Neutral Mask is to highlight where and when the student is physically blocking. The mask seems to require of the student that 'the body be integrated in a single image' (Eldredge & Huston, 1995: 128). Eldredge and Huston assume that, as a result, 'The dichotomies of physical and emotional technique are united in a single experience' (Eldredge & Huston, 1995: 128). In fact this may only happen intermittently, as students may well initially experience a sense of disorientation and alienation from their actions whilst wearing a mask, a sensation they will be unlikely to admit to as it will be clearly identified with failure. The effect of the mask is thus also to heighten the student's sense of vulnerability and scrutiny: 'As the actor is identified with the mask, the self becomes an external attribute that can be studied' (Mitter, 1992: 85). The Neutral Mask is then disciplining as well as liberating. It aims to integrate the body and present movement as a single image for scrutiny. In doing so, it forces the student into making choices with regard to the presentation and construction of their physical self, and into a construction of the self as primarily physical. The process is invigorating, provocative, and informative for the student. But as we shall see later, the process cannot entirely remove the student from the historically, socially and culturally contingent theatre practices that also function to shape them. Returning to the paradigms of the 'natural' body, we can now examine the extent to which the production of the 'neutral' body of the student actor builds on the discursive foundations which these paradigms provide.

THE NEUTRAL BODY AND ANATOMY

In line with the praxis of the 'natural' body, and in keeping with the attitudes of the early twentieth century theatrical avantgarde, there was a growing emphasis within the new systems of movement training on the rejection and removal of traditional artifice. In movement terms this meant that training stressed the development of a body which was freely expressive rather than one which communicated through well-established, formally categorized, languages of gestures. Emphasis was consequently placed on rediscovering the body's innate movement capabilities. Jacques Copeau, for instance, sought a movement training which would encourage a natural approach to the body, collaborating first with Emile Jaques-Dalcroze and his pupil Jessmin Howarth, and later with Georges Hébert and Suzanne Bing, to develop an actor's body which was pliant, expressive, and able to take on any necessary imprimatur. Stanislavski turned to Isadora Duncan and also to Dalcroze for movement training for his Moscow Arts Theatre Studio, influences which informed his own teaching and his theories of acting and performance. In all cases, the aim was to develop regimes where the body's movement was constrained only by limitations determined by rigorous movement analysis.

Lea Logie (1995b) draws our attention to the tendency of key twentieth century movement practitioners (she includes Meyerhold, Copeau, Decroux, Dalcroze, Laban, Lecoq and Barba) to segment movement and the body in order to identify an 'anatomy' of actions. Though influenced by developments in scientific movement analysis, physiology and anatomy, these practitioners were more interested in a somatic anatomizing—categorizing movements in relation to their psychophysical, emotional or spiritual significance. Logie is particularly drawn to the tripartite structure of actions which she suggests all the movement approaches are based on—a structure composed around a sequence from preparation (stillness, filled with intention, as the actor 'addresses' the action), to realization of the action, and finishing with completion of the action (with a return to stillness and relaxation after the release of the action). Such similarities should not surprise us unduly; the common influence of Delsarte is clear, as is the shared knowledge many of these practitioners have had of the work of each other and of other movement theorists.

In its relationship to performance (as with sport or health) the 'natural' body was not simply an escape from 'culture' towards some 'pure' ideal based on nothing more than anatomy. The efforts to return movement practice to a sound scientific basis were valuable and important, but in seeking to link anatomy and physiology to the emotional and spiritual life of the student the practitioners were attempting something more profound—to bridge the nature/culture divide. Into a body conceived as disciplined and culturally 'consecrated' would be inserted a renewed sense of the worth of the organic experience of the body, the joyfulness of the body in motion, and the possibility of transforming physical instinct and immediacy into art. The 'natural' body of the actor was a way in which the craft of acting could be ennobled and spiritually enriched at the same time as the actor's tools of physical expression were being developed, invigorated and refined according to contemporary knowledge of the body. The concept of the 'natural' body typically encompasses the possession of innate capacities for efficient performance, or as Lorna Marshall argues, 'movement work is 'natural' in the sense that it follows the body's anatomical design' (Marshall, 2001: 114). Since Isadora Duncan's successes with her 'natural' dance movements at the start of the twentieth century, the 'natural' body in performance has been idealized as both efficient and graceful—it moves 'harmoniously' and with an organic sense of wavelike motion (Daly, 1995: 99). 'Neutral' movement is also defined as 'effortless', and thus operates to associate the actor with both the 'natural' and the 'efficient'. This kind of effortless efficiency has increasingly been associated with the correct use of the human anatomy and physiology—what Eugenio Barba has called 'organic integrity', a quality which he believes young actors need to acquire before 'attempting to learn the language of stage training' (Sellers-Young, 1999: 89), but which also marks one site of the actor's claim to 'truthfulness'.

BODY KNOWLEDGE

If we acknowledge that the body owns innate anatomical and physiological capacities then this is also suggestive of the existence of body 'intelligence'. Implicit in the work of many of the innovators in movement training is an assumption that the body is capable of holding its own knowledge and may even 'know' what is good for it. Such assumptions are, for instance, often built into the language of movement teaching:

> [T]he body remembers things that the mind forgets. So that once you've learnt how to release and/or drop your weight or find your centre, once the body's learnt to do it, you don't need to remind yourself to do it.
> (Morris, 1999)

Looking more closely at this statement, we can note several things. Firstly, there is the assumption that the body's 'knowledge' is built on repeated practice which eventually bypasses conscious control and establishes conditioned responses. Secondly, it is suggested that body 'knowledge' is mediated through the body, through physical experience, and cannot be as successfully mediated in any other way. Thirdly, we can see that body 'intelligence' is here perceived as operating at a more profound level than knowledge associated with the mind.

There is still very little research available on the nature and operation of 'muscle memory' and body 'knowledge', what research is available is generally within the field of social, psychological and neurophysiological enquiry. Despite the pioneering work of early neuropsychologists such as Karl Lashley (1890–1958), who attempted to identify 'engrams', or movement traces in the body, limited research has been conducted to explore the actual manner in which movement training leaves its traces on/in the body. The available research is only generally accessible through texts on bodywork such as Juhan's *Job's Body* (2003), and is only visible on the margins of theatre scholarship (for example Pradier, 1990; and, Bloch, Orthous & Santibañez-H, 1987). As such, its impact on movement training within the drama schools has inevitably been limited. Whereas athletes and sports people have been quick to respond to developments in scientific understanding of the body, actors and performers have shown a reluctance to engage with science in the same way. Clearly the kind of mechanical efficiency required by athletes and sportspeople is not what is required by performers; the actor's achievement is not measured by speed, distance, height, accuracy of aim or stamina, rather it is more closely related to the effective expression of an impulse: '[I]t's about making it natural, making it come from the gut inside' (Rose Bruford first year student).

We can see that the 'natural' body is perceived as being driven by the inner impulses of the actor's 'self'. The student actor's body should 'learn' to facilitate the expression of such impulses with freshness and a lack of inhibition. Lea Logie (1995a) identifies the time-lapse between impulse and action as a key problem for the actor in performance where action should 'occur as instantaneous reaction' (Logie, 1995a: 256). In another sense however, the time-lapse which Logie seeks to erase is a crucial space for the student actor in movement class—a space for awareness, choice, feeling and reflection. If that moment is not taken an impulse might all too quickly collapse into a habitual response; such a time-lapse provides a crucial space for conscious control within the Alexander Technique for instance. Field observation confirmed that movement tutors make use of 'side coaching' to continually remind students, during exercises, of the choices available to them, and to encourage non-habitual responses. The 'neutral' body training seeks to enable the impulse to become visceral, physical and 'lived-in', to become 'natural': '[If the movement]'s not natural, it's not on an impulse, it's . . . become cold' (Rose Bruford second year student), but the movement tutor and the students themselves continually reflect on that 'naturalness' and interrogate it against other choices made and not made. Thus we can see the paradoxical role of muscle memory in enabling the spontaneous impulse. But for Logie, muscle memory also represents 'some process of internal association which leads from one movement sequence to the next', such that 'internal imagery can be built up by the body's spontaneous suggestions' (Logie, 1995b: 238)—a process which she associates with George Lewes' ideas on the body and memory. Through this facility, the actor is enabled to release psychological inhibitions and to play. Playfulness may certainly be one way of keeping movement options open.

Pradier (1990) compares the effect of repetitive physical activity to that of a dream state:

> Sporting activities are equivalent to the dream state, but for the sensory-motor system: they stimulate motor schemes while cognitive functions are at rest.
>
> (Pradier, 1990: 93)

He goes on to suggest that repetitive activity, through organizing and patterning behavior, may also play an important part in sustaining the body in a balanced and integrated state:

> OHPB's [organized human performing behaviours] participate in the holistic maintenance of the individual's integrity—cognitive, emotional, sensorial, and motor.
>
> (Pradier, 1990: 93)

At first this appears at odds with 'play' and spontaneity. But, reading Pradier's theory onto the 'neutral' body, we can identify a function of movement training that is, through the efficient alignment of the actor's physical resources, to enable and release the imagination and assist in the integration of their faculties. Thus the actor is helped to identify 'where emotions and experiences are held in the body' (Manchester Metropolitan second year student). Pradier further suggests that it is the performative aspects of movement training that play a major part in the integrated development of mind, consciousness, body and movement:

> Performance illustrates the holistic aspect of human behaviour: the most elaborate types of behaviour always include a component of sensory and motor responses (i.e., body memory, movements involved with language activity, etc.). The physiological processes of stabilization, development, and preservation of the integrity of the central nervous system (CNS) always include a performing aspect. Unlike actual computers, CNS activity has an effect on the whole biological system which influences the CNS production.
>
> (Pradier, 1990: 88)

This kind of play within technique, Yarrow argues,

> is how the body accedes to its own resources, how it discovers that it can be, say, do, understand and transmit, with and to anything and anyone.
>
> (Yarrow, 1986: 12)

'Neutral' movement training, operating at the level of an embodied consciousness, can function to bring into balance the human ecosystem. Or as Shona Morris more succinctly puts it: 'the body's (. . .) organized through the mind working through the body' (Morris, 1999). Neuropsychological research and scholarship is not then perhaps as out of touch with the aims of professional actor training as the language in which it is written might seem to suggest. Bloch, Orthous and Santibañez-H (1987) aimed within their research to explore techniques for recreating normal behavior patterns: 'The actor must learn to use his (*sic*) body in order to express emotions (. . .) This requires mastering a series of technical abilities' (Bloch, Orthous

& Santibañez-H, 1987: 198). Such training could be seen as more in line with the needs of the actor than, for instance, a ballet-trained body. Ballet survives within actor training for its discipline, its precision, its cultural capital and its association with artistic heritage. But its authority within movement training has been long usurped by the 'neutral' body. The role of body knowledge and muscle memory in the socio-cultural construction of the actor's self will be further examined in the next chapter.

A NEUTRAL MIND IN A NEUTRAL BODY

> [T]he movement element of actor training is not limited to the manipulation of muscles for in the act of manipulating the muscles one is influencing the actor's brain and mental imagery, and consequently his mind.
> (Sellers-Young, 1999: 90)

'Mind' and 'body' are two terms frequently engaged, from the late nineteenth century onwards, in attempts to understand and describe the processes and problems inherent in physical training for artistic expression. Historically the distinction between mind and body represents the intellectual dominance of Cartesian dualism and was also used to give authority to the perceived nature/culture divide between women and men. However, during the twentieth century both were increasingly recognized as culturally determined abstractions that could no longer be taken simply to refer to objective materialities. The distinction between 'mind' and 'body' also seemed increasingly out of touch with the developing interest in the human subject as an integrated organic whole. The use of terms such as 'body intelligence' represents an attempt to bridge the 'mind/body' divide and to do so in a manner which both allows of the conventional functions of 'mind' and 'body' and also includes those we understand as neurophysiological. It implies not control, but awareness.

Post Stanislavski, the challenge for the actor has been to achieve a kind of sincerity in performance whereby emotion is related to action and is released through a body that is open, flexible and responsive. Dominant Stanislavskian naturalism demands that actors are able to communicate believable emotion and to signal the action of the psychophysical generation of emotion. The aim of 'neutral' body training is, through improving physical alignment, to open up the body to respond as directly, physically, spontaneously and 'naively' as possible to emotion. Pradier suggests that the *fictive* nature of movement training for actors is important as it allows the work to function as an 'effective and safe stimulator of emotions' (Pradier, 1990: 90). Student interviewees seemed to feel an increasing sense of control, as their training progressed, over their ability to use physical activity to provoke feelings and emotional responses, as well as an increasing sensitivity to the emotions generated by the movement processes and activities which they are exploring. As the students develop confidence they seem able to manipulate the relationship between action and emotion, learning 'how to make a connected movement, so that your emotions are connected throughout your whole entire body' (Rose Bruford second year student). For Pradier, this ability to make specific connections between their movement and specific emotions is a mark of the quality of the students' training:

> There is (. . .) a difference between general emotional stimulation made by 'naïve' actors, and specific emotional stimulation by actors who are trained to perform the respiratory-postural-facial effector patterns of basic emotions.
> (Pradier, 1990: 94)

For the student this skill is about awareness and connectedness:

> I suddenly became aware of (. . .) all the different parts (. . .) and there's connections between one and each one . . . it's weird, it's . . . gives you such an awareness of each relation to the body.
> (Manchester Metropolitan first year student)

It is this 'connectedness' which highlights the fluidity of a body, or an action, which simultaneously signifies an emotion and is the emotion it signifies. Student actors therefore consider the flow between intention and action, between 'inner' and 'outer', between what is commonly referred to as 'mind' and 'body', as a valuable facility to develop:

> the connection between the thought and the physicality (. . .) that's what I'm getting from it at the moment. I think that's what we're encouraged to pick up at this stage. To get that connection.
> (Manchester Metropolitan first year student)

This mind/body connectedness is conceptualized by Ralph Yarrow as 'neutral' consciousness (Yarrow, 1986). Yarrow understands consciousness as 'integral to all knowing' (1986: 1), but is specifically interested in the extent to which it may, under specific circumstances, occur physiologically, opening out consciousness into a 'universality of awareness' (1986: 2). Implicit in this conception is a suspension of judgment and an openness and readiness for experience and action, what Lecoq calls *'disponibilité'*, a condition in which the student aims to, in Grotowski's words, 'eliminate his organism's resistance to [the] psychic process' (Grotowski, 1968: 16). For both students and teachers, rationalization obstructs the operation of this flow of psychophysical energies. There is a consequent move away from a dominantly rational and intellectual approach, towards one that prioritizes readiness, availability and openness above premeditation:

> At the moment of neutral action, one does not know what one will do next, because anticipation is a mark of personality; one cannot describe how one feels because introspection intrudes on simplicity; one reacts in a sensory way, because when the mind stops defining experience, the senses still function. Economy demands that both motion and rest be unpremeditated. Neutral activity withholds nothing; it is an energized condition, like the moment of inspiration before speech. The neutrality that the mask seeks is *an economy of mind and body, evidenced at rest, in motion, and in the relationship between them.*
>
> (Eldredge & Huston, 1995: 123)

By focusing on unpremeditated action, the 'neutral' body is respecting the flow and physicality of the acting process: 'They don't learn intellectually (. . .) They learn through experience. I think. Through doing' (Morris, 1999).

Both students and teachers find it difficult to describe movement training in words; those teachers who have written about movement training struggle to communicate in words anything more than the basic mechanics of an exercise. Imagery seems to provide the most effective linguistic means for tutors to communicate practical skills, techniques and experiences to students. Images seem able to operate psychosomatically through emotional and physical associations, functioning far more effectively for the students than objective description or instruction:

> I found that what helps me is . . . using mental images (. . .) when I'm working with an idea of releasing a certain part of the body, just work on releasing the head and seeing it as a beach ball and volumes of water shifting around to help the weight.
>
> (Manchester Metropolitan first year student)

Teachers also agree that the imagination can function to transform the body. Shona Morris affirms that,

> you actually see it happening, if you say to a student, you know, "You're light, the character's light, you know, there isn't weight, just imagine the upper spine floating away from the lower spine", you'll actually . . . you'll actually see that body change.
>
> (Morris, 1999)

In a manner similar to Lulu Sweigard's work on ideokinesis, it seems that images work because 'brain images can influence muscles to realign themselves in more economical patterns of use' (Sellers-Young, 1999: 90). For Pradier there is a clear relationship between the ability of the consciousness to imaginatively engage with movement and the manipulation of posture necessary to achieve efficient physical activity:

> The human brain (. . .) dynamically 'programs' its distributed subsystems in anticipation of the need to process certain types of action (. . .) Consequently, motor imagination can modify tonic postural activity.
>
> (Pradier, 1990: 93)

For Dowling the reverse is also true. Postural problems block the functioning of the imagination: 'when you hold your shoulders or your hips like that, what you're actually doing is you're stopping your imagination' (Dowling, 2000). The role of imagery and the relationship between imagination and movement training thus imply a different level of consciousness than the strictly rational or the impulsively emotional or physical, whilst maintaining the best qualities of all three. Both student actors and their tutors are, as a consequence, generally more comfortable with language which uses images and process words (such as 'energy', 'rhythm', 'flow', 'action', 'impulse' and 'intention'), all of which conjure a subtler, more dynamic and more complex relationship between the 'inner' and the 'outer' self than the oversimplifying distinction between 'mind' and 'body'. Vanessa Ewan (Central School) uses the idea of 'actions', for instance, as a concept to conflate the 'inner'/'outer' divide in relation to the acting process:

> If an actor can put everything in action, life is so much easier, if everything is to do with that action drive. I mean thinking is action, and if everything has a movement (. . .) it's all based on action—thinking is an action, feeling is an action and movements are feelings then it's all a lot easier.
>
> (Ewan, 1999a)

Equally, the idea of 'flow' is a useful metaphor for an experience obtained through the transfer of physical energy through action, and the relationships between action, energy-uptake and physical pleasure (see Pradier (1990) and Csikszentmihalyi [2002]). 'Flow' has an emotional quality, created as certain physical actions, reactions and energy transfers produce in the actor a heightened sense of elation. Both muscular release and the flow of energy within the performer, usually occurring simultaneously, communicate to the audience and engage them in a way that restrictive tension does not. It is as if the performer, in the act of moving, signals to the onlooker that the movement will be more efficient, that it will 'perform' better and expose the spectator to a more complete (and hence more pleasurable?) experience of the human body in expressive action. The work of Rudolf Laban has had a powerful influence within the development of this kind of language, and Laban's own work on character analysis through movement, together with the later work of his pupils Warren Lamb and Yat Malmgren, are attempts to create a language and a way of working through movement which avoid the problems of the 'mind'/'body' divide. Such a language is again predicated on the assumption that the body has its own form of intelligence. For methods such as Laban's to work we must also assume that the body has its own form of memory. If we were to say that the 'body' has no memory, and therefore cannot learn, then we would have to accept that the physical memory to perform spontaneous actions must be located elsewhere, presumably prioritizing the 'mind' over the 'body' again—exactly the kind of displacement which we have seen that actor training seeks to resist. What Bloch, Orthous and Santibañez-H (1987) and Pradier (1990) seem to be suggesting is that we reconsider the notion of 'mind' and 'body' and focus instead on the brain and the body's neurological functioning, reconfiguring theatre as 'a fundamental *biological* event' (Pradier, 1990: 86). In this way, it becomes easier to allow for notions of 'body intelligence' and 'body learning', and the link between patterns of social and/or extra-daily behavior and repeated muscular contraction seems clearer and, importantly, still not over simplified. In this way, the Neutral Mask and body training is not 'anti-thought', but constructs thought as something produced by and through the body.

The neurophysiologist, Antonio Damasio, provides us with a sense of how this works at a neurological level. For Damasio, 'the inescapable and remarkable fact about these three phenomena—emotion, feeling, consciousness—is their body relatedness' (Damasio, 2000: 284). Consciousness is thus profoundly linked to the emotions and to the body: 'the body is the main stage for emotions, either directly or via its representation in somatosensory structures in the brain' (Damasio, 2000: 287). Damasio's conceptualization of the process of exchange between the body and the brain resonates with the processes discussed above, adding further weight to a model of the mind/body relationship which is fluid and inter-dependent. Damasio's model challenges the actor to learn to feel their feelings, through a looping of changes in the 'body landscape' and changes in the somatosensory structures of the central nervous system. The student actor learns to acquire an experiential awareness of the flow between body and brain that creates the feeling of feeling. Even more intriguingly, Damasio also suggests an alternative mechanism that he calls the 'as if body loop' (2000: 281), in which emotions emerge within the brain's sensory body maps, 'as if' they had emerged from body-related changes. It is perhaps here that we can neurologically locate the processes through which the student actor learns to experience, model and re-model the relationship between their body, their emotions and their consciousness that physiologically constitutes their neutral body training.

THE NEUTRAL MASK AND THE CHILD— RELEARNING THE BODY

Actor training is, and has been during the last century, preoccupied with the development and presentation of the actor's self. This self is required to achieve the effective stimulation of emotions appropriate to the fictive character being portrayed and the sensitive and alert monitoring of this very process *whilst in action*. The student actor is encouraged to explore the 'neutral' state as a site within which their psychophysical responses to stimuli are able to take place with less socially conditioned physical inhibition and which simultaneously distances them from their everyday selves and familiar patterns of behavior. This idea of 're-learning' aligns the student with the child, an important paradigm of the 'natural' body. From John Locke's *Essay Concerning Human Understanding* (1690), through Rousseau's theories of natural education, to the liberal education experiments at the start of the twentieth century we can see the rise of the child as an image of physical, intellectual and moral purity and innocence. Ruby Ginner was only one of many to argue the significance of the child's supposedly unsullied approach to movement:

> The simplicity of a child's thought, the purity of its untouched emotions, its faith in the beautiful, give it a power and exquisiteness of expression which a teacher must reverence and guard as a pearl of great price.
> (Ginner, 1933: 147)

We can see these same themes in the comments of some of the student interviewees. For one student, 'neutral' body work was all about 'getting your body back to its neutral state on the day you were born' (Rose Bruford second year student), and for another, it was about 'being like a child again and learning how to walk and move properly' (Manchester Metropolitan first year student). Lorna Marshall has written that,

> Performers should be able to be as true and direct as a child in expressing their feelings, if this is required by the role. Not to have childish feelings, but to be as honest and transparent and as emotionally mobile as a child.
> (Marshall, 2001: 7)

For Jacques Copeau, work with children formed an important part of the development of his teaching (Evans, 2006: 57–62). For Copeau, working with the young was essential, he could see no other way of achieving the kind of new actor of which he dreamed. The 'uneducated', open body of the child was, through the influence of Copeau and of Duncan, Alexander and Dalcroze, to become a powerful paradigm for the 'neutral' body. However, at least from Alexander's point of view, such a picture would be an incomplete representation of his position. In 'Child Training and Education' (Alexander, 1986: 91–107), although he accepts that children at an early age are 'the most plastic and adaptable of living things' (1986: 95), Alexander makes his belief quite clear that far from children being 'blank slates', 'Every child is born into the world with a predisposition to certain habits' (1986: 91). Further, because for Alexander, progress and civilization are closely aligned to the improvement of conscious control, he remained suspicious of children's 'original savage instincts' (1986: 95). For Alexander then, it is the *potential* for (re)learning and achieving conscious control which the child embodies, which makes the child a paradigmatic site for movement training.

THE NEUTRAL MASK AND THE ANIMAL

For Michel St. Denis, the movement study of animals was another vital aspect of the student actor's training, which he himself had studied as a student with Copeau and Bing. It was to inform his own ideas on the training of actors (St. Denis, 1982) and his teaching at both the London Theatre Studio and the Old Vic Theatre School (Wardle, 1978). Animal study has subsequently remained a central part of movement and acting training at all of the major drama schools (McEvenue, 2001: 120) and is referred to in many of the books on movement training (Dennis, 1995: 154–155; McEvenue, 2001: 120–125; Marshall, 2001: 164 and Pisk, 1975: 78–80). Its importance lies in the nature of the very particular challenge it offers to actors:

> there's a huge transformation (. . .) it's a major technical jump, big, big change of breath, change of life, change of backbone, change of . . . I mean everything!
>
> (Ewan, 1999a)

It is a challenge that implicitly takes them on a journey away from the socialized and urbanized 'everyday' body to which they have become accustomed. The 'animal' body represents a body freed from the inhibitions of reason and the pressures of urban living, it associates it once again with the 'primitive' (or even with the child) as being in some important respect prehuman. In entering into the physical world of the animal, the student actor is also learning to let go of self-consciousness, of rationality and of their 'civilized' knowledge of the world. The 'pre-human' animal body is understood as a spontaneous body, enabling the actor who explores it to let go of the conscious self and 'play', facilitating a different experience of touch and of movement and gesture—they experience both their own bodies and the bodies of others differently. In this respect, the 'pre-human' body is actually given status, re-appropriated as culturally valuable, and 'recognized' as sophisticated in its own right and important in our construction of ourselves as human subjects.

For Alexander teachers, the animal in movement also represents an important model of postural, skeletal, muscular and neurophysiological organization (Park, 2000: 93–95). George Coghill, a biologist who researched movement and posture in animals in the early twentieth century, saw Alexander's work as enabling a person to remove inherited and conditioned conflicts in the nervous system (Coghill in Alexander, 1986: 190), thus emphasizing the importance of both the 'total pattern' of the organism and the efficiency and economy of action gained through the re-education of the reflex mechanism. Animals are sometimes presented as offering models for the study of this 'total patterning' of the organism.

> When we look at a cat waiting to pounce (. . .) we get an instinctive impression of organic perfection before the action itself is achieved. Trained performers express stored traces of this specific skill in their daily posture and gestures.
> (Pradier, 1990: 90)

Fundamental differences and similarities between the anatomy of humans and animals are also highlighted by the student's animal study, reinforcing the emphasis placed on the spine, the pelvis and the head/neck relationship by the tutors. Animal study may involve the student in sustaining the physical impersonation of an animal for forty five minutes or even up to an hour. This durational activity encourages them in traversing that vital stage Dowling identifies as 'making the jump from just the physical into the imaginative' (Dowling, 2000). The act of transformation so strongly associated with acting, and mythologized in the protean ideal, is embedded into movement training through these exercises. Of course, the student's body cannot materially become that of the animal, but the student can observe how the animal moves and attempt imaginatively to enter into the ways in which the animal comes to knowledge of its self and its world. The emphasis is thus placed once again on action words that enable the subject to express and explore the way in which the world becomes known to them. In this sense, rhythm changes for instance do not change material weight (mass), but change the way in which we experience it:

> if you are naturally a solid young man with slow rhythms, transforming the body is how do you make that body light? How do you make it quick, energetic, 'Quixotic'? So that you can be anybody, because everybody's rhythm is different.
> (Allnutt, 1999)

By experiencing the rhythms of the world around them as directly as possible, through physical imitation, the student is able more clearly to identify and manipulate their own rhythms.

> you can find the rhythm of something else, like an animal, like an element. Something that's fired by the imagination. Then rhythms seem to come more naturally.
> (Allnutt, 1999)

In this context, a 'natural' rhythm appears to be one which is 'fired' through the imagination, and in this way the student, whilst retaining conscious control of the exercise is not inhibited by self-consciousness. 'Natural' physical rhythm is then a spontaneous negotiation between internal psychophysical processes, external sensory stimuli and external socio-cultural stimuli, and can be representative of and thus used to interrogate all three (it is certainly *not* acultural). For these reasons, student actors are usually exposed to the animal study exercise within the first year of their studies.

THE 'NEUTRAL' BODY AND 'PURE' MOVEMENT

Abstract expressive movement work in actor training is commonly referred to as 'pure movement' by movement tutors in order to distinguish it from dance improvisation.

> Pure movement is technical; it's really the craft of movement. The technique of standing up straight, the technique of walking, the technique of raising your arms, of being relaxed, of not having what we call 'parasites'.
>
> (Allnutt, 1999)

'Pure movement' is seen by the students as movement which connects the body directly and without interference to the actor's imaginative and emotional impulses. The term also associates the 'neutral' body with movement which is uncontaminated by the everyday: 'you have to be able to leave behind your baggage' (Guildhall first year student). This idea has its own history in the twentieth century, extending from Stanislavski for example, who believed that, 'Extra gestures are the equivalent of trash, dirt, spots' (Stanislavski, 1979: 73), to Sears Eldredge, for whom 'the pursuit of neutrality purifies [the actor], making his (*sic*) very errors more commanding' (Eldredge & Huston, 1995: 128). Eldredge (1996: 53) actually identifies six principal characteristics of the 'neutral body': it should have symmetry, be centered, integrated and focused, energized, relaxed, and be about being and not doing; and he also identifies two further characteristics of the neutral body in motion: that its movement should be economical and co-coordinated (1996: 56). Purity and neutrality of movement can then, in his terms, be measured against the ability to express intention without tension, inhibition, imbalance, awkwardness or excess. Ultimately, within the trained actor, 'intention will organize the body' (Morris, 1999), and the actor's intentions will be transcendent, projecting the subject towards the object. The body will 'become' the intention. This efficient, trained, flexible and responsive body is then a 'body-as-conduit', supposedly eliminating any contamination of the character and the text by the actor's personality. The 'neutral' body in this manner contributes to an economy which gives

The 'Neutral' Body, the 'Natural' Body and Movement Training 95

value to the erasure of self and affirms the actor's physicality as malleable and docile. The theatre economy values such qualities only in respect of their participation in the efficient production of marketable performance, yet at the same time it tacitly gives greater value to the non-'neutral' qualities of personality, originality, excess and virtuosity (as and when it sees fit). We can see clearly in this discrepancy how easily a 'neutral' body can become a 'docile' body.

The aim is a body that is balanced, 'gathered' physiologically and spatially, the weight and energy related so that the actor can react to or follow an impulse in any direction, without noticeable pause. But to what extent is this accompanied by a disengagement of critical awareness? The actor has to achieve something that the character they are aiming to play does not. Blocks that are unconscious in everyday life are either overcome, removed or consciously applied in performance. It is not a simple naturalism that is thus achieved, but rather a heightened and polished naturalism; one in which everyday behavior is transformed into 'acting' behavior, identifiable as such through its economy and efficiency, through its 'performance'. As one Manchester student expresses it, if you allow

> your mind and your body to be . . . inhibited (. . .) you'll never be able to lose that and to free that to let something else come in (. . .) or for you to take on another character's experience.
>
> (Manchester Metropolitan first year student)

For early twentieth century movement theorists, in order to 'purify' movement they sought to abstract the body into 'pure', geometrical space. Movement was decontextualized from the everyday world into a space which was geometric, 'scientific' and had no directly apparent social significance. The early movement analysis of Delsarte, Marey and Demeny began this trend, but we can see it clearly in Laban's kinesphere (Laban, 1966: 18–26), in Oskar Schlemmer's triadic ballets (Fiedler & Feierabend, 1999: 541–542) and his drawing of man in three dimensional space (Schlemmer in Huxley & Witts, 1996: 332), perhaps also in Lecoq's 'effort-rose' (Lecoq, 2000: 82). In locating it in space in this way, the body was also becoming objectified—understood in relation to abstract geometry rather than creating understanding through the application of its own capacities. These conceptions of the body, when represented visually, typically take the form of a generalized (usually male) figure placed centrally within a network of converging lines through a passive, receptive and geometrically bordered space. Within this 'objective' space, the body and its movement could, it was suggested, be imagined in its 'purest' form. Clearly for the actor to respond to the challenges offered by such a framework for movement, they must bring their body to a point where it can respond with a similar 'purity' of intent. It is for this reason that the 'neutral body' is often conceived of by staff and students as a *tabula rasa* (see Locke, 1975 [1690]: 89), 'it's as if you're trying to get rid of your physical patterns, so that you've then got a blank canvas to work on' (Rose Bruford second year student). The blankness is iconical for abstract geometrical space, configuring the body as a series of 'possibilities' for movement in space. Some teachers use a Neutral Mask to encourage the student to 'depersonalize' in this way. The mask attempts to abstract the human face into a group of simple features in a state of open readiness.

> It highlights you, what it is about you that makes you you. Because you can't then hide things behind your face, it's just completely what is in the body.
>
> (Rose Bruford second year student)

If movement is understood in relation to a set of mathematical abstractions then that which movement represents can also be understood in the same way. Emotions, intentions, and other social and psychophysical functions should be able to be understood in terms of mechanical functions and spatial abstractions. In this sense, for instance, emotions can be included within the frame of abstracted movement knowledge. Jacques Lecoq's work on movement, space and structures within his Laboratoire d'Étude du Mouvement [LEM] sets out deliberately to explore these kinds of possibilities. The neutral body can thus be seen as an attempt, through purification and abstraction, to avoid what Roland Barthes describes as the 'adjectival' (Barthes, 1977:179–189); if the body can be described as having a quality then it is not neutral. Of course, in performing the exercises the student can never achieve abstraction, for the body is always asserting its presence and always present in the experiencing of movement. The student does not, indeed cannot, simply experience the body in motion within an abstract space, in phenomenological terms what they more exactly have is a sense of their body moving and coordinating the space which they interpret only consequently as abstract.

'AN AWFUL LOT OF MOVEMENT'—
PARADIGMS AND PERFORMATIVITY

We have seen then, that the 'natural' body is performative—constructing its 'naturalness' through the citation of movements and methods of training which are conventionally and paradigmatically associated with 'Nature', and which are understood as antithetical to industrialized and commercialized norms of movement. Efficient and economical movement bridges this divide; it sits comfortably within the analysis of movements in nature provided by the observations and analysis of Marey, Muybridge, Demeny and Souriau, whilst at the same time satisfying the needs of the capitalist economy for a system of production where superfluous and excessive movement is policed and eliminated. Body knowledge such as that acquired by the acting student is performative in that it is achieved through the repeated 'performance' or enactment of physical actions, exercises and gestures.

> I think it's Litz [Pisk] said that you have to do an awful lot of movement to understand how to stand still. So that in fact the more capable you are of moving your body in a controlled fashion, not just hurling it about, but the more flexible your body becomes the more that you can just stand still and speak the text if that's what's required.
>
> (Allnutt, 1999)

The 'neutral' body is in this sense a body compelled to 'give up its truth' through repeated physical performance. Pisk's 'awful lot of movement' operates as a subtle but repeated 'interrogation of the body to force it to yield its secrets' (McConnell, 1997: 218). It is not simply the body that learns to stand still, but the student who learns to configure 'standing still' as an important and valuable part of her subjectivity as a performer. In repeatedly seeking physical simplicity and efficiency, the student's body reveals itself to itself whilst simultaneously struggling to construct itself anew. In attempting to perform itself as 'natural' and 'neutral' it reveals the respects in which it is neither, performing its own difference through seeking its own absence. (In a later chapter this performative construction of the actor's body will be examined in greater detail.) The performative construction of the 'neutral' body has then inherent contradictions. It seeks to configure the student actor's self as a knowing subject which is at the same time somehow not actually fully present, the actor's self *is* constructed, but as a 'gateway' for the acquisition of a kind of 'pure' experience. In these senses, 'neutral' body training offers a phenomenological conception of mind and consciousness, a conception which is open to Judith Butler's criticism that it 'appears to assume the existence of a choosing and constituting agent prior to language' (Butler, 1990b: 270). In so far as the 'neutral' subject seems required 'to experience everything as if for the first time and [live] in the flow of the immediate present, in the here and now' (Eldredge, 1996: 58), it is required to pre-exist language. For Judith Butler language is paradigmatic discourse, we not only understand the body by 'reading' it, we live it in its textuality. If, as Butler implies, we can only read the body as sign(s), then the material body has no intelligence or memory of its own, knowledge exists only through the knowing subject and the 'neutral' body is no more than a shell. However, as Vicky Kirby argues in *Telling Flesh* (1997), if movement training seeks to enable students to 'know' the exercises through their flesh, muscles and nerves, then the body must be able to communicate directly and non-discursively and if it can do so then such practice would shake the very edifice of social constructionism. For Judith Butler, the 'matter' of the body is unintelligible to itself, and can only become so through thought/language (Kirby, 1997: 115). If our flesh has memory, can 'read' and 'write' and thus perhaps 'know' itself, then the primacy of thought/language is fractured and problematized (Kirby, 1997: 127) and we would need to re-evaluate the body-as-sign.

A naïve understanding of the 'neutral' body might consider it as an actual and achievable physical state, as if it were an object in the world. But we can best consider the 'neutral' body not as a material reality, but as a way of understanding the body's relationship to the world. We can furthermore suggest that the 'neutral' body's meanings may inevitably be discursively framed but will also be variously, multiply and fluidly produced. By considering the 'neutral' body phenomenologically, as a way of knowing the world, we can conceive more usefully of 'neutral' actor training as a process and the 'neutral' body training as a journey:

> [I]t's getting there that's the important bit, not the end result, in something like a movement class, really. 'Cause you can just continue the journey the whole time.
> (Rose Bruford second year student)

Even if we accept the body as socially constructed, it is never finished (even after death). It is always in the process of construction, of remaking, even of demolition or decay. Understanding the body is therefore a process of understanding not only how it has been, but also how it is and how it might be. Such an understanding has direct relevance for the training of actors. Movement classes for actors are 'lessons in expanding your awareness of how you do move, how you could move, and how other people do move' (Central School BA Acting for Stage and Screen second year student). Movement training seeks to place the student in a state of heightened psychophysical awareness with regard to these processes. This particular awareness reveals itself in practice through a condition of 'readiness' or what Jacques Lecoq called *disponibilité*: 'a state of discovery, of openness, of freedom to receive' (Lecoq, 2000: 38). This state, like 'the condition of a runner in the moment before his race' (Eldredge & Huston, 1995: 121), is broadly comparable to 'the basic level of organisation common to all performers' which Eugenio Barba defines as 'pre-expressive' (Barba & Savarese, 1991: 187). For Pradier, the pre-expressive draws on the notion of a body which is distinguished as a 'performing' body through, at least in part, its 'total patterning' and physical efficiency:

> What we see is a special organization of sensory-motor tensions which gives us the feeling that the action will be successfully carried out.
> (Pradier, 1990: 90)

Though movement tutors and students may not describe it in the same manner as Barba, Savarese and Pradier, nonetheless, as Shona Morris asserts, the state of being 'ready, alert' (Morris, 1999) is accepted as central to movement training: 'everybody who works in movement knows exactly what it means' (Morris, 1999). It is a body open to and aware of its own transmutability.

THE 'NEUTRAL' BODY AS PRAXIS

If we accept that the 'neutral' body is not an object, but a process, and a process which seeks performatively to expose and manipulate the social construction of the body, then we must also acknowledge that it is a process developed for specific theatrical purposes, purposes which in part define its nature. Professional acting makes very particular demands upon the body of the actor and on their ability to use their physical resources creatively, spontaneously, expressively and responsibly. To view the 'neutral' body as simply an ideological construct is potentially to individualize it in relation to voice and acting, and to marginalize its role in praxis. This is a mistake that Sarah Werner makes, for instance, in her criticism of 'neutral' voice training (Werner, 1996). Despite the shifting relationship between movement, voice and acting over the century, movement tutors have consistently seen their practice as in all important senses specifically working within the context of a coherent system of actor training. The development of 'neutral' body training has been driven by a pragmatic impulse—how best to provide the modern actor with the physical skills necessary for the interpretation of dramatic roles and the development of a successful career.

> [I]f I was to be writing about this rather than thinking about it as an actor, I would find it very hard to say, 'Yes, we can reduce ourselves down to this thing which is neutral', 'cause I don't believe that . . . I think everyone brings their own baggage and stuff. But, it's incredibly useful to be able to think like that for the purposes of acting.
> (Guildhall first year student)

THE SIGNIFYING BODY

> [A]n actor has to link the body with text and meaning. Learning with the body for an actor is creating meaning.
> (Morris, 1999)

The actor's body has to respond to the need to communicate clearly with the spectators who peruse it. In this respect it is required to signify meaning, intention, presence and resonance. For professional actors in the traditional theatre, important choices and decisions about the signifying functions of their bodies and their physical movements are not in their hands alone, but in the hands of the director who has employed them, of the writer who has written the play, and of the (hopefully) many and (possibly) varied spectators who will make multiple meanings out of the actions, gestures and movements they produce. The physical awareness and control developed through the 'neutral' body must then be viewed within the context of its participation in this complex economy of performance. The actor needs to be confident that they can respond to the demands of their employers, the requirements of the play, and the expectations of the audience. To this end, the actor learns about the construction of his or her self in order to learn not only about the creation but also more importantly about the communication of a fictional character.

> You have to be able to think about how you look and analyse how you look, and how you walk and move. But without worrying about it. You have to be able to look at it objectively. And . . . and just say, "Look, this is how I'm moving. This is how I need to move . . . to give off this image to create this character."
>
> (Rose Bruford second year student)

In learning to 'acknowledge your body a lot more' (Manchester Metropolitan second year student), the student actor is not only learning body awareness, but also how the body signifies to others and to the self. Student actors, in rediscovering their own bodies, acknowledge the performative and communicative potential of their own bodies both to others and to themselves. Posture is identified as a major signifier in this context. 'Neutral' posture represents not only the ability to adjust and change postural alignment, but also the alignment of the body in such a way that physical co-ordination, sensory awareness and physical 'presence' are enhanced. As a result of the development of systems of movement therapy and physical education over the last century, posture operates not only as a means for improving efficient body use and as a source of pleasurable experiences of integrated movement but also as a signifier of the same, placing posture within discourses of anatomy, physiology, aesthetics and the vocational. The 'neutral' body signifies (thus giving and communicating) a form of social status: 'if (. . .) you start to stand up, apart from anything else you're taking status' (Allnutt, 1999). In so far as it is possible to tell whether a student is trained or not, the audience in a performance may be able to read the actor's physical alignment, movement and gesture as indicative of efficiency, suggestive of performance, and as kinesthetically pleasurable. At the same time, of course, the audience read and construct themselves as participants in the culture which constructs the actors' bodies. In so far as the audience participate in this way, the training becomes invisible to them, either taken for granted or simply ignored—Pavis theorizes that the audience may even derive pleasure from the process of 'understanding, accepting and finally becoming accustomed to' (1993: 55) the conventions and movement regimes which they see being employed.

The 'Neutral' Body, the 'Natural' Body and Movement Training 101

The potential of the student actor's body to signify is in this sense partially circumscribed by the nature of its training. Movement training describes 'limits' and narratives for the body, which inevitably both create and control the communicative potential of the student actor's movement. The movement tutor has an onerous responsibility here, as it is they who set 'the bench mark about what is clear and what isn't in the space' (Morris, 1999). For some classes it might be that voice is excluded, for others it might be included; particular parts of the body might be given special attention (face, hands, spine, or centre of gravity). This selective focus within the training represents not just a convenient schema for the students' training, but is also representative of the training's attempts to organize the spectators' attention, to identify the modes of meaning-making and to establish their permissible inter-relationships. Further, the movement of the actor must operate to construct a convincing illusion of character for the spectator. For a post-Freudian culture that means that the actor's movement must signify its origins in the impulsive and subconscious mind of the character. The 'neutral' body training is thus seen as helping the actor to convey as clearly as possible a sense that movement is expressive of 'mind' and emotion, of intention. Certain emphases are given to the physicality of the performance from which the observer is encouraged to derive the *perception* of mind.

In conceiving of the neutral body as a 'blank page', acting students are also indicating that movements and gestures should be able to be both 'written' and 'read' more clearly on the body:

> you do notice with actors (. . .) if they're inhibited in some way you don't accept what they're trying to present you with. You don't believe them. Whereas if their whole body's in tune with what they're trying to give you, you do believe, and you accept it because their body is reacting to how their experience has affected them.
> (Manchester Metropolitan first year student)

Because abstractions such as 'self' and 'mind' cannot be directly read in performance, the 'neutral' body is valued by the actor, and incidentally by the director, for its ability to communicate 'groundedness' (a form of psychophysical sincerity) and 'presence', and for the extent to which it seems to be more easily readable. These qualities focus the spectator on the intentionality and significance of the actor's movement, such that we are able to understand the actor/character's psychic 'self' as *physically* produced in performance training (and in rehearsal/performance) and read it accordingly. Theatre-literate audiences are then able to assess an actor's performance in terms of its 'connectedness' and 'groundedness'. The success of the performative production of 'self' can be interrogated against a culturally constructed ideal vision of an 'efficient' performance of self where movement *directly* fulfils intention. Student actors grow in confidence in their ability to make these kinds of distinctions: 'You can see who's more in the body (. . .) You've got a vocabulary to express that' (Manchester Metropolitan second year student). Tutors and students feel that it is possible to tell intuitively when a movement is not 'true', is not connected; but, at the same time, this 'truth' is decentered—residing both with the person watching, and with the student observed. However as economic power lies with the observers, regardless of the student's own feelings of honesty, in this instance 'it is to do with (. . .) what we [the onlooker] perceive to be true' (Morris, 1999).

So there is a complex problem evident here. If we allow that the body operates as a sign, then we imply the material body as a signifier and must determine what it is that is signified. If the signified is identified as the 'self' then we potentially create a difference (however small) between the signifying body and the signified self, which works as if to confirm the mind/body dualism we have already sought to dismiss. Alternatively we could collapse the signifier and the signified so that the body somehow stands for itself, as a way of knowing itself. In such a configuration, those more aware of their bodies as signifiers may experience more distance between the body and the 'self'—the distance between intention and physical action is consequently increased—and less control over the function of that signification. Student actors are however required to operate within a dual configuration: bodies as signifiers (objects in a visual frame producing meanings); and bodies as intentional and active (impressing meaning on the world around them). How can students learn both to be and to become? Let us suppose that 'neutral' body training allows the actor to develop what might be termed an 'active consciousness'—a state in which the actor can engage spontaneously in the dramatic moment and at the same time maintain the level of consciousness required to allow the body to signify to itself. 'Active consciousness' is in this sense a distinctively theatrical form of consciousness. Without consciousness the mind and body would be one, operating in immediate response to the surrounding environment, but would not be capable of grappling with meaning. The actor seeks lively spontaneous action, which must simultaneously be brought to their consciousness to begin to give it significance. This complex set of contradictions also reveals important ways in which movement and the experience of the body in performance can be a site for difference, a subject that will be examined in the final part of this chapter.

ONE BODY/MANY BODIES

'Since bodies are unique, each person's neutrality is his own: there is no single pattern.'

(Eldredge & Huston, 1995: 124)

'[E]veryone's different obviously.'

(Rose Bruford second year student)

The 'Neutral' Body, the 'Natural' Body and Movement Training 103

Although Lecoq describes the 'neutral' body as having 'no character' and existing only as 'a neutral generic being' (Lecoq, 2000: 38), it would be misleading to take this as implying that for Lecoq, or for other teachers, there is just one generic 'neutral' body. Lecoq's humanism, informed perhaps by his war-time experiences and his training as a physiotherapist, predisposed him towards the recognition of common features of the body's operation at distinctive socio-physiological boundary points, such as 'walking', 'waking', 'the farewell' and 'the meeting', and to recognizing each student's individuality (and gender, age and ethnicity). At the same time as movement training for actors explores that which apparently cannot be detached from each of these common actions, it also teaches the nature and effect of various differences. When students put on the Neutral Mask and explore the process of waking, what the teacher identifies is the individuality of each student's response to the task. Lecoq was keenly aware of the tension which exists at this point: 'The idea that everyone is alike is both true and totally false' (Lecoq, 2000: 40). It might then seem plausible that 'neutral' body training acts democratically as a process whereby all students are both compared and differentiated on an equal basis against criteria related not to specific, ideal, material bodies, but to the processes through which those bodies move, make meaning and communicate. In this section I will seek to examine in greater detail the extent to which this aim is achievable. Clearly it is at the points of physical difference prioritized by our culture(s) where the arguments and issues are most acutely realized. I will therefore examine bodies that can be described as 'different' within the specific contexts of class, gender, ethnicity and disability, with regard to the effects of enculturation and the possibilities for resistance and empowerment.

Norms of physical appearance and facility for acting students have in part been sustained by processes of audition wherein the body is subjected to disciplined and detailed surveillance, and inspected for weakness or deformity. The audition process understandably mirrors the industry model for job selection, and with drama schools seeking to ensure that their graduating students get work it is hardly surprising that there is at this time only limited recruitment of students who do not fit a white, middle class, ablebodied norm. Such a scenario tends to perpetuate the status quo, making it harder for 'role models' to arise and for industry attitudes to be encouraged to change. 'Other bodies' have in the past been dismissed within our culture as inefficient because they have not matched criteria, which though seemingly essentialized are actually constructed with very specific cultural purposes in mind. Against the paradigms of the 'pure and innocent child', the 'organic and spontaneous animal', the 'noble Ancient Greek' and the 'virile gymnast', we can see the inevitable marginalization of the disabled, the feminine, the ethnic and the working class. If we accept that, 'Our experience of our bodies is always culturally determined; the very way we stand and sit varies from culture to culture.' (Gilbert & Pearson, 1999:

48); and that there are, within dominant economies, vested interests in the active maintenance of this distinction, then it follows that,

> Modes of experience which make obvious the problematic nature of this division (. . .) are therefore among the most prohibited and policed modes of experience within western culture.
>
> (Gilbert & Pearson, 1999: 48)

Despite its liberal and subversive traditions as an art form, theatre in this country has been particularly sensitive to the intervention of 'other bodies' into its most hallowed places. The attention given to Nabil Shaban's Mosca (Graeae, 1996), Fiona Shaw's Richard II (National Theatre, 1995) and the casting of the black actor Adrian Lester as Henry V (National Theatre, 2003), provide evidence of the assumptions informing the classical actor's body and the notice generated when those assumptions are challenged. Movement (and dance in particular) has stereotypical associations with the physical activity (and enjoyment) of black people, gays and women, and is simultaneously perceived as problematic for disabled people. In a number of ways then, it is already marked out as an important site for the construction of cultural identities. Paul Siegel's argument that 'gays and lesbians are more likely to be seen as communicating a message through their dance' (Siegel, 2001: 267) can thus be extended, opening up 'otherness' as particularly eloquent in movement training. This section will examine the implications of 'otherness' for our understanding of the 'neutral'/'natural' body in performance.

DIS/ABILITY

> Many of our ideas about autonomy, health, and self-determination in this late-twentieth-century culture are based on a model of the body as an efficient machine over which we should have total control.
>
> (Allbright, 1998: 65)

Disability provides an excellent example of a field in which certain bodies are deemed incapable of reaching socially accepted levels of efficiency. In a very contemporary sense, the disabled body is discriminated against by being positioned as a body which cannot 'perform'—it cannot supposedly achieve the levels of efficiency that post-Fordist western economies demand, and as a result it is conceived of as simultaneously invisible, asexual and outcast—and further, denied the opportunity to represent itself. For Allbright,

> The issue of control is (. . .) key to understanding not only the specific issues of prejudice against the disabled, but also the larger symbolic place that disability now holds in our culture's psychic imagination.
>
> (Allbright, 1998: 62)

The 'Neutral' Body, the 'Natural' Body and Movement Training 105

In so far as the disabled actor is culturally perceived as clumsy, awkward, inefficient, weak, or in any other sense incomplete, then that actor is a cause of anxiety for an industry which assumes bodies which are beautiful, graceful, responsive and efficient. Vanessa Ewan (Central School) highlights the dilemma that student actors and drama schools face now, whereby the training is moving faster to address inequality and discrimination than is the industry at large:

> I see no problem with an actual physical disability (. . .) you know, it's just going to have the same problems for them as in any other part of their life. I don't see a problem with them doing the acting. I see a problem with them getting the work, that might be extremely frustrating . . .
> (Ewan, 1999a)

The disabled acting student faces the biggest hurdle when, having trained, they attempt to engage with the disciplining powers of the theatre economy. Some students will go to great lengths to disguise or conceal disabilities during their training. Today drama schools are much more aware of the rights of disabled students and are quite clear that the 'neutral' and efficient, trained body should not be used as a source of discriminatory criteria. Some movement techniques, such as ballet, present particular problems with respect to perceptions of body image and dis/ability, and movement tutors are typically very alert to these issues. It is these concerns that have, in part, contributed to a shift of focus in many drama schools away from ballet towards the more flexible and expressive 'neutral' body and 'pure' movement training.

In the past the lack of access to professional actor training for disabled people has meant that training provision has happened mainly within the state education sector (for example Hereward College in Coventry), or 'on-the-job' within disabled companies such as Graeae. Before the increase in social awareness of disability issues from the 1970s onwards, disabled actors who found success in the theatre did so largely by concealing their disability (until perhaps their fame made it less of an encumbrance). In 1985 the Attenborough Report on Arts and Disabled People recommended that 'There is an urgent need for full-time training for disabled students in the performing arts' (Carnegie Trust, 1985: 16). Three years later a follow-up review identified only one course specifically training disabled people for the theatre (a diploma course for deaf students at Bulmershe College of Higher Education, Reading) and commented that although 'a deaf student may be successful at one of the Drama Colleges with special facilities provided; this is a splendid, though sadly rare, achievement' (Carnegie, 1988: 80). The Disability Discrimination Act should now mean that access to actor training should be easier for disabled students. The movement training of disabled student actors is clearly also an area that needs further research and development. The therapeutic value of the work for students with disabilities is clear:

I've got things wrong with my legs, so . . . the Laban and the Alexander just helps sort of free everything up. And gives me a lot more mobility. Before I came here, I couldn't (. . .) stay rolled down for more than a minute, whereas now I can happily stay there for ages if I have to.

(Rose Bruford second year student)

However it is equally important that this does not distort the perception of the students' abilities within certain exercises. Certainly, in a training culture increasingly obsessed with assessment and 'bench-marking', the criteria for movement performance as applied to both able and disable bodied students will need very careful consideration. It may be necessary to revisit in detail the idea of the organic and integrated body, the actor's ability to commit directly to an intention, the connection between emotion and action, and the signification of the body, when disabled bodies so directly challenge the value and importance that is put on an able-bodied interpretation of these factors. As Ann Cooper Allbright writes, observing disabled performers forces a double vision upon us, helping us to recognize that a performance both is and is more than a question of physical capability (Allbright, 1998: 58).

GENDER

'Women in sexist society are physically handicapped'
(Young, 1990b: 269)

One of the core principles of 'neutral' body training, as we have seen earlier in this chapter, is that the student actor should be enabled to experience the body not as a site of alienation, but as a site for 'wholeness' where the body participates in the understanding and realization of self-hood. This next section will examine the extent to which access to such experience of the body in actor training is gender-specific, and the implications for an understanding of movement training as potentially gender-productive.

In Iris Young's 1990 essay, 'Throwing like a Girl' (Young, 1990b), which will be examined as a key contribution to understanding the gendered phenomenology of the 'neutral' body and its training, she identifies the importance of physical activity for women in enabling them to develop physical freedom, strength and confidence. In her article Young contests Erwin Straus' suggestion (Straus, 1966: 157) that differences in the physical abilities of men and women (in particular, with regard to the action of throwing) are biologically determined. She argues that if one takes 'body comportment and movement as definitive for the structure and meaning of human lived experience' (Young, 1990b: 260) then the difference between masculine and feminine body comportment and style of movement must surely be significant. Thus, if '[e]very human existence is defined by its situation; the particular existence of the female person is no less defined by the historical, cultural, social, and economic limits of her situation' (Young, 1990b: 260). Young looks specifically at bodily activities that entail what she describes as 'gross movement', movements that 'require the enlistment of strength and the confrontation of the body's capacities and possibilities with the resistance and malleability of things', movements in which 'the body aims to accomplish a definite purpose or task' (Young, 1990b: 261). Such movement activity is central to the 'pure' and 'neutral' movement exercises the student actors are asked to perform: 'When an actor throws a stone, each part of his body should throw the stone, and no part should do anything else' (Eldredge & Huston, 1995: 128). What Straus observed was that, in the act of throwing, females did not tend to engage the whole of their bodies in the action with the same ease and confidence as males did. As a result, throwing seemed less 'natural' for women. Young views this physical tentativeness as indicative of a lack of confidence in the ability to perform tasks, and perhaps of a fear of getting hurt. For Young, the body is often experienced by women as 'a fragile encumbrance, rather than the media for the enactment of our aims' (Young, 1990b: 264); in her analysis,

> feminine movement exhibits an ambiguous transcendence, an inhibited intentionality, and a discontinuous unity with its surroundings. A source of these contradictory modalities is the bodily self-reference of feminine comportment, which derives from the woman's experience of her body as a thing at the same time that she experiences it as a capacity.
> (Young, 1990b: 264)

Young argues that under socio-cultural pressure to consider herself as a thing, like other things in the world, woman as a result remains immanent, under-using her real physical capacity and experiencing an 'inhibited intentionality' (Young, 1990b: 265). In this sense, 'women tend to locate their motion in part of the body only, leaving the rest of the body relatively immobile' (Young, 1990b: 266), learning to restrict their own movements. Accepting Merleau-Ponty's proposition that it is the body that constitutes space—'there would be no space at all for me if I had no body' (Merleau-Ponty, 2000: 102)—and that it is the body's movement which extends ourselves into the space around us, we can see the importance of body unity and integration in immediately linking the body and the space around it so that, '[t]he body's movement and orientation organizes the surrounding space as a continuous extension of its own being' (Young, 1990b: 266).

We have seen already how early twentieth century movement practitioners sought to 'purify' movement by abstracting it into geometric space. Though they may have initially intended, through abstraction, to avoid issues such as gender, applying Young's phenomenological analysis helps us to identify the manner in which space and movement is implicitly gendered through the moving body. Drawing on Merleau-Ponty's distinction between 'external space' (or the 'spatiality of position') and 'bodily space' (or the 'spatiality of situation') (Merleau-Ponty, 2000: 100), Young argues that, as women are forced to relate differently to space, then 'it must follow that there are also particular modalities of feminine spatiality' (Young, 1990b: 267). The culture/nature dichotomy proposed by Simone de Beauvoir and accepted by Young, further functions to denigrate 'embodiment and nurturing activity' and celebrate 'abstraction and fabrication' (Young, 1998: 287), sustaining a gendered hierarchy which prioritizes the abstraction of the body and movement.

'Neutral' body training produces changes in/on the body and to the experience of the body, changes in 'body use'. These are changes that have a significant and gendered effect on all student actors. Posture feels improved, the body lengthens, and feels more open: 'If you hold yourself the way we've been taught, then you kind of . . . you do feel taller and more open' (Rose Bruford second year student). The neutral body is a body reconfigured as an integrated whole. Male students seem to respond very positively to this—perhaps they are already confident in the ability of their body to engage with the world: 'I was thinking of the movements as me, as a composite being, doing a movement with everything' (Guildhall second year student—male)—but they also come to relish the sense in which their bodies become more than instruments, become a more sensitive and integrated part of how they understand the world and locate themselves socially. For the female student, the 'neutral' body process must also represent a liberating and empowering experience. It raises her awareness of the manner and extent to which she has learnt to acquire 'the many subtle habits of feminine body comportment' (Young, 1990b: 270), as well as allowing her to bring all her physical capacities to bear on the world and project herself with greater confidence into a space within which 'she can exist as a free subject' (Young, 1990b: 271). Interestingly, the voice tutor Patsy Rodenburg refers to similar experiences in voice training, in which:

> Male communication habits revolve around taking up space. Not giving in. Standing feet apart, sitting legs open. Chest open or puffed out. Energy forward, probing. Head held high. Choosing to look or not look without apology. Breathing slowly and deeply into the body. Speaking when they want to and not rushing. Driving the voice. Often being too pushy without apology. Not falling off a line, but sustaining an idea.
> (Rodenburg, 2000: 100–101)

The potential for a new physical awareness appears understandably to be motivational and exciting for female acting students. One Central School student expresses this new awareness as a strange mixture of generosity and selfishness:

When it comes down to it I do what I want with my body so . . . so I'm OK because I know that that's OK (. . .) I give you the whole of my body and everything into it. I think you need to have . . . you need to have that generosity, but then a kind of selfishness that goes along with it as well.

(Central School BA Acting for Stage and Screen second year student)

What all students, both female and male, seem to value from movement training is the connectedness, not only of the body parts but also of movement and intention—students even feel that they are able to distinguish this quality; it is, for them, a part of what makes 'good' movement. The exercises clearly go beyond work on the body at a physical level and introduce the students to the inter-connection of the body and the emotions. For male students, their movement becomes more emotionally expressive than they may have been used to, more clearly related to their presentation of and location of a performed social self (or 'character'). They begin to show evidence of an awareness of each other and of their own bodies, their movement work becomes softer—'more tactile, more sensuous, less focused round sexual gratification' (McRobbie, 1994: 168), they also experience an increased sense of 'being watched'. Though the gaze here is not (necessarily) as sexualized as the 'male gaze' (Mulvey, 1975), it does seem to operate to heighten the male student's awareness of his presentation of masculinity. Initially male students may feel a little exposed: 'they're not sure if it's all a bit . . . sissy' (Dowling, 2000), but for some students the training provides important insights to gendered behavior patterns:

you realise that you walk around every day (. . .) like that because, you know, it's a male thing and . . . you stick your chest out because you're a man and . . . it's all bollocks and it just makes you realise that.
(Guildhall first year student—male)

Some feminist theorists argue that men who 'toy' with the experience of femininity (i.e. feminine experiences of the body in movement) are 'gender tourists', in that the appreciation of women's experience is only partial. Nonetheless, such a critique need not lead us away from recognizing the value of a training regime which is able to construct the disorientation of the psychophysical self, the destabilization of the students' normal experience of themselves and their bodies, as a source of enjoyment and confidence rather than confusion and panic (Gilbert & Pearson, 1999: 107). For female students, they are encouraged to move beyond constricted space, into the 'yonder', through physical risk and purposive engagement with the world generating a sense of empowerment—'You work with blokes, have to pick blokes up, roll around with each other' (Guildhall first year student—female)—as well as sustaining a connection to the intimate personal space which is their physical and emotional centre: '[Y]ou're sort of there, ready for your self, rather than getting in the way of yourself . . . ' (Guildhall second year student—female). Of course social pressures don't disappear, especially for women entering the theatre profession, simply as the result of a movement class. Movement tutors need to heed Elaine Aston's warning that many women's persistent anxieties about body weight and size mean that: 'many of the games or exercises that might be encountered in the theatre workshop impede rather than facilitate women's 'self-acceptance" (Aston, 1999: 44).

Properly applied, 'neutral' body training could nonetheless play a valuable part in revealing the operation of essentialist discourses on the actor's body, whilst also promoting the possibility of purposeful and integrated physical engagement. In these senses 'neutral' body training accepts Young's argument and moves beyond it. Implicit in Young's argument is an idealization of masculine movement (Grimshaw: 1999: 105–106). 'Neutral' body training, in so far as it predicates the body as 'a free and effortless conduit, directly connecting ourselves with the world in a constant and fluid interchange' (Marshall, 2001: 3), would seem to be in danger of a similar idealization. Where 'neutral' body training does manage to evade idealizing the male body is in its 'undoing' of any familiar experience of direct engagement with the world for *all* students. In the proliferation of identifications suggested by the 'neutral' body training, it aligns itself with William Havers' analysis of Deborah Britzman's 'queer pedagogy', which he describes as,

> a technique (. . .) which does not make the world familiar or comfortable (. . .) but which defamiliarizes, or makes strange, queer or even cruel what we had thought to be a world.
>
> (Havers, 1997: 291)

This proliferation is embedded into the movement training experiences of all students.

Grimshaw also suggests that a level of 'objectification' of or distance from the body may be necessary 'as a transitional process whenever previous body limits are extended in some way' (Grimshaw, 1999: 110)—a description that, as we shall see more clearly in a later chapter, mirrors the learning trajectory of the student actor. Young does usefully identify that concepts of 'normal' body use do need to be problematized, and that within any 'category of the 'normal'" (Grimshaw, 1999: 108) we need to make space for a variety of modalities. It is these assumptions around 'neutral' movement training (as this section of the chapter seeks to argue) that drama schools may need to address with greater rigor. As Sue Ellen Case has argued (Case in Goodman, 1998: 145–146) this may mean examining critically the extent to which Stanislavskian approaches can truly represent women's experiences (and implicitly those of other marginalized

The 'Neutral' Body, the 'Natural' Body and Movement Training 111

communities). In a later reflection on her 1990 essay, Young suggests that the embodiment of pregnancy questions the extent to which an 'awareness of the body's thingness distracts from active transcendence through the body' (Young, 1998: 288). It could also be argued that the pregnant body can, in a similar sense, operate as an image for the trained actor. Both actor and mother-to-be experience awareness of themselves as object *and* as subject: as weighty, corporeal and observed as well as transcendent and purposive; as within the temporary process of being both one person and another; and, as an emotional centre and a receptor for the emotional responses of others. For the female actor this association functions positively to validate specifically feminine qualities of their movement. For male students it functions to open up their conditioned unified instrumentalism to a more complex awareness of the body as situated, whilst offering complex associations which are perhaps too strongly linked to conventional male/female domestic roles and biological determinism. The idea of pregnancy is a radical challenge to many men's gendered self-image and may go some way to explaining male preference for an instrumentalist attitude to the body. It is the deployment of such complex re-configurations of gendered bodies and their movements, which Paul Franklin suggests marks the actor as marginalized in respect of sexuality, gender and socio-sexual status (Franklin, 2001: 63). Such deployment may even feature as part of what Marjorie Garber refers to as 'the inherent bisexuality of celebrity' (Garber, cited in Franklin, 2001: 63), in that, 'All great stars are bisexual in the performative mode' in so far as they embody the condition of 'having two genders in one body' (Garber, cited in Franklin, 2001: 64). Heterosexual body norms are in this manner quite directly challenged through the students' movement learning: '[W]ith the neutral it's like an asexualness. You could be (. . .) girl, boy, man, woman or anything, 'cause that's the way they've trained us now' (Rose Bruford second year student—female). More recently some movement tutors have included work on gender and movement within their classes, explicitly exploring how and in what ways movement is gendered.

It is important to note that 'neutral' body training does not privilege the 'camp' body over the 'straight' body. Each student still has to take care, as it were, of their own sexuality; in so far as there is a 'queering' of the actor's body and movement it is on a subtle level and is allowed visibility only in proportion to its marketability, its value within the wider theatre economy, and its relevance to the dominant dramatic canon. Expressive movement training only displaces the genito-centric sexuality of social body language in favor of a more polymorphous body. The body is expressive in space and time (Laban) and expressive in relation to its physiological functioning (Alexander and Feldenkrais) and sexuality is partially displaced into a general sense of the body's sensuality and, as a result, partially sublimated. In this sense, the 'neutral' body training does encourage the gay or lesbian actor aspiring for a varied West End or classical career to conceal several aspects of a physicality they might otherwise wish to celebrate. Perhaps part of the significance of plays by writers such as Mark Ravenhill since the mid 1990s has been in the opportunity they have presented for bodies to perform in unashamedly queer ways on stage.

Actor training then offers both female and male students a site for the active development of movement which, in line with Young's thesis, engages with the world. The majority of young actors enter drama school well aware of acting's particular gendered characteristics, content to be looked at, confident in their physicality and eager to express themselves as fully as possible through movement. Yet in proving resistant and exceptional to Young's gendered analysis of everyday movement, the students are actively engaging in the construction of an exciting, expressive, potent if marginal, gender norm of the 'actor'.

> If the body in its very materiality is an effect of repeated practices (. . .) [then a body] which organises its pleasures through an interplay of elements 'masculine' and 'feminine', both and neither, might offer scope for modes of experience which would have potentially deconstructive implications for anybody, male or female, gay or straight.
>
> (Gilbert & Pearson, 1999: 102)

ETHNICITY

Despite the gradual improvement of access to actor training for students from black ethnic groups over the last century, the models for movement training in drama schools have all been predominantly white European. The veteran black British actor, Norman Beaton, reflecting on his experiences as an actor in one of the early television soap operas aimed specifically for a black audience (*Empire Road*), indicates some of the subtle and pervasive ways in which black actors found that industry norms (and by implication actor training) tended to emphasize reserved and 'neutral' English physicality and to encourage the repression of patterns of gesture and action with resonance for black culture as if these were in some important sense less 'neutral' than white English social behavior:

> *Empire Road* really [was], I suppose, the most important black soap that there has been in this country . . . [it] took race relations into a wholly different area . . . When Horace Ové came in to direct some episodes in the second series, that immediately introduced a different voice . . . All the structures of English acting that we had been using went out the window and, suddenly, we were doing big arm movements and using West Indian language in the same way we do back home. That was a wonderful experience. So when Horace came to direct the

episodes, we had a black soap written by a black man, directed by a black director, with a black cast ... The humour was there, the comedy was there, but now we had the opportunity to take the characters and the situation a lot further, because we had a black director who understood the cultural setting and who could guide us when we were missing certain things.

(Norman Beaton in Pines, 1992: 116)

This clearly illustrates the danger of the 'neutral' body becoming an objective reality, rather than a process. Movement training methods have historically been drawn from a wide range of cultural traditions—martial arts, yoga and capoiera for instance—such richness should provide constant challenges to the student actor's body, highlighting the cultural as well as social influences which they will need to be alert to. Asian influences have continued both within conventional training (for example Kenneth Rea's work at Guildhall School) and in mid-career training and open workshops (such as classes offered by Phillip Zarrilli, Yoshi Oida and the International Workshop Festival). Perhaps the longevity of Asian performance techniques (which often stretch back in unbroken lines of apprenticeship for several centuries) is attractive to a western culture which is constantly changing and which increasingly offers heritage instead of tradition. Though heavily codified, Asian theatre techniques seem to suggest a core of rigorous technique and an appreciation of the flow of energies and rhythms, which strike a chord with some contemporary training. For the theatre director Jatinder Verma, it is impossible to remove the cultural from theatrical production; he sees a positive future for British theatre practice and training in recognizing the richness which this potentially unlocks:

Language in the theatre (i.e. spoken words) is inherently physical. In theatre, therefore, cultural "signs" emanate from how the actor uses language (i.e. his body). For me, this is a fundamental axiom. In addition, English movement training proceeds from within a tradition that emphasises the dominance of the toe over the heel: in essence, the exploration of vertical space. Asian and African movement, in contrast, emphasises the heel over the toe: essentially, an exploration of the horizontal dimension. On a more prosaic level, European movement can be simplistically characterised as "airy" whilst non-European is "earthy".

I think the future of the theatre lies in the marriage, or the dialogue, between the vertical and the horizontal. Inevitably, therefore, I would wish to see more training in Kathakali, in Beijing Opera and in the popular Garba and Bhangra incorporated in our Drama Schools. BUT, this has to be in conjunction with the expansion of the syllabus to incorporate Asian and African texts.

(Jatinder Verma, e-mail correspondence with
Mark Evans, 16 July 2002)

During a master class at the Almeida Theatre in 1990, the Japanese actor Yoshi Oida instructed the class to adopt a pose in which the pelvis was held in a forward tilt. One participant remarked that such a position was surely 'bad posture', to which Yoshi replied that from the cultural traditions within which he had been trained this position represented good posture. This exchange reveals the profound extent of the cultural encoding of our bodies and our understanding of them. While western actor training fails to acknowledge the cultural construction of the norms it takes as 'neutral', such practices as Verma identifies above will remain exotic marginal extras, rather than become integrated and employed in offering the student new positions from which to understand their own cultural physicality and new perspectives on the multiple, various and fluid ways in which they can experience and communicate with their bodies.

Training institutions have become increasingly open to the opportunities and challenges of the international theatre economy. Cheap travel, increased cross-border mobility (especially within the expanded European Union) and the success and growth of festivals such as the London International Festival of Theatre have meant that new physicalities are increasingly seen and experienced in the theatres of London and the larger conurbations. This exposure can only work to reveal in more detail the cultural flavor of movement training for actors. Students at MMU commented that Polish theatre practitioners that they have worked with recognized the 'Englishness' of their movement work, characterized by a certain reserve. The challenge for movement training is to take advantage of the opportunities offered by increasing internationalism whilst avoiding uncritical acceptance of the exotic and alien or its blanket rejection. Global economic forces mean that the theatre economies of the West still function to prioritize the Western body and its patterns of movement, however at the start of the twenty-first century we are seeing the beginning of economic power shifts which may see the balance shift. Various international knowledges and practices have already found their way into university drama departments; this is surely an area where higher education institutions and drama schools could work more closely to explore transfers of new knowledges into the industry.

CLASS

Within the professional theatre industry of the twentieth century the 'well-bred, public school actor, often from a professional family background' (Sanderson, 1984: 292) remained dominant until after the Second World War. After the War, shifts in policy at the drama schools, increases in the grants available from local authorities, an increase in plays which dealt with working class experience, and a general enthusiasm for the democratization of culture and higher education all meant that an increasing number of students from working class backgrounds felt encouraged to become actors and actresses (Sanderson, 1984: 292–304). Notwithstanding the fact that by the last third of the century an increasing number of working class students were getting in to drama schools, the training took time to catch up and could still sometimes resemble a 'genteel finishing school' (Ronald Harwood in Sanderson, 1984: 295). Despite some changes in content and focus during the Sixties, movement training continued to rely on practices such as modern dance, ballet, fencing, calisthenics, martial arts and postural adjustment—all commonly associated with middle class education and leisure. Just as working class movement-based performance modes such as circus, variety and music hall are still generally ignored by the cultural elite, so working class movement traditions such as games, sport, folk dancing and tumbling were for the most part overlooked by the drama schools. For many working class actors this meant that they were forced not only to abandon their regional accent in favor of the (supposedly) neutral 'Received Pronunciation' (or 'RP') but also to erase their working class physicality for a (comparatively) reserved neutral body and what television critic Martin James has called an 'ineradicable gentility' (James, 2002). Between the Wars, the dominant acting style of the likes of Gerald du Maurier and Charles Hawtrey was based largely on the exploitation of personality and the manners of the upper middle class drawing room. The working class actor was required to assimilate and change or be reduced to a career of small character parts. Ewan MacColl recalls how:

> the theatre that we saw around us, the theatre of the West End and to some extent the theatre that was reflected in British films, for example, was so unreal, and the acting styles were so false, they typified what Stanislavsky called 'rubber-stamp' acting, a series of codified gestures, and codified grimaces, and to some extent codified dialogue.
> (Ewan MacColl in Samuel, MacColl & Cosgrove, 1985: 244)

It was to take the intervention of socialist theatre groups such as the Workers' Theatre Movement, Theatre of Action and Unity Theatre (all formed in the years after the General Strike in 1926) and later the Theatre Workshop to reassert the importance and vitality of working class physicality:

> An actor (. . .) should be like an athlete, he should be in complete control of his body, he should be able to make his body do anything that he calls upon it to do.
> (Ewan MacColl in Samuel, MacColl & Cosgrove, 1985: 244)

Joan Littlewood allowed and indeed encouraged her actors to make use of working class performance traditions—perhaps most memorably in *Oh What a Lovely War* (1963). Her own background, like that of many of her actors, was working class. As a scholarship student at RADA between the

Wars she found little that seemed relevant to her own needs and interests. As a result she was suspicious of drama school trained actors; instead, 'Littlewood preferred amateurs because they had not been spoiled by a drama school training with its accompanying mannerisms, fitting them for the West End, but little else' (Bradby & McCormick, 1978: 147).

By drawing together European theatre practice, agit-prop methods, cabaret, music hall, pantomime and revue, Theatre Workshop generated a robust and popular style of performance with its roots in traditional physical skills and in routines well known in working class entertainments. The visit to London of Bertolt Brecht's Berliner Ensemble in 1956 helped to further reinforce the value and importance of a vigorous and critical realism, in which Brecht's direction emphasized the use of actions and gestures which fitted their purpose. Nonetheless, since the mid-1980s, both a decline in adequate funding for working class student actors and a period of theatre production dominated by middle-class tastes have affected a gentle reverse. The model Littlewood provided for a theatre that was not afraid to engage either with the vibrancy of popular culture or with the challenge of European theatre innovation was allowed to fade away. The pride in class accent and physicality which marked the 1960s has all but given way to a more malleable and docile attitude, where it is employability and success that matters. As a result physical skills and ways of working developed by many committed touring groups (7:84, Foco Novo, CAST)—drawn frequently from the pioneering work of Meyerhold, Brecht, Littlewood and others (Samuel, MacColl & Cosgrove, 1985: 243–244)—have been submerged again beneath the waves of conventional practice. Peter Cheeseman, former director of the NCDT and former artistic director at the New Vic Theatre, Stoke-on-Trent, laments the prejudices which keep traditional popular or folk forms of movement practice hidden:

> [W]hen I was running the theatre at Stoke I got very involved with using folk forms (. . .) I was very interested to discover how accessible the forms of English traditional dance were to the average actor. (. . .) I was amazed by how many forms of movement could be built out of the language of traditional English folk dancing. There are rather peculiar prejudices against it, which I don't understand because the tradition is so rich. (. . .) I think this is one of the great treasures of this country.
> (Peter Cheeseman in NCDT, 2001: 33)

It may not be possible to turn back the prejudices Cheeseman identifies, prejudices which tend to categorize such practices as quaint and no longer meaningful, as artisanal rather than artistic. On the other hand, the success of Clive Barker's *Theatre Games* (1977) can be placed in direct relation to his success in recognizing the needs of actors less at ease with ballet, fencing and deportment classes by drawing on activities (such as popular, 'everyday' games) with rich roots in working class social history. Such an approach provides a valuable model for the manner in which the very exercises for movement training must be understood as socio-culturally situated, and reminds us that such situatedness can be turned to political advantage and eventually used to enrich the development of actor training.

CONCLUSION

During this chapter we have seen how social and cultural paradigms have influenced the development of the 'natural' body, how this in turn influenced the development of what is known as 'neutral' body training. The dominant paradigms continue to have a strong association with white, male/heterosexual, able-bodied culture, though I have shown that there are possibilities for current 'neutral' body training to re-examine and to re-construct its practice in ways which will offer resistances to this hegemony. All the movement tutors interviewed were sensitive to these issues and approached their teaching with a constant sense of the need for review, awareness and development. After all, the very nature of their job necessitates a developed sensitivity to the bodies within, and which constitute, our culture. Our society (for in a democracy we must at least assume that it belongs to all of us) can only benefit from the richness and vitality of contemporary cultural diversity. As Jatinder Verma suggests, 'We are, in a quite real sense (. . .) living in times of *dis*continuous narratives, where other lands, cultures, times and tastes seep into our present at a remarkable rate' (Verma, 1999: 197). The drama schools can play an important role in leading professional theatre towards a better recognition of the possibilities this osmosis offers for the theatre of the future.

The 'neutral' body, in its most abstract sense, is unattainable—it is quite literally and metaphorically a 'no-man's-land'. But 'neutrality', I have argued, is not a 'place', nor an external material quality (a 'perfect' physique); but rather a practical process, developing the uninhibited flow of impulses and energies. Nonetheless, the idea of a perfectible body is a powerful influence on the student. The acting profession has long been associated with the promotion of norms of physical beauty (looks, weight, posture, size, dimensions), which creates unenviable tensions for drama school staff in addressing issues around body use and movement. Reference to efficient physical process as opposed to aesthetics of physical expression can help to distance the students from a negative perception of their body. Such an approach reinforces the significance of 'efficiency' within movement training, whilst simultaneously signaling the industrially and culturally constructed nature of the relationship between the efficient body and the 'beautiful' body. However, the tendency to focus on efficiency in this way can, the more rigorously it is applied, distance the training from its complex social contexts by configuring its problems as purely technical. Such distancing is unfortunate, if it occurs, as it is the social contexts which not only enable physical techniques to negotiate meaning, but which also function in the discursive construction of these techniques no less than in the discursive construction of the bodies that engage in them.

Any 'neutral' training that is predominantly technical serves to individuate the students' bodies according to their technical facility, and the social structures that bind them and their actions together are given less importance. Such a 'technical' and individuated approach implicitly infers the 'natural/ neutral' body as pre-social, facilitating re-education from the contaminating forces of modern society and industrial culture. It is a naïve neutrality which assumes that it is by stepping outside the social structures that the student actor is to be able to grasp the socially situated nature of their movement. There is a real danger that the neutral body becomes only another middle class English pattern of movement, unless it is fully understood as a constant process that must be repeatedly applied in order to effectively and meaningfully reveal difference and engage its expressive potential. Whilst the 'neutral' body forms a useful tool for movement analysis, it is important that movement tutors also continue to enable and encourage students to analyze movement socially and culturally. Improvements in movement technique may enable students to engage more purposively with the world (see Young, 1990b), but we must understand that that engagement is socially situated, political and potentially empowering. Equally, it is important not to take any direct and positive engagement with the world for granted. Kate Paterson reminds us of Drew Leder's observation that:

> in everyday life our body 'disappears' from awareness, it is 'taken-for-granted': 'While in one sense the body is the most abiding and inescapable presence in our lives, it is also essentially characterized by absence. That is, one's own body is rarely the thematic object of experience' (Leder 1990: 1)'
>
> (Paterson, 2001: 88)

The 'absent' body is potentially dangerous because it is not available for critical interrogation, we are not able to bring its functions directly into our consideration. It is in striving for a physical spontaneity in which the body becomes only the shadow of the subject's will, that we may create the very circumstances in which we ignore important differences. The journey for the student actor must then involve repeated reflexivity, learning again and again not to take their body for granted.

Neutrality is valued as a concept of the body which simultaneously allows the individual student to consider their movement activity from 'inside' (in terms of locating and expressing psychophysical impulses) and from 'outside' (in terms of the economical and efficient performance of physical actions). On the surface it is often presented as de-politicized. The student actor is not generally encouraged in movement classes to look in depth and detail at the socio-political significance of movement and gesture. Within most drama schools issues of socio-political significance are seen as the job of the acting tutors if they are dealt with at all. Movement classes have tended to focus on the dynamics and the sensory experience of physical action. Despite middle class British culture's historical resistance to a theatre of ideas such as that seen elsewhere on the European mainland—a resistance built on a steadfast belief that ideas hinder action—and despite the consequent tardiness in developing socially and politically aware approaches to actor training, there is nonetheless a willingness to offer a micro-political engagement with the movement training of the actor's body.

> The concept of neutral is an intellectual and imaginative construct. Once it is consciously, or unconsciously, applied, like any concept it conditions how we look at the world: through its lens we notice things that we might not see otherwise.
> (Eldredge, 1996: 49)

In disrupting the student actor's habitual perspective on his/her body, in provoking changes in body use and in presenting the student actor with physical exercises which aim to transform the ways in which the student experiences the body, 'neutral' body training can be transgressive, involving liminal practices which offer a semi-ritualized separation of the performer from their everyday self and everyday behavior towards an 'acting' self and 'acting' behavior. By continuing to engage with bodies which are at the 'margins' of the historical norms of the performer's body, movement training for actors can develop new sites from which to disrupt the students' perspectives on their physical behavior. In this manner it can respond flexibly and sympathetically to the social and cultural complexities of early twenty-first century life.

Though the 'natural/neutral' body is as much a cultural construct as any other 'body' of which we might conceive, and although it may occasionally be misunderstood as an idealized point of refuge from the socio-cultural forces at work on our bodies rather than as a pprocess, yet it is important at the same time to recognize that it has had and continues to have real potential as a point of resistance against those forces. I will seek to show in the chapters which follow that those very tensions which make the 'natural'/'neutral' body such a focus for discourses around race, gender, age and dis/ability, operate not only to normalize the body (see Chapter 3), but have also been put to use in resisting, subverting, challenging and transgressing body 'norms' (see Chapter 4). Further, 'neutral' training, in helping to return the actor to the body and denying the pre-eminence of the voice, has, as John Wright suggests (Wright, 2002), helped to create a healthy and provocative imbalance in a theatre industry in danger of becoming dominated by text and the spoken word.

3 Movement Training for Actors and the Docile Body

> Oh my god, you're standing like an actor.
>
> (Rose Bruford first year student)

> A body is docile that may be subjected, used, transformed, and improved.
>
> (Foucault, 1984: 180)

> [Y]ou kind of give in to your training, 'cause you do . . .
>
> (Central School BA Acting for Stage and Screen second year student)

Training the body for a particular purpose, whether that purpose be for performance or not, involves the 'lived' body of the student passing through disciplining practices which claim to produce useful effects on and for that body. This chapter will examine the nature of these disciplining practices in relation to the physical training of the professional actor and to the discourses through which they operate. Drama schools obviously operate to integrate the student actor into the profession, to make him/her 'absorbable'. A key question then is the extent to which not just the skills but the values of the industry will also have been received (see Foucault in McKenzie, 2001: 50–51). The chapter will examine the pedagogy of the movement class in terms of its 'ability to produce codes of signification' (Meyer in Goodman, 1998: 257). My analysis will draw on the work of Michel Foucault and Judith Butler (Foucault, 1984 & Butler; 1990a, 1993, 1997), Foucault's later concept of the 'care of the self' will also be examined for its potential as an alternative conceptual model for physical training—a model not simply productive of docile and receptive bodies. In a very straightforward sense, clearly the function and purpose of movement training for actors is to 'produce' the body of an actor. Power shows itself through its inscription of knowledges on the actor's body; inscriptions which are not often noticed or considered, which are 'not clearly available to sight and categorization' (Melrose, 1994: 210). The two previous chapters have sought to examine the nature of these 'knowledges'; the aim of this chapter will therefore be to elucidate the nature and effects of these productive powers. Since the late 1960s both the body and the voice have increasingly been seen as important sites for literal and metaphorical resistance to social structures and practices which have been perceived as limiting the rights of individuals to self-expression (Boston, 1997). An initial reading of twentieth century texts on movement training for actors can suggest an essentialist tendency, a desire to position the body as a source of 'original' truth. This chapter, and the subsequent chapter on the 'unruly' body, set out to critique such assumptions and examine the extent to which movement training both embodies institutional values and the naturalization of the social order and offers a potential process for their interrogation.

STARTING AT DRAMA SCHOOL

For the student actor newly arrived at Drama School, there is often little in their previous experience that will have prepared them for much of what is to come. For most students, whatever previous physical education they have had will have focused on the sports and dance activities provided by their colleges or schools. Since the start of the twentieth century secondary level physical education has tended to prioritize the improvement of physical fitness levels rather than the development of expressive movement. As a result physical activity in schools is conventionally framed within larger discourses of health, discipline, 'team-work', and physical pleasure/leisure through movement (Hargreaves, 1994). Students from all four Drama Schools reported that their previous physical education had not prepared them for the movement training they were now experiencing. The new demands made on their bodies seemed to result not only in the physical pain associated with unfamiliar muscle activity, but also in a significant degree of emotional vulnerability: 'not being co-ordinated can make you feel very vulnerable' (Morris: 1999). The students feel 'exposed' in a manner which they identify as both disconcerting and stimulating: 'Out of all the lessons I saw on our syllabus it was the one I was dreading the most, and it's now the one I enjoy the most' (Rose Bruford first year student).

The categories within which they had previously understood their bodies had seemed to them as stable and meaningful. The new reality for them is that these categories are now subject to transformation, as new forms of knowledge operate upon their bodies. As they experience the changes this new knowledge produces on their bodies, they also realize (more or less explicitly) the extent to which their bodies (and those of others) are socially constructed (though constructed without a significant level of awareness, or consensuality). The students rationalize the process of transformation to which they are subjected as appropriate preparation for the professional actor's work in generating a fictional stage character. The 'disorder' of the new students' untrained bodies provokes a pedagogical desire both to 'explain disorder and restore order' (Turner, 1991: 5), and to restore stability through 'systematic classification: the creation of ordered categories' (ibid). But this is a classification which is not simply linguistic or symbolic; this 're-ordering' is intended to operate at the level of the body's materiality and its physical movements. The student's body is not just anatomically and physiologically reclassified, it is also materially reorganized in the light of this new knowledge—posture is adjusted, gesture is clarified, the quality of movement is enhanced: 'They stripped us right down to the very basics. Literally we stood still for probably about three lessons. We were just getting our posture right, standing up straight' (Rose Bruford first year student). Previous movement training (particularly dance) is perceived by the students as a hindrance, or as a cause of feelings of vulnerability. Students are quick to identify differences between dance and movement training for actors. Although both approaches to training make technical demands on the body, in seeing movement as more predominantly expressive students are attempting to conceive of their movement training as constructing an expressive rather than a docile body. The emphasis is on 'purging' the body of technique, in order that resistances to patterns of movement which will fulfill the actor's intentions (Barker, 1977: 12) can be removed: 'It's not technical in the same way that dance is. It's much more about you expressing yourself through your physical shape, rather than sort of imposing a particular movement on yourself in the way that you would in dance' (Guildhall first year student).

The 'assault' of actor training on the bodily inscription of their previous movement experience, the attempt at a form of 'erasure' or 'stripping down', rather than building a sense of resentment or animosity towards their new teachers is perceived by the students as a necessary part of their learning. The students actively work to create a distance from their past experiences of movement training, dance, theatre and theatre training. It is their pasts that now separate them, and they therefore seek to validate the new experiences which bind them together as a group. The rapidity and intensity of this process heightens self-awareness, promotes the rigor of the training, and gives value to the close observation of self and others. If students have anxieties about this process they tend to conceal them, possibly in response to an understandable desire to conform. In general terms, the new student, through the 'neutral' training process, initially identifies the body as the 'problem'; it, and most of its previously acquired patterns of behavior, become the barrier that must be overcome, even transcended, for the sake of artistic expression:

> The right school is making the body a very closely concerned, free instrument through which an acting impulse—the acting imagination—can pass and not be blocked on the way.
>
> (Peter Brook in Eldredge, 1996: vii)

VOCATIONAL BODIES

> [T]he body becomes a useful force only if it is both a productive body and a subjected body.
>
> (Foucault, 1984: 173)

The vocational purpose of actor training, present since the founding of the first Drama Schools, has been reinforced both by the increasing need to distinguish their courses from university drama degrees, and by the pressure on all higher education towards greater vocationality. Though there has been some recent questioning of the dominance of professionalism (Brown, 1996: 213) this has yet to make a significant impact on the practice of actor training in most Drama Schools. The NCDT, through its accreditation of courses, has a regulatory function to maintain acceptable levels of vocational relevance and, in pursuit of this aim, to prescribe certain physical skills as required features of any accredited professional actor training program. The students likewise locate any self-development achieved within the course against a perception of their eventual needs as professional actors. The concept of professionalism is used both to rationalize any physical discomfort and to validate their movement training: 'all actors have is their body, voice and their imagination, things like that . . . and it's just an element that a lot of people in normal life don't have to really think about too much, but we have to because that's what our job is' (Central School BA Acting for Stage and Screen second year student). In this sense notions of what constitutes a professional actor become sites for 'truth' within the training. The Drama School tutors are important to the students as 'gate-keepers' to the profession, and much authority is consequently invested in them. The proliferation of acting and movement methodologies over the last forty years of the twentieth century has created a 'confusion of choice' (Barker, 1995: 101); consequently, for the student, the acting or movement tutor has become a necessary guide and counselor in the labyrinth of training approaches—advising on professional relevance. The commitment of the student to their tutor's vision is marked by the assimilation of key words, phrases and expressions into the student's language and vocabulary. The act of 'naming' their new experiences in class helps students to engage with the exercises; and it constitutes the acceptance of a new 'truth', a new way of knowing the body: '[T]hey teach it to you first and then they start giving you the terminology so you know what this movement is called, you know where it's coming from' (Rose Bruford first year student).

Towards the end of their courses, the students seem to position themselves more and more confidently as 'professional'. At this point the connection between training and performing seems to become problematic for them. They need to view themselves as 'finished' within their training, and tutors often fear that third year students may begin to belittle the importance of voice and movement in relation to the 'real' job of acting. The students seem less willing to remain vulnerable; a condition associated more with training than with professional status. Equally they recognize the need for resilience, for a process robust enough to protect them in a ruthless and competitive industry: '[T]hey've become different people and they lose the ability to be vulnerable in a class situation. I used to get upset about that and think, "No, they've lost it" but in fact they haven't, they've just changed into what they have to be, which is a more resilient actor' (Ewan: 1999a). Embedded within the training process is a tension produced between, on the one hand, the students' desire for and the tutors' encouragement of professional independence and the development of personal process, and, on the other hand, the 'docility' of a training which requires the actor to produce a particular product to order, an actor who can do anything demanded of them. In preparing students for professional employment, 'neutral' body training appears to have the advantage of enabling actors to offer employers a malleability, an emptiness and receptivity which is generally less problematic in relation to the processes of theatrical production: 'I think it's kind of taught me to go in to the rehearsal room on the first day and just be a clean piece of paper, do you know what I mean. Fold it, shape it, anyway you want' (Guildhall first year student). The 'neutral' body is here revealed as a commodity within the theatre economy. The students' ability to suppress or erase from their rehearsal and performance work any inappropriate and unnecessary elements of their habitual physical behavior is part of what they can offer 'for sale'; it is an indication of their professionalism. The drama schools typically operate a final year program of performances presented by a 'repertory' company of student actors, including a showcase of audition pieces. Such a system confirms for the student the value of professional flexibility, and the importance and relevance of the skills they have been taught, whilst enabling them to present those skills to the market place. The student actors seem to feel that they have little control over their careers—'at the end of the day, you know, to an extent, you're going to be stereotyped and play as cast' (Guildhall first year student). Directors are often perceived as having little or no knowledge or experience of movement training. Choreographers have specific needs to do with setting dance routines within short rehearsal spans and dealing with a range of dance abilities. Both seem to expect a no-nonsense approach to movement from the actor; it is left to the actor to warm-up, keep fit and attend necessary classes. The time and eventually the inclination to develop movement 'from within' inevitably become harder to find outside Drama School. The body as 'instrument' is thus professionally validated, a position reinforced as the student progresses into the profession.

As it is the very tensions between their vocational skill development and their creative self-development that effectively produce them as actors, the students are unlikely to criticize the system that places them in this position. They accept these tensions as implicit in the socio-economics of the theatre industry. Vocational education increasingly operates to compound the student's experience of such tensions; government policy places the concepts of personal learning and process within a discourse of results, achievement, assessment and professional goals. Assessment creates significant pressures, which some students see as the whole point of actor training and which other students see as getting in the way of a deep learning process. Assessment also works to inscribe benchmark vocational standards of physical aptitude on the students' bodies. The operations of economic power then are inherent within the actor training provided by the Drama Schools, within the acting profession at large, and within the student actor's body.

MAKING ACTORS/MAKING SELVES

Students spoke frequently in interview about the relationship between an 'inner' and an 'outer' self. Generally the 'inner' self signifies for them the subconscious, the impulses that drive movement; the 'outer' signifies the physical activity perceived by the audience. Students perceive the value of movement training as facilitating the flow of impulses and intentions from the 'inner' self to the 'outer' body in an unmediated way. At the start of the training, the dualism in this conception of the mind/body relationship works to maintain the 'purity' of the 'inner' self and tends to locate any problems in the ('outer') body's inability to respond obediently to the impulses it receives. This dualism reflects the operation of social conditioning (prior to training) in the construction of the body as 'flawed', 'unreliable' and problematic in relation to a rational, unitary and coherent inner self. However, the training, as it progresses, develops its own internal paradox. In the early stages of the training, the pedagogy operates to create a specific sense of an 'inner space' which is inhabited by a personal 'self' (and which exists in a distinctive relationship to the 'outer space'); and yet by the end of the training it has functioned, intentionally, to create a sense of a self which *is* the outer space. Though the relationship between these spaces is complex, the students perceive the difference as both useful and vulnerable. The student's 'self' can be exploited *and* protected, revealed *and* concealed, all simultaneously, within this oscillating construction of the psyche.

Students look for ways to protect their sense of a private and personal self whilst also opening up that self to scrutiny. They learn to be vulnerable but to conceal it: 'Because this is what we're going to do, we've got to get used to that, bearing yourself' (Rose Bruford second year student). The student's body is taught both to 'master' its vulnerability to stimuli, scrutiny and criticism, and to heighten its awareness of its own functioning. Acting students learn the value of vulnerability—which is ennobled as central to their craft and identity as an actor. The training in this manner constructs the student's subjectivity in the context of this 'mastery'. The value of such 'mastery' is reinforced through the ritual and ceremony surrounding movement classes and exercises (e.g. dress, preparation/warm-up, possible use of masks, silence). The criteria for effective self-mastery relate closely to general cultural criteria for professionalism and self-development, which in turn validate the processes, the learning and the craft of acting. Such a training also eventually leads the student to desire the situation of 'performance' as the set of circumstances which allows her or him to achieve identity iteratively, through coping with vulnerability and scrutiny, and through exerting self-denial and 'self-mastery' (from within and without). The paradox for the actor is conventionally understood as a conflict between the technical representation of emotion and the imaginative expression of emotion; it is the central thesis of Denis Diderot's *The Paradox of the Actor* (1957 [1773]) and of a number of subsequent theories, books and articles (see Roach, 1993). Conventionally this might imply a simple dichotomy between ('inner') passion on the one hand and ('outer') technique on the other. What is already evident is that a more complex image for the relationship between the 'inner' and the 'outer' self is required. 'Neutral' body training has been examined earlier as an approach to training which offers to collapse the distance between 'inner' and 'outer' for the student actor. The 'neutral' body might in this respect be usefully compared to a Mobius strip (Grosz, 1994). It may appear that there are two selves, but there is actually only one—the inner self constantly becoming the outer and vice-versa. Both separation and unity are required for the actor to achieve 'mastery' and for that 'mastery' to enable effective expression. The actor needs to master the body to two purposes: firstly to develop a technique able to protect the self in performance, and secondly to develop and sustain an openness and vulnerability in performance which will enable the representations of a fictional self to seem spontaneous and communicative. This is a complex and delicate balance to negotiate and emotions can at times run high as a result. Crying seems to be a common occurrence for some students at this stage, though they can be understandably reserved about discussing it. The dual need for protection and scrutiny is most tellingly symbolized in the 'uniform' used for movement classes.

BLACK TIGHTS AND LEOTARDS

> [M]ost of them don't have a good relationship with their body, and you're asking them to stand up in tights and leotard.
> (Morris: 1999)

The 'uniform' of black leotard or black T-shirt and leggings (referred to as 'blacks'), which is required for movement lessons at all four Drama Schools surveyed, operates as a frame in which the students' bodies are 'presented' for scrutiny, submitted to the teacher's gaze, and to that of other students.

The uniform has some relationship to dance class outfits and those students with previous dance experience may feel more confident about wearing it: 'if you've got people who dance they'll stand up in leotard and tights and not think anything about it' (Allnutt: 1999). Historical evidence of the use of 'blacks' is scant, it is an area which would not normally warrant much attention. Mary Clarke refers to a report of Dalcroze students performing in 'plain black bathing costumes' at the start of the twentieth century (Clarke, 1962: 13). As early as pre-World War Two movement tutors seem to have insisted on only the most basic of outfits for their lessons, Joan Littlewood recalls cobbling together a pair of tights and a bathing costume for her classes with Annie Fligg at RADA (Littlewood, 1994: 68–69), and later Wendy Allnutt (GSMD) recalls much the same attitude to dress for movement classes in her own training under Litz Pisk at Central School. Jacques Lecoq used to wear a tracksuit for teaching, which covered his whole body leaving only face and hands uncovered. Etienne Decroux, on the other hand, favored a body that was often virtually nude and openly revealed for view. For Lecoq, the 'inside' is revealed, through movement, as transformative; for Decroux, the 'inside' is revealed as muscular and skeletal. The history of the uniform reveals its importance in defining the trainee professional actor's body. It is also interesting to note that as the concept of efficiency transformed from the mechanical efficiency of the nineteenth century towards the psychophysical efficiency of the twentieth century, the body became more naked and revealed rather than less.

The 'uniform' is quite strictly imposed in drama schools and failure to bring the right clothes to a class may result in a sense of isolation from the group and sometimes exclusion from the class activity. The uniform is intended to reveal not the flesh of the body (which is mostly covered), nor the mundane signification of fashionable decoration (which is discarded), but the movement of the body. The uniform thus implies a notion of a body (or more precisely an embodied self) which is concealed or hidden in everyday life, but which represents the expressive starting point for the actor, as it becomes selectively unhidden: '[I]t's basically as much covered up as possible, bare feet—*always*—black, no nail varnish, hair right off the face—you know, all that hiding nonsense' (Ewan: 1999b). Paradoxically the 'uniform', whilst it prevents the student from hiding behind 'decoration', simultaneously provides protection through a sense of group anonymity, establishing an atmosphere with no personality issues. Within this uniformity, aesthetic value is placed on the 'clarity' and 'purity' of the resultant images: 'When you take away all that tat and rubbish they look beautiful' (Ewan: 1999b). Such aesthetic values work to validate exposure and 'naturalness', and to reinforce the importance of physical control—all part of the student's personal journey towards a 'neutral' body and creative self-awareness. The uniformity of the 'blacks', whilst depersonalizing the student on the level of decoration, emphasizes that individualization will take place at the level of the body and its movement.

SCRUTINY AND PROFESSIONALIZATION

> Having people look at you is horrible.
> (Central School BA Acting for Stage and Screen second year student)

The uniform facilitates the disciplining of the body through close scrutiny. It acts to protect but also to reveal. The tutor's detailed observation and analysis of student movement begins as early as the moment of audition. Subsequently, in the early stages of their training, the scrutiny seems to them particularly intense: 'everyone's just looking at you, and there's nothing you can do, they're just looking at you' (Central School BA Acting for Stage and Screen second year student). Students are initially unused to the attention given to every subtle detail and nuance of body movement: 'How specific everything was was the big surprise' (Rose Bruford first year student). Descending individualization (Danaher, Schirato & Webb, 2000) works to focus the visibility of power not on the tutor but on the student. Scrutiny isolates individual students; however they accept this scrutiny as necessary for the development of flexibility, self-knowledge and sensitivity—ultimately for their construction as actors. For Wilshire, this is an important part of the phenomenological process through which we come to know ourselves: 'I must experience myself as a body identifiable by others, so my identity must include how I experience others' identifying and experiencing my body' (Wilshire, 1982: 149). Eventually the students volunteer for individual attention, and in this way, the tutor's scrutiny becomes partially internalized. The pedagogy functions to encourage the students to become critically aware of their own movement, and that of others. Such systems of self-scrutiny create a strong sense of mutual group supervision: 'I think that more than any other class perhaps, you can't get away with not working. If you're not putting it all in (. . .) I think it's very transparent for everybody' (Guildhall first year student). One other function of such scrutiny is to encourage or even coercively to compel the student to commit to the work. Despite the fact that some students may find particular exercises difficult or awkward, the general ethos reinforces the belief that it is necessary to 'go with' a movement, rather than be inhibited about it: 'you're learning inevitably about movement you've just got to go with it no matter what' (Central School BA Acting for Stage and Screen second year student). Effective physical expression is constructed around this concept of physical honesty and commitment.

A key teaching and assessment mechanism is the 'crit', an assessment method with a long tradition within schools of Art and Design, in which students present work for critical scrutiny by their tutors (and sometimes also their peers). The 'crit' represents institutionalized scrutiny; it formalizes tutor observation. It has a significant function in dividing practices, creating 'norms' of categorization: actor/non-actor, talented/untalented, co-coordinated/clumsy. Its by-product however is to create a tension between the 'outer' self and the 'inner' self. Students comment on the fact that praise is limited and selective. This operates to maintain discipline and focus within the class, sustaining the tutor as knowledge-holder and maintaining an attitude that the work is never finished. Some students *prefer* limited praise; the prospect of perfection, in themselves or in others, actually seems quite frightening: 'If somebody says, "Oh look, they're doing it right. Watch them do it." You just tense' (Central School BA Acting for Stage and Screen second year student).

By the second year the scrutiny is accepted. In line with the students' increased professional focus the scrutiny is no longer related to a personal body image but to a 'professionalized' body, a body which looks more or less professional in its ability to 'perform' in a particular way and to accept criticism. Student actors learn to see the scrutiny of the class and the crit, not as a risk or a danger (onlookers as voyeurs, judges, or critics), but as a necessary part of their social being as actors. The students' submission to scrutiny places them in an economy of looks—physical/visual effects are valued (physical skills, physical expressivity, physical attractiveness), success is measured by what the tutor 'sees', and knowledge is conceived of in terms of insight, vision, seeing what the body is trying to do. The student actor learns to be looked at, and then learns to construct their body and their movement to present for scrutiny that which is valued. When the student is looked at by the tutor, they can know *that* they are perceived but they cannot initially know *how* they are perceived. Their only access to this knowledge is through learning to 'align' themselves discursively with the onlooker, the tutor. They learn in this way to perceive their movements, through the tutor's eyes, as representing the journey of 'inner' intentions towards 'outer' expression. The student resolves the 'inner'/'outer' self into a psychic construction, shaped by dominant discourses, appropriate for the processes required by the professional actor. What the tutors look *at*, in this way, becomes what the students look *for*.

The scrutinizing gaze of the movement tutor prioritizes the physical expression of the student actor. The tutor looks for evidence of the student committing to expression through the body. The student learns to have their bodily surface read by the tutor who acts as an informed expert and surrogate audience. We have already seen in the previous chapter that this reading cannot be any more neutral than is the reader, suggesting the difficulty faced by the tutor in framing their responses to the students' work. Ultimately there is not, nor can there be a unitary onlooker—neither in the academy, nor in the public theatre audience—but rather there are always many perspectives from which the students are watched. The commitment to the movement work that the students learn through the gaze(s) of the tutor should not be seen as in and of itself meaningful, but it is more appropriately understood as evocative of meaning. If we understand scrutiny as 'a searching gaze' (OED), we implicitly produce, through that gaze, a desire for inner meaning and intention. The actor's presence and the tutor's scrutiny create a *need* for meaning. In learning to be physically present and in resisting a simple representation of meaning, the student may be able to learn to evoke multiple and challenging readings of their movement performance that need not rely on essentialist conceptions of the 'self'.

A PROTECTIVE PARADOX

The tension the concept of an 'inner' and an 'outer' self creates for the students represents in some respects the difficulty they face in their attempts to construct a model of themselves as agents of their own learning. Whether the tutors' criticisms are perceived by the students as accurate or not, the effect is the same—the student recognizes a gap between the 'inner' and the 'outer' self, between intention and achievement. They learn to disassociate their 'outer' physical work from their 'inner' self in order to sustain and protect a sense of coherent identity unchallenged by criticism. For some students the gap between the 'inner' and 'outer' self may be 'the reason they got into acting', because 'they liked the moment when they were not themselves anymore' (Ewan: 1999b). The student then is encouraged to construct a distinct 'self-as-performer', a professional self able to accept the criticisms, and to absorb the physical training. The 'self-as-performer' is caught between the need to associate self and body, and to disassociate the two. The students experience a continuous struggle to resolve this paradox. One second year student was led to resolve this tension by trying to develop a 'healthy disregard', from which it might be possible both to take the work seriously, but also to laugh at it and 'just [not] get so obsessive about it' (Central School BA Acting for Stage and Screen second year student). For these students, it would seem that the problems that perplexed Diderot in the Eighteenth century still remain pertinent and unresolved. In many respects, as we shall see, contemporary acting students are going through the same problems and exploring similar processes as solutions.

TECHNIQUE, THE 'TOOLBOX' AND INSTRUMENTALITY

> I *do* believe that the body is the instrument.
> (Morris: 1999)

> Everyone has toolboxes.
> (Guildhall second year student)

Technique is associated with the development of 'technical' skills. The learning of a technical 'jargon' of psychophysical acting process represents one operation of Foucauldian power/knowledge to configure the student's body within a discourse of professional functionality. The rational dominance of the 'inner' self is represented within the technical discourse through a mechanical conception of the mind/body relationship. Through the concept of the actor's 'toolbox' the student is permitted to see themselves as taking distance from their physical skills, making objective choices, and operating some control within the process: 'you can identify what you need in your toolbox' (Guildhall second year student). However both the process of choosing and the 'toolbox' contents are effectively defined and prescribed by the exercises the student has assimilated. Movement tutors see the relationship between the mind and the body in more complex terms, but similar themes also emerge. Vanessa Ewan at Central School of Speech and Drama believes that 'the body is an instrument' (Ewan: 1999b), but she also identifies a sense in which movement training for actors needs to go beyond a simple program of skills acquisition. The training is aiming to take place on levels that engage more than the functional aspects of movement skills: 'Skills you can get anywhere, you can go anywhere and get a skill and you can't go too far wrong. But it's the core stuff that is problematical. And that's what we try to teach here' (Ewan: 1999b).

The 'toolbox' operates to disassociate the student as 'subject' from their body's pain or discomfort, or from the psychic pressure of the tutor's 'crits', through configuring the body (and its actions) as instrumental. The 'toolbox' in this sense represents a professional value system, where the 'effect' to be achieved is valued as highly as the personal expressivity of the performer. Thus it functions discursively to assist in the construction of the students' bodies as 'professional'. The 'instrumentality' implicit in the notion of the actor's toolbox also suggests a specifically masculine modality, in which the qualities of professionalism, choice, objective distance and discipline are appropriated within a male value system:

> The instrumentalist-purposive model of action privileges plan, intention, and control. These are attributes of action most typical of masculine-coded comportment and activities. Modern Western culture may have elevated such a model of action to the paradigm of creative action, but clearly such a model does not cover the full scope of modes of action.
> (Young, 1998: 288–9)

However, the 'toolbox' can also be associated with the construction of a process as opposed to a system. A system is configured as disciplining the student, whereas a process is taken to imply choice and decision by the student:

> some of the colleges you're working on a system . . . you know . . . it's a way of working. It's handed down, and it's too restrictive. I like it here because we're working on a process.
> (Ewan: 1999b)

And in this sense, both tutors and students value the 'toolbox' as a site for resisting docility through flux and change, through choice, and through positioning exercises as available for selection rather than essential and universal, or prescribed and systematized:

> I always have to keep trying different methods. And because we've had a big variety of things to look at, ways to think of our movement—whether it's images or anything—that's good because it keeps you awake. (. . .) You've got to learn something all the time, soon as you start to get a rigid system, and, "This is what I do all of the time," I think it stops being useful, because it's not personal . . . it's not real.
> (Manchester Metropolitan second year student)

The 'rules' of the training, the 'system', are, in this sense, made to be challenged; if not: 'you have your stage where you learn your rules, and then quite often what happens is people take the rules and they become precious' (Ewan: 1999a). The emphasis on the reflexive self-reliance of the professional acts to justify the avoidance of rigid systems or theories. The lack of, or failure to make use of, a metalanguage of technique should not be taken in itself however as an indication of docility.

The desire to maintain and control a unified sense of self and to resist the productive forces of the pedagogy is evident in the students' belief that the tutors supply the exercises, the techniques, which it is then their responsibility to evaluate and to use creatively. This desire encourages the students to value situations in which they are able to see themselves as self-learners: 'they let you fill the movement yourself, and leave it up to your own imaginations, your own motivations' (Guildhall first year student). At the same time, they also view their teachers with a high level of respect, even reverence, despite the inevitable jokes and occasional critical comments. Students value their movement tutors, specifically for the high level of interest and attention given to work in class. Particular respect was evident for the tutors' impressively detailed knowledge of the students' physical achievement and progression: 'They spot like every little detail as well (. . .) Twelve of us in the room and she'll notice, she'll just home in on my little finger' (Guildhall first year student).

THE TUTOR AS 'EXPERT'

The authority of the tutor derives from a personal mix of subject expertise; institutional, national, or international status; personal 'charisma'; and historical association. From the mid-nineteenth to the mid-twentieth century key movement practitioners (e.g. Dalcroze, Delsarte, Laban, and Lecoq) strove to establish movement studies as a field of specific knowledge and expertise. Their influence is reflected in the institutional recognition now given to movement training within Drama Schools. The *'master* teacher' (with all its gendered connotations) is an interesting paradigm to examine. Rudolf Laban and Michel St. Denis were part of this pedagogical tradition of training the artist through intense and disciplined examination of their subject. Laban was also influenced by the esoteric and mystical theories of eastern philosophies such as Sufism and the teachings of the occultist and mystic Georges Ivanovitch Gurdjieff (1877–1949). Such mystical influences promote the notion of the teacher as a possessor of profound knowledges, which can be used to awaken others in the search for meaning in life (Foster, 1977: 26). Teaching theory has moved on from this kind of approach, but the sense of exercises repeated under close supervision and instruction as part of a guided journey to self-knowledge still remains within most somatic exercise and therapy regimes. The dominance and significance of key practitioner/pedagogues, such as Laban and Copeau, is the result of their control over the signification of movement, their 'mastership' is represented by the nomination of their codes as 'original':

> The 'original', then, is the signifier of dominant presence and, because dominance can be defined as such only by exercising control over signification, it is only through the 'original' that we can know and touch that power.
> (Meyer in Goodman, 1998: 257–258)

The habit of authority understandably comes easily to movement tutors; it is rooted in their passion for their subject, their own detailed knowledge and experience, and their sense of participation (as a student themselves) in the direct transmission of this knowledge from some form of source. Tutors have been students themselves at some time, they are aware of the pedagogical influence of their own teachers. They recognize the significance of 'master' teachers, and the time it takes to move away from their influence: 'I found that to begin with, that I always had a gallery of my master teachers watching me (. . .) I would find myself doing an exercise like [Philippe] Gaulier, or an exercise like Lecoq' (Morris, 1999). This process is not a matter of 'blind faith' in the original practice of the master. The tutor has to 'make the exercises their own' as part of the process through which they become a tutor. The knowledge has to be critically challenged, possessed and reconstructed (Barker, 1977: 8). The 'expertise' of the tutor cannot therefore simply be judged on the intellectual acquisition of knowledge, it must be assessed against the extent to which that knowledge has been tested and embodied through the tutor's own experience. Students' respect for their tutors can be positioned in relation to these factors. Several features of the movement training function to situate the tutors' practice in this sociological context.

The 'contract' between teacher and student is in part negotiated around the possession of knowledge: 'You have to be an expert in what you're practising'

(Morris: 1999). Teaching can sometimes necessitate physical demonstration and students admire the ability of their tutors. Tutor authority also operates to provide psychological security for the students' personal exploration. The tutors' teaching is organic, unintrusive and yet critical—affirming that learning is both available and necessary. The students seem to lose themselves in the uncertainty of the movement work sometimes—the 'vagueness', the slow (and secondary) process towards a conceptual understanding of the work, can be disconcerting. It is in this state that they find security in the certainties offered by the tutor, which are often highly valued, remembered as 'wise words', and distilled into anecdotes.

The students' vulnerability with regard to their bodies constructs the movement tutors' physical knowledge of them as a particularly intimate or secret form of knowledge. The tutor's attention 'probes' under the students' skins like a body scanner; they use their knowledge of anatomy, building 'objective facts' in the students' knowledge about the workings of the human body. Whether consciously or not the teaching also gives permission for certain activities and modes of physical behavior—establishing what is allowed or permissible within the healthy use of the body and the sociocultural constraints of the theatre industry. This knowledge is not always viewed uncritically, tutors are required to practice careful self-reflection if their knowledge of the students is not to be perceived as intrusive or manipulative. Knowledge operates here in a Foucauldian sense to confirm the authority of the teacher. In part this is an inevitable function of the role the movement tutors play in helping the students to 'make sense' of their movement training; a part which is working on the borders of intellect and body, language and action. One movement tutor describes herself as 'the link-pin, being the movement-for-actors person, who actually makes it make sense for them' (Ewan: 1999b). There is a sense of 'initiation' implicit in the learning of a specific vocabulary, marking another part of the students' professionalization.

For some students, their enthusiasm can lead to an apostolic enthusiasm for the training and its effects: 'I always wish that everyone, all my friends, all my family could do this' (Manchester Metropolitan first year student); though this is tempered by an ability to detach from the disciplining process, and to take a 'quick reality check (. . .) a quick time to go, "OK. It's only movement" (Central School BA Acting for Stage and Screen second year student). At first sight the pedagogy of the movement class may then seem to resemble that of the 'master/pupil' relationship familiar in martial arts. Certainly some elements seem similar: intense, repetitive training; emphasis on the non-verbal, on 'thinking with the body'; loyalty to the school; specific sets of practical techniques with little reference to theory (cf. Levine, 1991). The students are vulnerable, spread throughout the space, silent, easily controlled and observed, eager for the tutor's feedback—all conditions which potentially offer significant power to the teacher (Smith, 1998: 128). Nonetheless students seldom seemed to express any sense of this power being abused. Acting students generally felt that they were encouraged by their tutors to reflect critically on their training, and to focus on developing their own ownership of a process rather than blind loyalty to a system. The important correspondences to martial arts teaching lie in the emphasis on the students' changing consciousness of their bodies, on the move away from end-gaining towards 'becoming', and on the sense in which these aspects are focused on an 'art of the self'.

DISCIPLINE

The disciplining effects of the courses are made more complete by their intensity, by the integration of skills, and by their overall coherence. In this manner, alternatives are more effectively excluded and scrutiny is more effectively sustained. Coherence helps the training to 'make sense' to the student. Physical discipline and construction of the self as professional are discursively linked; Trevor Jackson, author of a report on Movement Training for Actors for the NCDT, laments that drama schools 'don't seem to want to drive students or be tough with them' (NCDT, 2001: 21). He wants students to see discipline as 'absolutely crucial to their futures' (NCDT, 2001: 22). On a basic level, discipline is understood by the students and tutors as a respect for professional levels of attendance and time keeping. Lateness is usually dealt with strictly; 'offenders' may be excluded from class or not allowed in for the rest of the day. Discipline is also identified with a professional level of physical competence and with a physical expressivity which emphasizes control, precision, technique and focused awareness. For some tutors, this discipline is initially understood in relation to dance and to their own dance training. Dance is valued for its ability to imprint certain qualities onto the student actor's body—co-ordination, rhythm, spatial awareness, and musicality—nonetheless tutors do recognize the limitations of the model of the dance class and of dance pedagogy in relation to the training of actors. The human topography of the typical movement class can also be used to challenge conventional spatial realizations of the relationship between tutor and student. Rather than starting with the students 'standing facing one direction' (Ewan: 1999b) in a manner reminiscent of the dance class, tutors are increasingly willing to explore more multi-centric configurations (e.g. 'find a space and face a wall').

Discipline brings together 'form'—the physical regimen for the body—and subjectivity—the construction of the self as subject/object. We need likewise to ask how effectively discipline functions in actor training to produce the desired professionalism for the twenty first century. Underlying the tutor's desire to create a disciplined actor's body is a realization that the normative ideal of the professional actor is not matched by the common practice of working actors who are drawn in to a working culture which may value talent over practice and discipline. In reality the trained actor's body cannot have been effectively disciplined if relatively few actors carry on a reasonable level of physical training after they've graduated.

The operation of technique and discipline is revealed through the students' practices in constructing characterizations. The actor's creative work is constrained within a technical 'vocabulary' drawn from an ideologically constructed conception of the formation of character. In many Drama Schools, a critical analysis of the process of characterization is omitted and thus, with respect to Drama School training, placed outside the requirements of the professional actor (who is implicitly positioned as reactive, responsive and uncritical). This has not always been the case, and some Drama Schools are more explicit about the political principles on which their acting teaching is based. The political ownership that students might seek to regain over their bodies is, and can only ever be, partial and contingent. It is created and sustained within the context of a desire to succeed in an industry that requires specific commercial uses of their bodies: 'You have to know what it is that you can do. So that you can sell it' (Rose Bruford second year student).

REMEMBERING THE LESSON

> It is not in the mind but in muscular memory that a performance is stored.
>
> (Harrop, 1992: 21)

The earlier section on 'Body Knowledge' has already addressed the extent to which movement training is capable of constructing, through muscle memory, an altered movement praxis. The very concept of muscle memory predicates a propensity on the part of the body to absorb impressions and patterns of movement. However, if muscle memory functions to embody knowledge, and if we accept Foucault's argument that knowledge is not neutral but is socially constructed, then it is clearly important to examine the manner in which muscle memory participates in the embedding of the discursive practices circulating around movement training into the student actor's body. Pedagogically, the scrutiny required at the start of the training is increasingly made less necessary as the student's body becomes accustomed to sensations it has learnt to register within its new system of signification. In this process we can read the performative (de/re)construction of the self:

> equally important is the repetitiveness of constantly doing the arm lift and the accuracy of it, just lifting your arm up, so when you do it on stage it's like blinking, it just comes.
>
> (Guildhall second year student)

The 'comfort' of movements which flow through muscle memory is both a physical sensation and a recognition of the practice as aligning the student socially, professionally and culturally with a particular scheme of movement practice. In this manner muscle memory configures emotional responses to movement across several levels. The discourses around 'the neutral body' mean that value is placed on an integrated relationship between these levels—a movement, for instance, can be justified because it 'feels' right against the learnt physical memory: 'I can feel when it's wrong. I can feel when it's right' (Central School BA Acting for Stage and Screen second year student). It can be justified because it feels right in relation to efficient and relaxed body use; students variously describe good movement as: 'released' (Rose Bruford first year student) and 'open and ready to adapt to a situation' (Rose Bruford first year student). It can be justified because it feels right in relation to its purpose, intention or function; it is seen as 'movement for a reason, not just movement for movement's sake' (Rose Bruford first year student). And finally of course, it can feel right because the student doing the movement is enabled to feel like an actor, the movement work 'ties in with acting' (Rose Bruford first year student), and 'what they are asking from our bodies is to listen and respond' (Rose Bruford first year student). Overall, students seemed to feel that movement work was good if '[the] movement was filled with something, which movement should be' (Guildhall first year student); implying that movement work will always be more than the purely physical, that the inscription of the body has not only a physical effect, but a social, psychological and cultural effect as well. The body does not remember immediately and without practice. It takes time for the inscription to work in such a way that the student can place the discourses inscribed on their bodies in relation to their own experiences of movement.

> I remember when they say to you, "Just do it. Don't ask any questions, and you'll get it. If you don't understand it, you will soon." And you stood there going, "Well I wanna know now." Well I was stood there going, "I wanna know now. Why are we doing this for God's sake." And in hindsight now, a couple of things that we did maybe a year ago, or just under a year ago, they sort of start clicking away now and you're sort of thinking, "Oh, I get it now."
> (Central School BA Acting for Stage and Screen second year student)

The teaching slowly shapes the body, creating it anew as a material response to the discourses within the classroom. Equally the student's experience of the body starts to become more closely aligned with those discourses and, in this manner, makes more sense, and becomes 'truer', for the student. Movement that fits the student's physical memory confirms that sense of self which their training is seeking to construct. The development from first year to second year is distinctive in this respect—the training moves from being a 'blur' (Central School BA Acting for Stage and Screen second year student) to being something which made sense and which could be incorporated into their acting.

Physical discipline operates on the body, through practice, in order to move the student to the point where acting is not deliberate and over intellectualized. For one student at least, 'that's the whole point of movement, isn't it. I mean to record it in your body, because if not you're acting just by intellectual abstraction' (Central School BA Acting for Stage and Screen second year student). In this respect the body is 'inscribed' by the training in order that it might engage more productively with the discourses around theatre performance. On one level, this is what conventional theatre acting is (or can be seen as). Movement training, in this respect, fits in with the other discursive practices around acting and theatre production. Memory exists, in relation to the body, both as a physical condition and as something akin to a 'dream'. It has reality for us, and yet its existence is cognitively diffuse, elusive and uncertain (Danaher, Shirato & Webb, 2000), always deferred in relation to the present moment. Our bodily sensations create the illusion for us that we are both being and becoming ourselves constantly, because in relation to this immediate and fleeting physical sensation of 'movement' our experience of memory is as something 'fixed' and yet past. Our memory's function is to place us in relation to our experience, giving our sensory experience meaning. In this sense it reinforces our notion of and experience of 'self'. Memory both stores and mediates our movement experience. Through the mechanisms of memory the student is introduced to new conceptions of how the body works, how it connects and communicates, and a new signification for bodily sensation is created—highlighting some formerly mundane physical functions and actions and giving them new importance. Movement and posture are placed within a system of theatrical signification that 'is meant to create perceptible relationships and effects of meaning' (Pavis, 1998: 335) between the stage, the spectator and the 'everyday'. The student's memory, in all its forms, is a psychophysical mapping of this process.

DONE TO YOU

In many ways then, through scrutiny, uniform, and muscle memory, we have seen that movement training is something that, however consensually, is 'done to you' in a number of ways. For the new student actor this aspect of the training can initially feel quite stressful, yet they recognize the value of being put under pressure and, in an important sense, these pressures and crises contribute to the process through which the training (re/de) constructs the student's body. The students do enjoy the emotional pressures and the dramas of the training process: 'I was like, 'Why am I here if like every other day I cry?' But I love it' (Central School BA Acting for Stage and Screen second year student). The emotionality of the training experience clearly has significance for the students. It must in part be a result of and reaction to the displacement of the actor's subjectivity and agency away from the rational control of the 'thinking' subject. In fact it seems simply not possible for the student to operate spontaneously in class or performance at that level of conscious rationality within such a complex field of human activity. The student feels 'crammed' with physical consciousness: 'It's just the whole training thing. I just feel full at the moment' (Guildhall second year student). The emotional significance of the body and of physical experience can in this manner effectively be prioritized over the rational—both for the actor, and for the 'subject'. The danger here is of an anti-intellectualism that might coalesce into a resistance to any theorization. There is a perception among some student actors that reason and intellect are not valuable in the learning of movement skills. In reality however, far from ignoring theory altogether, student actors are very aware of the manner in which their training is part of a larger theoretically structured approach to acting and theatre. The interview data gathered in the research for this book reveals an interest in and enthusiasm for abstract and critical discussion around the practical work of their training (in the context of a group interview). Any assumption that theory and practice are inimical (Callery, 2001: 13–16) in many ways undermines efforts to critique body/mind dualism through praxis.

The changes that happen in the students' bodies and in the students' conceptions of their bodies are not the result of a simple and direct imposition by the tutor. Interview responses indicate that the perceived level of 'intrusion' or 'imposition' by the tutors is low, allowing students to retain a strong sense of their own self-construction as active learners and subjects.

> [T]hey're not changing the person you are—in some Drama Schools or whatever people are getting stripped down and everybody comes and acts the same way. Do you know what I mean? But it's like they're adding to you rather than taking away.
> (Central first year student)

> [Y]ou are left very much to make your own journey of self-discovery within your head and your imagination work. It's never dictated to you.
> (Manchester Metropolitan first year student)

This resistance to docility might seem at odds with a professional training that requires them to make changes to their bodies. However, the discursive practices which work to construct their bodies as flexible and malleable (as 'professional'), simultaneously encourage them to glimpse the very mechanisms through which the social construction of their bodies has already operated and continues now to operate. Though students willingly take on board the skills and practices perceived as requirements for entry into the acting profession, by the end of the second year they show an increasing awareness of the imprint their training has made upon them.

One student talks of the difficulty in disconnecting from the 'ways of seeing' developed in class when outside the training environment: 'I mean if somebody strikes me on the tube as a very awkward, odd person, I start analysing them (. . .) instinctively I start deconstructing his body' (Central School BA Acting for Stage and Screen second year student).

They are keenly aware of the ways their bodies have been changed by their training: 'like when we first came for example, how physically we were all very different, I think, than we are now' (Central School BA Acting for Stage and Screen second year student). Nonetheless, students voiced concern that actor training can involve a level of psychological intrusion— 'you know you have all of these terrible stories about people knocking you down, people . . . dissecting, everything like that' (Central first year student)—a concern that indicates an awareness of the potential for abuse. The process is complex and requires more than just the control or manipulation of the students' bodies, it requires positive acquiescence. The student enters into the pedagogical relationship under little coercion and is encouraged to maintain a critical alertness. Tutors introduce the student to the embodied discursive practices which will effectively take them much of the way to being able to recognize themselves as actors, and at the same time they will open the students' critical faculties and provide them with insights into the creative potential of the processes through which those discourses are operating.

> [Y]our role is not to tell them when it's right or wrong, but actually to provide a vocabulary and an experience that matches that vocabulary, so that they can understand for themselves. To help them develop their own critical faculties when they're watching other people, so that they're aware of why something works physically and why it doesn't work physically. I mean in a very general sense to empower them to learn for themselves.
>
> (Morris: 1999)

Movement tutors make claims (as do voice tutors, see Berry, Linklater & Rodenburg [1997]) to be in the process of discovering and liberating a 'true self' for the student. Achieved through a process of 'breaking down' the student, actor training is supposed to involve:

> the systematic stripping away (. . .) of all inauthentic action to find the core of the person from which all authentic action springs.
>
> (Barker, 1995: 108)

Poststructuralist theory critiques the ability of such a process to locate a metaphysically 'true' self. What could though be changed through movement training is the epistemology of the body, the students' way of knowing what 'right' behavior might be. Within such a reconstruction of knowledge, it would be necessary to re-imagine the body; 'stripping away' physical practices from the body implies a 'flayed' body, understood as anatomized in layers, like the bodies in children's 'peel-back' picture books of anatomy from the 1950s. Could it be that instead we should see the body not as passive, inert and dissected, so much as active, present and accumulating. Such a body would be moving/dancing to several different choreographies—sometimes conflicting and contradictory—and such movement training would teach the student actor to watch, select, align and repeat the choreographies of the bodies most appropriate to their perception of the theatre industry, the art of acting and their own journey of self-discovery: 'It's all about trying to just make the next step for yourself. Because it's your body' (Rose Bruford first year student).

CONCLUSION—LOOKING THE PART

This chapter argues that the physical training process is inscribed into the psyche of the student actor, they learn not only techniques but cultural behavior—how to *be* an actor, how to *look* like an actor. The student actor learns to give out a 'body gloss' (Goffman, 1971: 11) that informs the public/audience that they are actors/acting. 'Being an actor' is constructed around ideas of 'craft' and 'self' that have traditional and conservative roots. Claiming to be a professional actor is often a difficult step for a student to negotiate. Who confers professionalism upon the student: teachers, directors, friends, family, peers, audiences or the Inland Revenue? The very claim to the name immerses them in the socio-economic discourses of the theatre industry. Professional techniques are 'made available' for the students and they conceptualize the techniques as 'tools' which they can choose—'You're aware of it, but none of it dictates to you' (Guildhall second year student)—constructing professionalism as providing a form of choice. But, within the discourses that inform the acting profession, larger socio-economic forces constrain and orientate actors' choices towards professional success and protection of 'self-hood'. Ultimately student actors' bodies are trained to be used as a medium to reflect fictionalized bodies constructed within a dominant system of economic production. To this extent, expressive and individual as their bodies are (or seek to become), they are not institutionally encouraged, or allowed, to reflect overt resistance or to engage with the 'less attractive' areas of cultural body practices (e.g. danger, nakedness, sex, and other 'taboo' practices). The conventions of professional commercial and subsidized theatre, television, and film, mean that those codes which replicate everyday physical behavior are the focus of attention and are prioritized over new and alternative codes:

> We're all following a set of rules as ourselves, everyday. We follow a set of rules, it's just that we don't know we're doing it anymore. We have code

rules. We have relationship rules. (. . .) we have so many rules. I mean we have rules about how to sit, where to be, who to face . . . you know.

(Ewan: 1999a)

Nonetheless the student actor does develop an 'art of the self' which may be able to offer opportunities, through the 'performance' of the self, for the student to become a self-determining agent and challenge some of the power structures which have been at work on them. The actor, after all, is seeking to be able to adapt their subjectivity, to make it fluid, to represent or inhabit the subjectivity of fictional others, in effect to expose the fictionality of subjectivity. The subjectivity of the actor is created, following the title of this chapter, through the naming of certain movements, postures and bodies as 'normal' within the context of the profession. Feminist theory has shown us that subjectivity is not a stable position, but one of change, transformation, and fictionality. 'Standing like an actor' is thus not *standing* at all, but a constant choreography of the self—redefining and recreating itself in action. Within this dance, the actor can certainly be transformed through the operation of dominant discourses; what the next chapter will examine in more detail is the extent to which the actor's transformation of self can also be liberating and empowering. We can admit that acting will not change the world, but to what extent does it offer ways of changing the self, and of exercising power within our networks?

4 Movement Training and the Unruly Body

> It's extraordinary, it's enjoyable, it's agony, it's depressing.
>
> (Central first year student)

> Even if the actor offers us a veritable bouquet of signs, an organised and satisfying discourse clearly related to the global system of stage signs; even if the actor is a perfect enunciator, that actor's role is nonetheless incomplete, and cannot be left at that.
>
> (Anne Ubersfeld in Melrose, 1994: 13)

Actors are always aware that the body 'is' more than we can ever consciously or rationally intend. Its multiple potential effects, its multiple potential meanings, all indicate its potency as an unruly source of inspiration. For even the most successful actor, the body can evade conscious control; Laurence Olivier thus describes the 'unruliness' of his big toes: 'I had not too happy a memory of Alfred Lunt's remark to me after *Oedipus*: "I was fascinated by your feet; the more intense you got, the more rigidly did your big toes stand straight up in the air!" I was horrified as well as disappointed' (Olivier, 1983: 270). To consider the body as only that which is intended or that which is discursively framed is akin to looking down the beam of a torch and claiming that everything that is lit is all that there is or can be. We must not be afraid of the darkness, of the unshapely materiality which will, despite our 'clear vision', eventually find its way into our consciousness. In this way new knowledges are possible. Elizabeth Grosz, in a discussion on body building in *Volatile Bodies* (1994), proposes the following relationship between the discursively inscribed body and the material body:

> [B]ody building does not simply add to an already functional, nonmuscular body; rather it operates according to a logic that Derrida describes as supplementary—in which the primary term, in this case the "natural", pre-inscriptive body, always makes possible, through the impossibility of its own full presence, its binary opposite, the term which has been expelled in order to constitute it, in this case the "worked-over" muscular body. There must be some shortfall of nature in order

to make possible the augmentation of nature; there must already be a plastic and pliable body in order for it to be possible to mold and sculpt it according to the canons and dictates of body-building protocols.

(Grosz, 1994: 143)

Grosz argues that, logically, the 'pre-inscriptive' body cannot be fully present, yet its existence is nonetheless and equally logically 'required'. The 'pre-inscriptive' body may, in this way, only be knowable through the ways in which it becomes inscribed—Grosz argues that any concept of the 'natural' body must take into account the 'extreme formlessness and plasticity' (Grosz, 1994: 144) necessary for it to be uninscribed. Such a position suggests that the only way we can know our bodies is through their inscription, but this argument can be inverted to suggest that we can know our bodies as inscribed only through an implicit acknowledgment of the 'pre-inscripted body'. It might seem problematic that we cannot directly *know* this 'pre-inscripted' body (how can we be sure of its existence, talk about it, without 'knowing' it), yet we can deduce its existence. In this context, it is useful to follow the lead of the phenomenologists and allow that 'knowledge' can be constructed not only as 'knowledge-of-the-body' but also as 'knowledge-through-the-body'. Further, in so far as the inscription of the body operates both to reveal the absence and produce the erasure or over-writing of the 'pre-inscripted body', it would appear that this very inscription also participates in creating the distance the subject experiences from his or her own corporeality. This chapter seeks to argue that such a distance is in itself oppressive and enables power to operate on our bodies more directly. The separation of the subject into a doing self and a knowing self is insidious and pervasive in many forms of educational practice. It enables the embodied self to be constructed as an object which is manipulated, as *merely* an instrument; the 'control' that the subject/agent maintains over the 'instrument' is limited by the extent to which discourses of labor and industry are allowed to circulate unresisted. In order to begin to experience the mind/body relationship in other ways the student has to be prepared to lose some sense of their existing rational subjectivity and of their emergent professional identity. Boundaries must be broken down; meaning associated with movement must become fluid, leaky, slippery and playful. The *sensations* that students experience in this process become very important in developing an understanding of that same process and its potential. We therefore now need (in contrast to the tenor of the previous chapter) to ask the following questions: how does the student's body become *unfixed* within the training; what purpose does the volatile, transformative and 'unruly' body of the trainee actor serve; how does an examination of the movement training of the actor help us to understand the relationship between the disciplining, subject-forming aspects of movement training and the corporeal unpredictability of the body?

AGAINST THE INTELLECT

[Y]our body carries you rather than your intellect.
(Manchester Metropolitan second year student)

Historically actor training has focused on developing the functional efficiency of the body in expressing the intentions of the mind (Pavis, 1998: 34–35, 223–224). Joseph Roach suggests that this mechanistic approach to the actor's body reflects the complex cultural and scientific developments of the Enlightenment (Roach, 1993). It is certainly possible, as Roach proposes, to view the techniques of improvisation, spontaneity and physicality developed through the work of early Twentieth century innovators (such as Jacques Copeau, Constantin Stanislavski, Vsevolod Meyerhold, Antonin Artaud, Peter Brook, Jerzy Grotowski) as responses to contemporaneous scientific understandings of the psychophysical processes. In identifying these processes in terms of the body as an instrument, science has certainly assisted in the understanding of the actor's craft but also, perhaps unintentionally, stripped that craft of some of its alchemy. The body as instrument or machine (even on a temporary basis) removes it as a site for physical pleasure, mystery, magic and delight. Somehow actors seem to require that some aspect of their art remains ineffable, beyond the reach of the conscious rational intellect. This begs the question: what is lost if the transformative process of the actor is made conscious, rational or formulaic? During their first year there is evidence that students come seriously to question the status of the intellect as part of the actor's equipment. Intellectual qualities such as consciousness and awareness are valued by the students only in so far as they are applied to the lived experience of the physical-emotional self and to the awareness and observation of the movement of others. Even in the second year, the students experience a strong sense in which an increased conscious awareness can inhibit their work. The pressure to demonstrate that they have learnt from the training exercises can make them unnecessarily conscious of their actions in rehearsal, and even in performance. Certainly they perceive their journey as a student actor as one in which they travel from ignorance, through physical experience and reflection, towards awareness and knowledge. Equally importantly they view it as a journey from predominantly mental activity towards holistic activity involving the mental, emotional and physical self: "it's just amazing how much your body also gets involved" (Guildhall first year student). Some students experience this transition as painful and uncertain, but the excitement, the intense sensation and the delight of new body learning often appears to compensate.

We have seen, in an earlier chapter, how muscle memory can help an exercise come to 'make sense' for students: 'There have been moments when suddenly . . . a movement becomes more organic for me, I don't have to force it anymore. And suddenly I find the key to what is inside me' (Rose Bruford first year student). It can also help the student to overcome the increased awareness of processes (an awareness that was previously operating at a subconscious level) which can now produce awkwardness and self-consciousness, a feeling of inhibition and ultimately lack of control over the body. The teaching is seeking instead to move the students towards an awareness that does not inhibit physical release: '[I]t's helped me to lose the kind of self-censorship and the third eye, you know, that thing which is always you looking at yourself and commenting the whole time' (Guildhall first year student). The teaching diverts the student from intellectualization in a number of ways: very few tutors provide reading lists or encourage reading around the subject of movement training (there are also very few relevant texts); practice far outweighs discussion within the division of class time; the tutor emphasizes physical results over what the student says about what they've done; the tutor engages with the students not simply through verbal instructions or criticisms and comments, but also through participation, demonstration, and hands-on correction. Just as we have previously determined that the intellect is never simply discarded, so we can also see that it is never entirely dominant.

Diverted from thinking too self-consciously about their movement, students begin to experience their bodies as capable of provoking emotions, images, and states of mind, as well as ideas. Pure, 'disengaged' intellectualization, or even mild interference by 'front brain' consciousness (Barker, 1977: 16–25), is associated by the students and tutors with inhibited physical response, manifested in the body through unnecessary physical tension. Students learn therefore that, paradoxically, expressive control comes not from a tense and heightened awareness, but from release into the lived body. 'One of the basic problems for the actor is not to let thinking get in the way of doing' (Harrop, 1992: 2). Control over the body has previously been associated with conscious front-brain mental activity, possibly related to commands and instructions from teachers and parents. An attempt to provide the actor with tactics to overcome the problems caused by conscious inhibition underpins several texts on acting, from Stanislavski (1980) to Barker (1977). The concept of 'release' or relaxation is central to most of these approaches, and is significantly opposed to the 'driving' attitude required for, say, sport.

> [T]he harder you work the fitter you get in football training and . . . even when we did contemporary dance . . . I don't know, the more you put into it the more you get out of it. It's the same but it's not. It's different. It's like releasing the movement instead (. . .) I freed myself up rather than working myself.
>
> (Guildhall first year student)

In this respect a different approach is initially a little confusing for students: 'You're relaxed and therefore you're in control. It sounds a bit contradictory because you're into, "OK, I'm in control, I'm in control." But you're not, no' (Central first year student). The physical and emotional sensations generated by this psychophysical release are sometimes quite powerful. Such sensations seem to form an important part of the students' developing sense of the processes at work within them and of their own increased ability to engage in these processes. The students begin to rediscover 'weight' and 'openness' as physical experiences, and to realize the emotional and psychophysical impact of this release: 'Dropping the pelvis . . . it took me a while to get that, 'cause I wasn't opening up myself to basically 'drop' the pelvis (. . .) You just feel yourself freeing up every time you do it' (Rose Bruford first year student). The release of weight is a key aim in the early part of many of the training schemes; the exploration and use of weight has been a central part of the influence of Alexander, Laban and Leeder. 'Weight' is constructed not as mass, but as a quality of strength and effort in relation to gravity, time and space—a physical quality with emotional resonances. It is not an objective reality as such, but a way of knowing the world. Tutors see it as a movement quality that works intuitively, informs our relationships with the world, and is not easily replicated: 'The weight is a big issue (. . .) You can fake nearly everything else, but you cannot fake weight' (Ewan, 1999b).

Although release is also used within voice teaching (see Berry, 1973), the students perceive it as a primary and central element within movement training, specifically within the 'pure movement' work. Release enables the student to let go of physical tensions, which act as physiological markers for inefficient habitual patterns of behavior, in effect the residue and deposits resulting from the process of everyday bodily inscription. Because these habitual patterns contribute to the construction of the student's sense of their own personality, release implicitly also addresses the psychophysical history of the student. This is both physically and culturally different from the constructive practices of, for instance, ballet and as such can produce strange feelings for the student: 'a lot of tension gets released from all over the body, you don't realize you're holding. Then you let go and, "Oh God"' (Rose Bruford first year student). The sensation is unusual but it is also clearly pleasurable. We are reminded that the enjoyment of movement *is* sensual, emotional and liberating: 'you feel good after you do it, or as you do it. It just gives you a really good feeling inside' (Rose Bruford first year student).

THE LEAP OF FAITH

The first year students who participated in the research for this book seemed to be poised, albeit somewhat precariously, on the cusp of learning and understanding—unsure at what distance or with what intimacy to engage with their new learning: 'Now I feel I'm ready. I'm increasingly ready. I'm not ready at all, but . . . you know . . . ' (Central first year student). New students are required to take a lot on trust as they begin work in a field almost entirely knew to them and a 'leap of faith' in the teaching is implicit in their attitudes. They are told to give themselves up wholeheartedly to the exercises, and yet the initial experience of those exercises is as unsettling and as frightening as it is pleasurable and stimulating. There are some parallels with games in the association of release with unforced but intensive physical engagement—'all this work that we're doing is not about forcing yourself all the time. It's about releasing and having fun and still working hard' (Rose Bruford first year student). The principle of physical release is used to provide a process for the controlled and focused engagement of the psychophysical self at a subconscious level, in a manner that can be seen as enabling the student to participate in and to enjoy the release of physical tensions (including psychosexual tensions). Training approaches have evolved over the last two or three decades in ways that have increasingly taken on board the value of this kind of release. An early influence on this development was the work of Clive Barker (1931—2005), who developed a systematic approach to the use of games in actor training in order to achieve a physical and mental state of active release which could provide the basis for a psychophysical acting technique. Barker's significance lies not solely in the vocational and educational value of his approach to actor training, but also in his formulation of a thorough theoretical underpinning to this approach, which he published in his seminal book *Theatre Games* (1977). The themes of delight and play in movement have multiple significances and will be re-visited later in this chapter.

THE VALUE OF CHANGE

The students' feelings of uncertainty and vulnerability confirm that the movement classes intentionally seek to make the students' selves, but most specifically their performance identities, more open, flexible and fluid. Yarrow suggests the significant role of 'defamiliarization' and 'hesitancy' in shifting the students' consciousnesses into a more fluid condition, where certain transformational qualities are more accessible. Yarrow identifies these as:

> sense of unity or wholeness (self + work/world, all aspects of work, organic understanding), modification of evaluation of self, potential for creating form (readiness for voluntary acts, awareness of multiple possibilities, spontaneity), and conjunction of distance and involvement.
> (Yarrow, 1986: 3)

In so far as these transformations take place at a level of consciousness that involves the body, Yarrow also suggests that the uncertainty and defamiliarization provoke a more profound 'articulation of the focal range of the body' (Yarrow, 1986: 5) and are, in a sense, the basis of the students' future ability to create and act. Yarrow connects this state of consciousness with Antonin Artaud's 'état d'incertitude et d'angoisse ineffable qui est le propre de la poèsie' (Yarrow, 1986: 8), thereby linking the history of this notion of neutral consciousness back again to the cultural revolutions taking place in early twentieth century Paris. Acting students, through this work on the neutral body, begin to realize the value of this fluidity—it is suggestive of the ability to extend and transform the self and through that same process to extend the range of characters that they can play. However, the idea of a physical self that is willing to become abject, unformed and plastic is not necessarily a comfortable one, compromising as it does the student's notions of self.

The difficulty for the student is compounded by two potentially conflicting requirements: to 'release' and 'let go' physically, but within a disciplined and assessed vocational training regime. Perplexingly for the student, it may sometimes be their ability to 'let go' that is actually being assessed. The student 'releases' into the psychophysical process—'You've just got to give yourself up to it' (Central first year student)—but this is not simply a collapse into sensuality. The mind does not give in to the body, nor does the student actor give up to a construction of the body imposed from outside; but quite specifically (because these two events can or do also happen), the student actor is giving up to the experience of the psychophysical process of acting. The students move towards knowledge, through the 'lived' body, of the particular ways in which the activities of acting draw upon 'lived' experience. Movement training, in this sense, seeks to become a 'processes of knowing' (Yarrow, 1986: 1), perhaps even a 'prelude to knowing' (Yarrow, 1986: 6), rather than a repository of knowledge. The precise effects of this release and their significance will be examined in more detail later.

One student associates 'release' with the image of 'flowing': 'you just come into natural flow. And that idea of moving can really take you away, and it's when you can do some of your best acting. You're just letting the movement take the flow of the line' (Manchester Metropolitan first year student). 'Flow' has a particular value and significance for students who have often experienced a disjuncture between the body and the mind at early stages in their training. 'Flow' also creates a sense of something sensuous, with its own momentum that is difficult to control. It opens up the possibility for a sense of communion, a more total and organic state of being for the actor. Such a notion is at odds with the objectivity and discipline of reason. In this manner the body is moving outside the strict logic of the mind: 'Movement I find is less logical' (Central first year student). Movement however, as we have seen, is not exactly positioned as 'irrational' in this respect, but rather as intuitive. Doing and abstract thinking are conceived of as happening on different levels—the doing is not experienced, does not come to consciousness, in the same way as the thinking. In fact the suggestion is that rational, logical, abstract thinking may impede the processes required for doing, even for 'learning-through-doing'. The qualities students identify in relation to movement training exercises align with the elements that Mihaly Csikszentmihalyi describes as central to the pleasurable experience he identifies with the notion of 'flow' (Csikszentmihalyi, 2002: 48–67); such as: the merging of action and awareness; focus on the task; relaxed control; loss of self-consciousness; transformation of experience of time.

If we accept Yarrow's notion of 'neutral' consciousness (similar to what I elsewhere refer to as 'active consciousness'), then perhaps movement training can usefully function to help bridge the 'doing/thinking' divide:

> you try and do things, but the way you think about them gets in the way so therefore it halts how far you can go or your progress. And I think a lot of the work tries to or aims to stop that in a way.
> (Central School BA Acting for Stage and Screen second year student)

This requires a high level of trust and a commitment, by both teacher and student, to a pedagogy of process. Pre-conceptions and expectations are considered distracting and restricting, resulting in 'end-gaining' where the outcome is prioritized over process and mental preparation over physical responsiveness. Such 'end-gaining' can have a direct and detrimental effect on the student's posture and body-use. It is not that the mind is not involved in the impulse to move, but that should the rational processes (the front brain) dominate, then the body will react physiologically in ways which inhibit free and relaxed general movement (Barker, 1977: 43–44). One student interviewee discussed how her training had caused a literal displacement of the source of her movement from her head to her torso, 'It's like thinking sometimes from there, that becomes your eye [indicates centre of the body]' (Central first year student). This can mean that tutors actively decide to deny or to refuse explanation: 'today in movement class we got into a discussion because we wanted to straightforwardly define things. And they won't tell you' (Central first year student).

The coherence of the students' sense of self and individuality becomes challenged in this new construction of the actor's psyche. They generally view the experience as positive, as if this learning trajectory acts to heighten their sense of individual physical self, rather than deny it: 'it doesn't neutralise your character. It just puts you in a situation where you can express your character more' (Guildhall first year student). The 'body-as-flesh' is seen as being re-animated by the movement training, brought into a new focus and a new relationship with the mind, one which the students can clearly associate with. In this context small successes can have big significance for the student: 'It's so hard to achieve things in movement. It's like we almost had orgasms the other day because we realized that we'd learnt how to roll down the spine with keeping legs straight' (Central first year student). The use of the sexual metaphor not only reveals again the sublimated sexual undertones of movement work, but also emphasizes the development of a mind/body relationship which prioritizes the physical.

Yarrow draws parallels between the 'neutral' consciousness and ritual, shamanism, meta-awareness and altered/heightened states of consciousness (Yarrow, 1986). Physical movement sits on the cusp of our ability to 'know ourselves', and the effects of movement work on the students' bodies can be difficult for them to explain and rationalize. Their 'awe' at the effects that movement training can have on the body should not be seen as simply a naive and passive reaction. Such a view would miss the sense in which students are recognizing the empowering effects of their training in a world where they perceive little opportunity for the body to be 'liberated' from its social construction. Given the inevitable difficulty in finding words to express the non-rational experience of movement, a reversion to quasi-religious metaphor is perhaps not surprising, as it represents a familiar and established register. Such 'mysticism' may also relate to the pleasurable relief they experience in releasing conscious control of aspects of their movement activity and engaging the psychophysical processes at a non-rational level.

> I was reading this book [Herrigel, 1985] and it was talking about the kind of spiritual sense you get when the art becomes artless, and it becomes, you know ... I think movement at its best is that. It's kind of ... it sounds a bit weird, but almost kind of spiritual. 'Cause it's very, you know, this is my body and I'm completely aware of everything that's going on. Do you know what I mean? Very kind of pure. Which is, you know, kind of like an amazing feeling.
> (Guildhall first year student)

JOUISSANCE—FORGETTING THE SELF/ BEING IN THE MOMENT

Students seem to experience a fluctuation between, on the one hand, the heightened technical awareness of the 'professional' actor, and, on the other, the *jouissance* (Barthes 1977) of the moment of performance, when the psychophysical process operates in a manner which by-passes the inhibiting effects of self-awareness. The idea that the physical can erupt through the rational and be present, even communicate, more directly and immediately is identified as an important effect of acting at a professional level. This is conceptualized as the condition of 'being in the moment'. This notion is only loosely defined in most of the literature. It draws on associations with states of mental alertness, what Lecoq calls *'disponibilité'* (Frost & Yarrow, 1990: 151–155), but students and tutors also relate it to posture, alignment and levels of tension or relaxation. Some students conceive of it as a state of self-forgetting, where the *jouissance* of the performance seems to by-pass the conscious application of exercises and techniques:

> I was just doing the story, and the movements all just sort of happened. And I came off, and I had one of those amazing experiences where you can't remember what happened (. . .) you just go, "Did I just do it?"
> (Guildhall second year student)

Conscious control over this kind of experience is of course, by definition, limited. This is a potential area of danger; the release of physical energies can be unnerving and can operate psychoanalytically to produce or bring to the surface unpredicted psychological effects. The released, unruly and volatile body could be just as easily manipulated as the rigorously trained docile body, both are eventually working on patterns of behavior which can operate below conscious intervention: 'when I've been working on a character, and I put the costume on, I'll find that my body has just gone into the position, and it's just like, "I didn't even mean to do that"' (Central School BA Acting for Stage and Screen second year student). Being in the moment is not an escape from history, culture, society and gender, though it may feel like it is. It is a 'forgetting', a 'sublimation' of awareness to the physical imperatives. The dangers in such an effect are clear—forgetting or ignoring context can be only one step from smiling acquiescence. The volatile and unruly body can only be understood in relation to the docile body; a politics of the body is a necessary context for work on physical release. The potency of theatre as a medium for the sharing and releasing of the psychophysical processes is strong; the results for audience and actor of such a communal experience are conventionally seen as empowering and beneficial. It means a lot to the students that such moments are both achievable, socially valued, and yet out of their immediate reach.

> Robert Stephens played Lear (. . .) He did this moment where he's fighting with the air and these petals fall down and it was one of the most amazing moments in theatre to date . . . well, which I've seen.
> (Central first year student)

If the body is, in the moment of *jouissance*, unknowable then it would seem that it is nonetheless capable of releasing meaning and of knowing itself as in action—even if that meaning and knowledge is on the edges of our conscious knowledge. In this respect, such unruliness of the body may seem at odds with the need for a trained and disciplined physical instrument. Yet the body's ability to store and release important but unpredictable elements of the students' experience can form a vital part of the process by which the students come to understand themselves, and specifically to understand themselves in relation to their embodied memories:

I've had a huge sort of psychological change through the first few months of being here. Of having a lot of things in my past that I've either shut off from or . . . Not particularly bad stuff, but just things that you forget about or you do shut away because you don't want to think about. And a lot of those came flooding back through dreams or whatever when I started this course. I think . . . you're made . . . or, you're not made to, but . . . you're sort of slowly realised to accept yourself. And I'd accepted things that I never thought I'd even think about ever again, or never thought I wanted to think about again. And sort of accepting who you actually are, instead of being this person that you think you are or that you think you're presenting.

(Manchester Metropolitan first year student)

Initially students may see the body as corresponding to the subconscious self; conventional binary divisions between the rational mind and the irrational body are potentially revealed through the references to dreams, fears, repressed memories and a lack of control. Thus, at first, releasing the body is a site of uncertainty and insecurity for the student. One first year student expressed an ambiguous mix of understanding and fear about connecting body and mind:

I think it's partly to do with fear as well . . . that's stopping you. Because it is . . . I think it's meant to be connected, and it makes so much sense to connect it. It's just your fear or your worry or . . . I don't know . . . worrying about what other people think that stops you from doing that.

(Manchester Metropolitan first year student)

By the second year however the fear seems to have subsided and the body is perceived as potent, as less irrational, and as capable of communication and 'intelligence' in its own terms:

[Our tutor] is always saying, you know, the most exciting moments happen when you just throw yourself into something, just see what happens (. . .) I can now just let go completely, just do something and let my emotions flow, and just give myself, more and more, to the work. And the thing is you start to trigger off or just establish a lot more down here [indicates the lower torso], more emotional, and more exciting and more dangerous.

(Guildhall second year student)

If movement training in the first year initially produces a heightened mental awareness which restricts the 'volatile' body, this would explain why first year students in particular can find that work designed to encourage release can sometimes operate to inhibit movement and produce the opposite effect. The difficulty thus posed is compounded by problems in measuring achievement in 'releasing' where conventionally objective benchmarks are hard to formulate:

> there are very few exercises with blueprints, if you know what I mean. There are very few exercises, in which we go, "This is how you do it. This is the correct way to do it. Now try and do it." There aren't any, because everyone's body's different, because it's all about your own personal exploration. So you'll never have a measuring stick really, except in your own body.
> (Central School BA Acting for Stage and Screen second year student)

The exercises are not measured in terms of exact body placement. As I have argued in Chapter 2, the 'neutral' body is not an objective physical state and as such cannot be assessed in this way. Tutors notice when someone is 'on the right track or if they're completely off' (Central School BA Acting for Stage and Screen second year student), but their comments are designed to deny the students opportunities to 'close the book' on an exercise. The students refer to the sense in which there is an 'essence' or a *total* experience of an exercise that is aimed for, but this state, if achieved/achievable, seems difficult to sustain; the body perhaps inevitably remains transient, temporary, in flux.

AUTHENTICITY, VITALITY AND PRESENCE

> You're giving something unliveable life.
> (Ewan, 1999b)

The work of the actor is commonly conceived of as the creation of 'natural life' for a shape, a movement, a posture or a character, as 'giving life' to a fictional construct. The requirement placed upon the student actor to construct an organic and dynamic relationship between the 'lifeless' parts, and to engender spontaneous life in the engagement of these parts in action, is reminiscent of the late nineteenth and early twentieth century theatrical interest in vitalism (Roach 1993). In this manner, and within the cultural historical context of the 'natural' and 'neutral' body (see Chapter 2), 'vitality' is constructed into and around the actions of the student. Both tutors and students attempt to evaluate evidence of this vital presence analytically, but more often than not the evaluation may be operating on an intuitive basis—an inevitable compromise in the face of the difficulties involved both in capturing transient and fleeting impressions of the student's movement and in identifying the nature and source of this 'vitality'. The transience and fluidity of the 'vital' body, a body spontaneously improvising new identity-fictions, tend to disrupt and defer the connection between signifier and signified, offering to collapse the conventional operation of the sign and release the potential for multiple meanings. By conceiving of the body as having meaning through its 'livedness', through its vitality and unruliness, we return to the 'neutral' body seeking to have its own form of absence, in which its existence is not contingent on an arbitrary, but 'fixed', relationship to other 'signifieds'. It is the body's 'way-of-knowing-the-world', the students' new sense of the experience of their bodies as bodies-in-the-world, the *process* of neutrality, which are emphasized. To 'do its job' the actor's body has to be both present and absent. The actor has to dissolve and defer some meanings in order to realize the potential for others.

A key focus of the training then becomes the question of how to generate 'a real, beautiful, breathing, live moment' (Ewan, 1999b) in movement. Tutors and students find this process, and its rationale, difficult to put into words. The students identify the body as trained not simply in relation to its ability to respond to instruction with precision and alacrity but also in relation to its vitality, strength and suppleness—to their sense of their own physicality, their experience of 'being-in-the-body':

> It makes you feel really powerful as well doesn't it. I feel much stronger in everything than I was last year. Just sort of walking around and just more present and more supple as well, because of all the acrobatics and everything. Less stodgy, do you know what I mean, just more spring in my step and sort of alive.
>
> (Guildhall second year student)

The authenticity of the body is here positioned in relation not to technical skill or to strength per se, but rather to a heightened sense of the lived body. As Iris Young (1990) suggests, the social conditioning of the body inhibits and blocks access to the vital and authentic body—particularly for those who feel alienated from their own subjectivity. Students see this authentic condition as situated around the limits and boundaries of their socially constructed bodies, and on the edges of their technical ability. They recall feelings of 'connection' with their bodies that emphasize the 'authenticity' of the physical work in relation to their experience of their 'everyday' bodies.

For many students this effect is associated with physical work which draws on ritualized or 'ecstatic' approaches to the body and its training—such as Grotowski-based work, Gabrielle Roth's 'Five Rhythms', and Asian martial arts based regimes. In these traditions, intense, focused and sustained physical activity is used to change the students' experience of their physical body: 'The more you dance, the more you sweat. The more you sweat, the more you pray. The more you pray, the closer you come to ecstasy' (Roth, 2002). For one group of Manchester Metropolitan students their experiences with a Polish Grotowski-based group were a formative experience: 'You were pushed into a point where you did work instinctively, through pain or exhaustion, you connect to a text from there [indicates torso], rather than from up there [indicates head]' (Manchester Metropolitan second year student). Niamh Dowling's occasional use of Gabrielle Roth's work on rhythm and movement in her classes at Manchester Metropolitan University seems to have fulfilled a similar function for some of her students:

> 'Five Rhythms', Gabrielle Roth's theory (. . .) is a bit like the Grotowski work, where you're just knackered by the end, but it's freeing yourself up and just dancing. It's like a natural high, when you do it. (Manchester Metropolitan second year student)

The nature of this work is such that it heightens the students' focus on their bodies *as experienced through movement*, to the point where they are connected to their bodies in a manner which defers conscious, rational self-awareness: 'Know it's a bit of a cliché, but it's just like you come off stage and go, "Oh, where've I been?"' (Manchester Metropolitan second year student). The experience of this sense of self-forgetting is similar to that described in relation to more general movement training work such as 'pure' movement, and the neutral mask work. Approaches such as those of Roth and Grotowski offer a heightened experience of this self-forgetting; the extreme physicality and the authenticity of exhaustion all contribute to a state of changed consciousness where their physical experience is predominant and at the core of their learning within the exercises. Culturally these approaches speak to a generation alert to the pleasures and excitement of physical practices such as clubbing, extreme sports and parkour. The danger of course is that the body becomes a place of refuge from the intellect, and immersion in the physicality of movement an end in itself.

FREEFALL

The sensation of that moment of release is clearly quite exhilarating and inherently contains an element of risk. Actors love to create a sense that their work is not serious, not adult, and not sane. Theatrical anecdotes frequently focus on the extent to which acting is dangerous and risky—physically, psychologically and in relation to the making of coherent meaning (which may, with one forgotten cue, collapse or fade). Actors have traditionally been licensed to be dangerous (Harrop, 1992: 110). There is an energy needed to overcome danger and inhibition, this energy creates a powerful 'aura' around them. Such an 'aura' is actually accentuated by the constant possibility of a technical (missed footing, slip, clumsiness) and/or professional (missed cue/entrance/line, lack of talent or skill) mistake.

As well as physical exhaustion then, risk and danger are the other elements which assert the authenticity of the body, and confirm the body-as-experienced as a key site of meaning for the actor. One group of students associated the image of freefall with the emotional risks of acting, for them this best captured the sensation of releasing the body through training into a world of psychophysically connected experience:

Student	You just take a risk.
Student	Freefall.
Student	Yeah.
Student	Freefall, that's such a good take on it.
Student	Just jump off a building.
Student	That's what it feels like when you go on stage, it just feels like you're diving in to something like off a cliff or something.
Student	Actually, yeah. It was last week wasn't it? We were doing release work in the legs. It was quite scary actually. It sounds really stupid now. But I had a habit holding in my legs, and I'm used to supporting myself with(. . .) yeah, we were releasing in the legs, and for the first time, and it was only a week ago, that's really bad . . . I felt like a real connection between emotion and physicality. I thought I was really quite . . .
Student	She was in stitches laughing.
Student	Scared and laughing and sort of frightened at the sametime. Because it physically felt like I was falling even though I was on the ground. It felt like I was actually moving somewhere. And it was really strange. That was probably the change, in the past two years.

(Manchester Metropolitan second year students)

Of course not all risk is necessarily so enhancing and pleasurable. The tutors are well aware of the delicate balance that needs to be struck between risk and danger in order to empower rather than inhibit students' ability to deal with the 'unruly':

> I think the more physically safe you can make it, the more emotionally people tend to be protected. You know, it always seems to happen that people have terrible, huge, emotional traumas when actually physically they don't feel very safe.
>
> (Morris, 1999)

Nonetheless, the risk element is important in imbuing the actor with decisiveness in movement, in achieving 'the ideal of a body that does not destroy the rhythms of a performance through allowing itself to be restrained by fears' (Logie, 1995a: 257).

THE PLEASURE OF MOVEMENT

> The performing arts are a source of pleasure most of the time for the actor.
>
> (Pradier, 1990: 92)

Central to the conceptions of the unruly body examined in this chapter is the notion of physical pleasure through movement—a notion which relates back to the physical pleasure of efficient movement discussed in the first chapter. When a student from MMU asserts that movement is pleasurable 'in the same way that a violin played very beautifully would be pleasurable' (Manchester Metropolitan second year student), we hear echoes of the aesthetic principles of Paul Souriau:

> It is unquestionable that under certain conditions the sight of bodies in motion gives us aesthetic pleasure; and we are not content with enjoying this kind of spectacle when nature chances to provide it; we also seek its display; we try to bring harmony and rhythm into our own movements.
>
> (Souriau, 1983: xxi)

By introducing the concept of the pleasure of movement, Souriau is introducing a sense, which Henri Bergson also picks up later (Matthews, 1996: 27–29), that movement can be experienced not only on a superficial level common to all human subjects (the external form of the movement), but also on a more deeply personal and individual level. This is an aesthetic of the body which gives pleasure not through form alone, but through kinesthetic experience.

> Movement also gives positive physical pleasure. When we take part in an activity in which we put a lot of energy, all our functions are accelerated, our hearts beat faster, we breathe faster and deeper, and we get a general feeling of well-being. We are living more and feel happy to be alive.
>
> (Souriau, 1983: 5)

Physical sensation, traditionally treated by aesthetic theory as suspect or as symptomatic of more important events in the mind, is, in Souriau's scheme, in this manner integrated into the aesthetics of movement. For the acting student, exercises are in this same sense perceived as 'right' or correctly executed in so far as they generate pleasurable sensations in situations of physical risk, intimacy and vulnerability. Pradier goes further, identifying performance as a source of pleasure through a form of 'neuro-hormonal reward auto-stimulation' (Pradier, 1990: 92). He suggests that: 'The physical phenomenon of thrills—tingling sensations—illustrates the biological aspect of pleasure in theatre and dance' (Pradier, 1990: 92). The same physical activity that helps students to develop the required spontaneous connection between impulse and action also generates the neurochemical reactions to produce physical pleasure and enhance the learning experience.

Student   And you have to work hard with your body, and you do as an actor. You forget sometimes, but you do have to work very hard, because you always sweat, sweating loads after . . .
Student   I feel good for it afterwards. I go down and think, "Oh, no . . . can I . . . ?" And you start getting into it and by the end, it's like, "Yeah. Yeah."
(Manchester Metropolitan first year students)

Student actors all profess enjoyment in their movement training class, which is itself a subculture within the larger culture of the Drama School, thus offering an experience that is exciting and pleasurable in its own marginality. Compared to other areas of study it must offer a particular potential for excitement, risk, danger, thrill and sublimated erotic pleasure. The movement work is not immediately experienced as sexually pleasurable or sexualized, even if the students are at least aware of its erotic potential. Close physical contact may suggest that students are likely to have to repress sexual arousal, but what is at operation here is a process to sublimate or transpose sexual energies. The focus of conscious attention is displaced and the student's engagement is with the psychophysical process, rather than with any overt sexual intention. Students claim to attend only to the general awareness of the physical self, to consciousness-*through*-sensation (as provoked by the exercises), rather than to the potential sexual associations for any close physical contact that occurs. Any translation of this general awareness into, for instance, sexualized awareness would then be seen, in the terms of the training, as a construction *on top of* a general physical awareness and thus as a contamination of the work. The psychophysical process is in this way prioritized over sexual pleasure or titillation; sex is at least partially and temporarily disassociated and deferred. Any energies generated as a result of suggestive physical relationships between bodies are certainly recognized, but then 'recycled' into the students' movement performances. This is another way in which the 'neutral' body training attempts to re-perform gender and sexuality, reconstructing the energies of interpersonal and intimate contact in ways which, through their absence/reconfiguration, potentially increase their significance for the spectator. The students experience release into the performance of movement which is intimate, but which they are also encouraged to perceive as not conventionally sexual or gendered. The lesson, in attempting to set aside the context of everyday sexualized behavior, can certainly allow for the playful and exploratory performance of movements and actions—the sexual implications of close physical contact are deferred—but then move on.

The discipline of the class means that the pleasures of movement, its sensual and erotic effects, unlike in social movement activities such as 'clubbing', have to be sublimated and then channeled into pre-defined creative outlets. The sublimation of the erotic and the attempt to disengage through pleasure from the verbal/symbolic operate in part through exercises which, in sensitizing the whole body, facilitate a polymorphous eroticism. Within such an eroticism, pleasure is expanded from precisely (and binary) gendered and socially located areas of the body surface, in a sense which is similar to the infant experience of physical pleasure suggested by Freud (Segal, 1999: 105). The danger is that such an approach to the body, reminiscent of Marcuse's call for the re-eroticization of the de-eroticized capitalist body (Marcuse 1969), lurches into a false sexual utopianism and an infantilization of the pleasure of movement. As Pradier warns, the physiological and psychological rewards of pleasure can 'succeed in silencing the critical senses' (Pradier, 1990: 92).

The generation of physical pleasure inevitably problematizes movement teaching. The erotic function of movement work can be difficult for some (younger) students to come to terms with at first:

> Some students come when they're very sexually inexperienced and yet we're asking them to move bits of their body in front of each other. Not sexually, but just to free bits of their body in front of each other, that they haven't even discovered in private . . . you know they haven't even discovered for themselves.
>
> (Morris, 1999)

For some students, coming to terms with movement work that may sometimes focus on or draw attention to sexualized body parts must make for an uncomfortable or awkward period of their studies. Set against this, they cannot help but feel some pleasurable effects of movement through the neurochemical 'high' of the endorphins generated by movement activity and the hormonal chemical activity generated through being in close physical contact with other students. This 'high' is potent enough to be capable of generating an 'addiction' to physical work—a phenomenon more commonly associated with dance and keep-fit students: Thus, if the sexual energies generated in movement are necessarily sublimated, they are nonetheless sustained by the pleasurable biological effect of movement. These effects operate on a subconscious level, balancing the student between the sexual structure of movement (its coded expressions), and the erotic effect of movement (its materiality, its voluptuousness).

The intimate nature of the movement class, and the pre-verbal level at which the exercises work, operate to create an element of mystery, even awe, around the subject. The classes often take place in a different manner, in a different kind of space, and at a different pace to classes in other subjects, as if to accentuate this distinctiveness, and each of these differences also functions to intensify the physical experience. The sublimated erotic pleasure generated by and within the performing body-in-movement functions to stimulate a 'voyeurism' in the spectator which invites both desire and empathetic kinesthetic pleasure. The achievement of a controlled and focused release of this pleasure may well operate as an indicator of professional competence, and certainly also functions as an important element in the socio-economics of desire within the theatre industry.

ABSENCE, ABJECTION AND THE UNTRAINED BODY

By contrast to the active, authentic body engaged in pleasurable physical activity, the untrained body is conceived of as 'helpless', 'detached', and lacking in definition:

> I'm really interested to look back on my fifteen year old self and to thinking on stage, 'I never know what to do with my hands', you know. And just thinking, 'OK. Now I . . . do'. Well not know exactly, but now I know how to get rid of that sense that your body is helpless.
> (Guildhall first year student)

The untrained body is here viewed as unresponsive, unruly and inhibited; it is unable to contain its intended meanings. As such, unable to contribute consciously, it is effectively 'absent' within the process of theatrically efficient signification demanded by the industry, yet simultaneously signifying excessively. Placed in a situation which heightens the need for a flexible, aware and expressive body, the untrained body desperately signals its lack of these qualities. For the actor it becomes a body of shame: abject, wasteful, worthless, but also potentially dangerous and in need of taming. Movement training not only intervenes in that excess, but also then imposes boundaries upon the body to enable it to 'contain' theatrical meaning. One student interviewee, for instance, argues the need to 'know where our bodies stop, so you know exactly what you are doing' (Rose Bruford first year student).

Jeliça Šumič-Riha (1997: 233) theorizes that there is body enjoyment in the process of purging what she calls the 'natural' (or in these terms, the 'untrained') body. In so far as that enjoyment operates to reassert the body's 'livedness', it also undermines the body's coherence and stability as a signifier. For Šumič-Riha, the process of training the body does not then simply institutionalize it within the acting profession, but subverts that institutionalization by re-injecting the unruly vitality of body enjoyment. As we have seen, 'neutral' training seeks to take the student through a process which reveals to them how their bodies have signified previously, and the multiple possibilities for future theatrical signification. They are required to offer themselves as 'empty vessels' for 'the dramatist's fine illocutionary wine' (Keir Elam in Aston & Savona,

1991: 103). This takes place through the construction of a defined and controlled psychophysical self, which operates within the demands of a particular performance, a particular dramatic genre, a particular audience/stage relationship, and a particular socio-economic model of the performing arts industries. At the same time however, students find the whole process productive of sometimes quite intense feelings of enjoyment, excitement and pleasure; they are invigorated by the opportunities to manipulate and play with the signs and boundaries which mark their bodies as theatrical.

PRESENCE/ABSENCE AND RESISTANCE

The binary oppositions revealed above leave the body's ontology 'undecided'. Some of the metaphors used by various writers to describe the presence of the actor evoke a sense of this instability. The images of lightning, fire and flame, for instance, as used by Harrop (1992: 112), Grotowski (1968: 34) and Brook (Heilpern, 1977: 147), conjure the body of the actor as transformative, fluid, neither present nor absent, and thus, like a flame, in a constant process of becoming and dying. Training functions to make the actor both present (the 'lived' body of the actor) and absent (an empty vessel for the writer). How then can we decide whether the actor's body is just a docile instrument functioning without question within the socio-economics of the performance industry, or whether its unruliness, its pleasurable vitality and 'livedness' potentially make it harder for power/knowledge to manipulate. What is the value of a training which whilst disciplining the body makes it less secure? For Donnalee Dox: 'the culturally inscribed body need not be viewed as a stable repository of displaced and deferred codes. The body may be intercepted in situations, or at moments, when signification dissolves and is reconfigured' (Dox, 1997: 150). The situations and moments of dissolution and reconfiguration are positioned at the 'edge of experience', where 'the codes or signifiers generally thought to identify the body as an object in culture are shown to be flexible and ephemeral' (Dox, 1997: 150). Judith Butler has also suggested that despite the fact that: 'We are, as it were, worked upon, and only through being worked upon do we become a "we", nonetheless the 'conditions for revolt [are] also occasioned by [this] submission' (Butler, 2002: 19). For Butler, it is also at the margins that revolt and resistance are possible. She argues that we can find release from the 'terms' or 'norms' which give form to our existence (similar to Šumič-Riha's 'institutions' [1997: 234]), which through our desires make us vulnerable to exploitation, by opening ourselves to desires which challenge the norms:

> The question Foucault opens (. . .) is how desire might become produced beyond the norms of recognition. And here he seems to find the

seeds of transformation in the life of a passion which lives and thrives at the borders of recognizability, which still has the limited freedom of not yet being false or true, which establishes a critical distance on the terms which decide our being.

(Butler, 2002: 19)

Though Butler's argument relates most clearly to her previous work on gender and sexuality, this argument is also supportive of the general notion that the unruly body is resistant and challenging to docility exactly because it does not immediately recognize 'the rules'. If the unruly body challenges recognizability (a function of semiotics), then it is to the unstable boundary between the 'body-as-sign' and 'the lived body' that we must turn our attention. The actor's body requires itself to operate both as a sign and as the context for knowing itself—to be simply a sign is to be no more than an object, to be immersed in 'livedness' evades the requirement to communicate or evoke meanings. How might this co-existence function? How might the actor open themselves up to new experiences, new physicalities, and new desires?

PHENOMENOLOGY AND THE 'GRAIN' OF THE MOVEMENT

The moving body is inextricably present. It forces us to deal with it—positioning us as both mover and moved, watcher and watched—but if it is to be capable of more than the social construction of its meaning then it must negotiate a new relationship to the discourses which form it. The body's materiality might be something which can extend outside our discursive relations as conscious subjects, but as Grosz suggests (1994: 143) it is always discursively immanent. Movement's presence as discourse is not simply a function of the subject being conscious of physical activity, as even when movement functions at a subconscious level it cannot simply evade discourse. As we have seen in the examination of muscle memory, discursive power can be placed and identified at the level of the subconscious. Williams and Bendelow further suggest that the unconscious cannot be disentangled from discourse as it 'is composed not of raw biological instincts, but of mental representations we attach to instincts' (Williams & Bendelow, 1998: 96). Harrop reminds us that, 'unlike philosophers and literary critics, actors are obliged to make a specific choice in the moment of action' (Harrop, 1992: 4) and in this moment, 'the actor is both himself and the character at the same time' (Harrop, 1992: 7). One might build on Harrop's suggestion and propose that both the actor and the fictional character do not exist as simple objective material realities, but that they are both inscriptions; they exist for our consciousness only as systems and codes of behavior. But, as I have argued in the previous section, this does not adequately allow for the *experience* and enjoyment of movement. If movement is to be able to operate at the edge of the body's 'un/decidedness' then we need an analysis of movement that takes account of the fluidity and the sensation of movement. It will be necessary to consider how the actor functions as an actor not solely by signifying a character's body, but by operating within the 'grain' of the body, within the 'livedness' of the physical performance.

THE 'GRAIN' OF MOVEMENT—JOUISSANCE AND THE BODY

For the actor, no matter how hard they attempt to control movement and determine its meaning, it will always be operating beyond what they can consciously control—partly because the meaning is not theirs alone but is also constructed by the audience, and partly because they will never be in complete control of the complex meaning-making mechanisms and impulses which function within the human subject. If this were not the case, movement would be little more than a conventional re-writing of existing signs. Like music, which on one level is constantly organizing pre-inscribed meanings and on another is dissolving them within the sensory experience of the sound, movement also exists as a site for the dissolution of meaning and experience (for both actor and spectator) into fluid and multiple interpretations. This dissolution is a result of the insistence of the 'raw data' of movement or music; the impression of such data upon our psyche is, according to Merleau-Ponty, a necessary pre-condition of our ability to 'make meaning'—our continual exposure to sensory experience means that meaning can (and must) remain contingent, that change is possible. To develop this position further and explore how the sensory experience of movement training might penetrate the operation of socio-economic power to construct the actor's body and control it, We can make use of Barthes' notions of *jouissance* and *plaisir* (Barthes, 1977), and of the *studium* and the *punctum* (Barthes, 2000). We can also draw on Gilbert and Pearson's (1999) analysis of the relationship between music and corporeality.

Theatre could be considered as, in certain respects, not unlike Gilbert and Pearson's view of the clubber's music/drug/dance experience—'waves of undifferentiated physical and emotional pleasure; a sense of immersion in a communal moment, wherein the parameters of one's individuality are broken down' (Gilbert & Pearson, 1999: 64). The theatre event, the acting experience, even 'neutral' body training, combine elements of sensuality, movement, inspiration, 'the child-like feeling of perfect safety at the edge of oblivion' (Gilbert & Pearson, 1999: 64). Gilbert and Pearson argue that it is at this marginal point that *jouissance* is possible. They describe *jouissance* as:

a type of extraordinary sensation which derives from the moment before the human child leaves its state of comfortable bliss (. . .) It is at the moment that it falls from this state of grace that the child enters into the symbolic order of social relationships, gendered identity and language.
(Gilbert & Pearson, 1999: 64)

In this sense it is conceived of as a moment outside signification, or at least where signification is deferred. Stephen Heath positions Barthes' notion of *jouissance* as a pleasure which 'shatters—dissipates, loses' cultural identity—a pleasure associated with rapture, bliss or transcendence (Heath in Barthes, 1977: 9). Its ability to bring together the sexual, the spiritual and the physical could thus be very relevant in any search to resolve the issues at the heart of this chapter. Club dance seeks to legitimize 'pure physical abandon in the company of others without requiring the narrative of sex or romance. The culture is one of childhood, of a pre-sexual, pre-oedipal stage' (McRobbie, 1994: 168). 'Pure' or 'neutral' body training for the actor similarly seeks to remove inhibitions to expressive movement, to evade the complications of sex and romance, and it can harbor nostalgia for the innocent, pre-adult body. Gilbert and Pearson's argument assumes a pre-linguistic, pre-subjective (unrecoverable) state, a state which, like Grosz's plastic body (Grosz, 1994: 143), can never be adequately described because it is pre-discursive. It can only be experienced 'in situations in which our normal relation to the symbolic is disrupted' (Gilbert & Pearson, 1999: 64–65). For them, as for Barthes, *jouissance* is not only associated with the body's materiality, but it is accessed at 'moments when the materiality of the means of signification interrupts meaning' (Gilbert & Pearson, 1999: 65). Movement practice should then be such that it 'actively foregrounds its materiality, its corporeality' (Gilbert & Pearson, 1999: 65), and consequently at least defers meaning.

The cultural identity, that which is shattered by *jouissance*, can be aligned with Barthes' conception of the *studium* (Barthes, 2000: 25). It is through the *studium*, the general taste of movement, that the actor culturally participates in the gestures and actions of the world around her, that her work is 'recognized'. When student actors use the cultural trappings of movement to make identities for themselves as actors, then they are indeed operating through the *studium* and 'articulating and reinforcing their identities rather than breaking them down' (Gilbert & Pearson, 1999: 65); they construct a fictional ego which participates in the cultural taste of the host society. *Jouissance* is by association aligned with what Barthes defines as the *punctum*, the puncturing of the fabric or skin of the social body. Gilbert and Pearson suggest that *jouissance* 'is actually often experienced as unbearable pain, as the eruption into subjective experience of that which subjectivity by definition cannot tolerate' (Gilbert & Pearson, 1999: 65). The exhausted body, the body impressing on itself its own physical experience of effort, fatigue, ecstasy, pain, distress or danger, is a body only on the *verge* of collapsing its social significance for itself and for others, but it is not free from recognizability. The 'puncture' operates at the moment of a new experience and relies on a simultaneous deferral of the urge to interpret. Thus movement training also seeks, indicates and values those 'disruptive' inexplicable experiences which are central to the 'alchemical', transformative and non-verbal/ritual experience of acting. Every acting student, every actor, knows that theatre survives ultimately on their ability, in collaboration with those others involved in the creation and presentation of the theatre event, both to recreate the known and to create the unknown. The intimate political power of theatre lies in part in the actor's ability not simply to enact but to re-configure, however subtly, human subjectivity. Movement training prepares for this at the most basic of levels, the actor's body.

Can we thus liberate ourselves so blithely from the symbolic order? Janet Wolff argues that we must be wary of the easy equation of expressive movement and freedom (Wolff in Goodman, 1998: 241). Though Wolff is principally concerned with dance, her point that by mistakenly prioritizing movement as 'intuitive, non-verbal, natural' (Wolff in Goodman, 1998: 241) we may abandon 'critical analysis for a vague and ill-conceived 'politics of the body'' (Wolff in Goodman, 1998: 241) is surely a valid one. Clearly then, whilst we may accept that in moments of movement 'the edges of things blur and terms such as mind/body, flesh/spirit, carnal/divine, male/female become labile and unmoored' (Dempster in Sheridan, 1988: 52), this mobility whilst providing playfulness and dissolving identities cannot and perhaps should not altogether sidestep language, and critical awareness. Wolff identifies some questionable assumptions often made about expressive dance: that it 'bypasses language', 'subverts (phal)logocentrism', and 'provides access to what is repressed in culture' (Wolff in Goodman, 1998: 244)—assumptions which it would be all too easy to make about movement training for actors. Certainly the perception of dance as 'creative' is too often used to differentiate it from other more commonplace movement activities as somehow articulating a particularly embodied 'authenticity'. Movement training for actors, whilst it extends itself to cover a wider range of physical activities (including, for instance, walking), cannot ultimately lay claim to any greater authenticity than dance if that authenticity is also to rely on the contentious idea of 'extra-linguistic experience' (Wolff in Goodman, 1998: 244).

Wolff is critical of Barthes' idea of *jouissance* as some sort of 'direct engagement with the corporeal' (Wolff in Goodman, 1998: 244–5). Certainly formal technique, in so far as it is mediated by cultural practices and recorded in books, cannot help but engage with the *studium*. For Wolff, 'bodies produced by different dance techniques—ballet, Duncan, Graham, Cunningham and contact improvisation—are specific to those techniques' (Wolff in Goodman, 1998: 245); for her, all movement is socially learnt, in that it is 'still coded, stylized and appropriated in social and cultural contexts' (Wolff in Goodman, 1998: 245), and thus just another kind of social practice. But is that what Barthes is suggesting? Surely *jouissance* works to provide moments of puncture, but not to remove the repressive structures. *Jouissance*, in so far as it is a moment of experience which is 'unrecognizable' to the subject, can be aligned with the 'unrecognizable' in Butler's analysis of the margins of desire as a site for revolt (Butler, 2002). It is perhaps then less a question of escaping discourse and more a question of the extent to which the actor can challenge dominant discourses. If movement training for actors is going to be, as it aspires to be, more than just a functional re-working of patterns of existing social behavior, then it has both to subvert those patterns and also to 'deal' with the dominant knowledges and economies of the body. The student actor's bewilderment in the midst of their training may thus be understood not simply as a sign of their critical ignorance, but as an inevitable consequence of the need to defer meaning in order to expand the creative potential of their work. Such a representation would certainly match the experiences of the students interviewed.

THE BODY NEVER LIES

We have seen in Chapter 2 how the paradigm of the child is privileged within the 'neutral' body training; we can now recognize its secondary metaphoric importance in its representation of the return of the body to a pre-symbolic state. The assumption that the 'neutral' (and childlike) body can be seen as more 'honest' belies a nostalgia for the non-rational and the pre-symbolic, for the pure expression of the body untrammeled by the 'interference' of the mind ('the body never lies'). The students interviewed seemed happy to identify with the statement that 'the body never lies', but we need to ask what it might mean as a claim to knowledge: that the body reveals things that the mind might not intend to have revealed; and, that the body cannot make a 'false' statement—what we read in the body is what is actually intended.

> They say that the body never lies, and I think a really, really important thing that we're taught in loads of the movement lessons is just to get rid of our habitual stuff and like the stuff that we show without meaning to.
> (Central School BA Acting for Stage and Screen second year student)

On one level, the purity of the 'body-which-never-lies', in the context of movement training, assumes a body which is then not inhibited by its physicality and materiality, where clumsiness, leakiness, hesitancy and fidgeting have all been cleared away. It proposes a body which represents without hindrance the impulses of the 'self', which is constructed as rational, 'mindful' (in every sense) and unitary. This conception is discursive in so far, for example, as it also introduces the idea of gender. Male bodies in expressive movement are conventionally constructed as awkward, clumsy and fidgety; female bodies are perceived as more contained and graceful, if more prone to weakness and to hesitancy. Movement training is deeply informed by discourses of dance and gender in locating 'truth' and 'authenticity' not in the clumsy and awkward body, nor in the tightly disciplined and trained body, but in the transcendently expressive body which combines both uninhibited movement energy with balance, co-ordination and purpose. Interestingly, contemporary physical theatre has also sought to avoid dance aesthetics and to assert what can be perceived as a more 'authentic' body through high intensity physicality. Exhaustion is seen as emphasizing the 'grain' of the physical (Evans, 2001). Parviainen (1998) draws on Dovey (1985) to argue that authenticity in movement is a property of process and relationship; the relationship between the form of a movement and the processes which produce it.

On another level, the 'body-which-never-lies' suggests a body which is always capable of being read (and therefore always in the process of inscription), though its meanings may be on the margins of consciousness. The perpetual 'readability' of such a body implies that it is constantly and repeatedly opened up both to itself and to others. Movement training likewise requires its 'truth' to be constructed not simply as a measure of compatibility with existing 'norms', but as an indication of the value which could be attributed to its *'unrecognisability'* (in Butler's terms). Perhaps it is for these reasons that many actors resist the systemization of their craft; if authenticity can only lie beyond conventional practice, then such practice can be seen as peripheral to the central art of acting. Movement training has moved away from ballet, dance and posture towards training which is less 'precise' but perhaps allows for greater 'authenticity' within these parameters. During their training student actors draw on coded indicators of authenticity—jargon, uniform, special spaces, inspirational teachers, provenance of subject, 'secret knowledge'—all of which assist in the students' construction of their identity as 'actors'. At the same time actors aver that it is the intensity of 'lived experience' which informs their best acting which is the real source of their authenticity as actors—something some actors insist is unrelated to warm-ups, mask-work and physical exercise: 'There is a whole philosophy of a kind of cool, the old actors who say, 'If you can't act then all the jumping up and down isn't going to make the slightest difference', and that attitude runs deep' (Peter Cheeseman in NCDT, 2001: 36). As we have seen, the students respond positively to elements of their training that allow them, through rhythm, through intense non-verbal expressive movement, and through physical engagement (sometimes to the point of near exhaustion), to reach towards states which problematize the simple communication of pre-inscribed meanings. Nonetheless, for a generation raised on popular social dance culture, such 'pre-symbolic' physical activity is linked to their social experiences and the socio-cultural associations attendant on those experiences. Students may thus use borrowed codes of authenticity to validate and understand even the most intense of movement experiences.

LEARNING TO LIKE THE EXPERIENCE OF THE BODY

Julia Buckroyd (2000) builds on Lacanian psychoanalytic theory to suggest that the ability to experience movement and the body positively at the non-verbal, pre-oedipal stage is crucial to a child's (and an adolescent's) development. For Buckroyd this also suggests the importance for the student dancer of achieving a related sense of 'physical indwelling' (Buckroyd, 2000: 20) in her work, which allows the student to feel that her physical experience is 'real' and 'substantial'. Buckroyd is here echoing the concerns of Young (1990) with regard to the gendered physicality of movement (see Chapter 2). The ability of the student to feel that she is able (in the absence of the parent/carer) to 'contain' and self-soothe her body is seen as important to the student's subject-development. Training seeks not only to release these pre-oedipal pleasures but also to control them, exercising them 'purposefully'. Professionalism demands that simple *free* adventures in pleasure are not available for the actor, whose pleasure should principally exist in relation to the pleasure of the audience if their acting is not to become self-indulgent. The actor's identity is generated out of pleasure (*plaisir*) or delight in pleasing others, which is sometimes seen as a subconscious reason for entering the acting profession. But the actor can offer the audience both the pleasure of the recognizable and the 'ecstasy' of the 'unrecognizable', thereby allowing that their skill can be measured against their ability to transport the audience beyond the simple construction and communication of meaning. For the student actor, such moments of release into a physical pleasure in movement also represent a limited release from the strictures of their training and the perpetual scrutiny of their tutors; movement training is thus subtly subversive in its positioning of the student between a conscious psychophysical system and an impulsive physicality. It also provides an important release from the physically inhibited nature of mundane, everyday, socio-physical behavior. In professional theatre of course, such pleasures are only available within the limits and demands of the part they are lucky enough to play, the text they must enact and the social parameters of the performance event. Nonetheless, in so far as the actor is able to share a released physical experience with the audience, they are also able to act subversively in revealing movement which is no longer constrained by existing patterns of behavior, but which may *necessitate* new meanings.

JUDITH BUTLER, THE PROBLEMS OF 'JOUISSANCE' AND THE ENACTMENT OF RESISTANCE

Judith Butler's work on gender, performativity and the formation of the subject has been widely used to argue that there is 'no well-spring of pure *jouissance* situated in the pre-history of the subject' (Gilbert & Pearson, 1999: 102). Gilbert and Pearson align Butler with Wolff in refuting the simple idea that it is only through momentary points of intense physical experience that we can challenge the dominant discourses (in her argument, discourses of gender):

> to restrict ourselves to these fleeting moments of intensity as the only real way to challenge the dominant discourses, is to accept the terms of these discourses, and thereby to have given up the struggle for real social change before it has even begun.
> (Gilbert & Pearson, 1999: 103)

For Butler, as we have seen earlier, the radical gesture is to occupy the spaces of our bodies in all their marginalities—seeking 'refuge' in oblivion is not the answer to challenging the dominant discourses, that can only come through an awareness of and willingness to inhabit the full and diverse potentialities of our embodiment. The answer as to how this might be achieved lies in Butler's notions around performativity. By repeatedly enacting our bodies and recognizing how that re-enactment (re)constructs us, as well as how it inevitably fails to repeat itself exactly, we may be able to explore new enactments or the opening of those gaps between enactments. Butler argues that we cannot simply turn mind/body dualism on its head and claim that the mindless body of the ecstatic performer is resistant or innovative. Turning the binary values on their heads still leaves the conceptual distinctions on which they rest intact (Gilbert & Pearson, 1999: 103):

> The task—if we follow through the logic of Butler's argument—is not either to reject or reverse terms or distinctions produced by the dominant discourses, but to *deconstruct* them, in doing so problematising the terms themselves.
> (Gilbert & Pearson, 1999: 104)

Deconstruction in practice might mean that movement does not simply describe character in terms of identifiable conventional social behavior, but that it destabilizes unitary notions of character and their socio-physical construction and provokes awareness of the assumptions around character and character construction.

NOT ONE BODY, BUT MANY—RESISTING DISCOURSE AND THE ART OF ACTING

Human subjectivity is not constituted by one single discourse, but by the intersection of many, overlapping discourses. In a manner represented by the structure of this book, the actor is constructed through not one body, but many. If we return to Grosz's suggestion of a 'pre-discursive' materiality with which this chapter opened, we can now perhaps recognize the importance and significance of this multiplicity. At any moment 'the body' is constructed out of many points of physicality, but never out of all of its potential points of physicality. *Jouissance* marks the possibility for the actor to absorb themselves in emotional and physical experience rather than its meaning and be thus enabled to 'inject' themselves into meeting points with new meanings. The sense of indeterminacy that is created at this point may be productive for the very de/construction of identity which is part of the actor's craft. The profound psychophysical experience of intense and intensive movement work can lead the student to a space where the potential discursive material reorganization of the body can take place. This is made possible not by removing the student from discourse, but by (re)interrupting its function. The possibility for (re)interrupting the function of the dominant discourses within the movement class (for both tutors and students) may then exist in the tension between *plaisir* and *jouissance*, where the training operates simultaneously both to construct and to deconstruct the body of the student.

Movement training which simply foregrounds its physicality, which focuses only on physical exercises and technical competence, and which does not address its relationship with the discourses surrounding actor training, may run the risk of simply confirming that movement: is 'about the body'; is (within patriarchal ideologies) predominantly a feminine activity; and, is extrinsic to significant human experience. By addressing the manner in which discourses create us as subjects through movement and the body, movement classes can provide students with insight into many other bodies. The common perception of actors and drama students as sexually ambivalent (already indicated as a possible by-product of 'neutral' body training—see Chapter 2) may be relevant here, revealing the actor's body as a potential site for sexual, as much as subjective, multiplicity. To move as an actor is both active and passive—the actor gives his/herself up to the director's instructions, the playwright's stage directions, the fictional character's objectives, and allows the character to 'move' his/her body; at the same time, the actor engages the whole body and its energies in the present moment through a purposeful decision to commit to movement (Gilbert & Pearson, 1999: 106). Both are 'meaningful', but one offers a stronger image of the liberated body than the other. The 'passive' actor certainly fulfils his/her contractual obligations, but it is the 'active' actor who engages us most directly in the performance event, in the act of perception which points us outwards (Williams & Bendelow, 1998: 53). For movement training to offer the potential for *empowerment* as well as expression, it must find a way in which it can engage students in movement practice which takes them beyond the parameters of the discourses which have produced them. But these parameters, and the moments of *jouissance* in which they transcend them, should not themselves be essentialized; they must be recognized as contingent and contextualized. Certainly some students express their understanding of their training in terms which suggest that the effects of movement training are always 'in process':

I enjoy most the vibrant sessions, where we get in touch with our emotions. When we're moving I do find too much Alexander technique without movement can make you switch off. And at the moment we have to do Alexander every morning which was voluntary before, but now we have to do it every morning. And after a while there is a downside to it. Because if it ever begins to get to work without making it interesting it'll allow the students to switch off. And as soon as you switch off it's not useful anymore. So, in a way it's up to the students to keep yourself interested in it, but it's a double edged sword, anything can be bad if you do too much of it.

(Manchester Metropolitan second year student)

Movement training can be resistant and even liberational, though not alone through its discipline nor through its danger and physicality. Intervention and empowerment may be possible through an approach which can combine the repeated (re)performing of the body, and through the simultaneous recognition of the body of the actor as, in important respects, 'undecided'.

CONCLUSION

Movement training for actors then valuably negotiates between the possibilities and the problems of body training as both professionally purposeful and personally empowering. As Grosz (1995) argues, the body itself refuses to be subsumed completely into the discursive. Against Butler's constructionism, she suggests that:

> The body that performs, however much Butler insists it is produced by performance itself, must nevertheless 'abide between performances, existing over and above the sum total of its performances' (Grosz, 1995: 212).
>
> (Williams and Bendelow, 1998: 128)

Furthermore, as Lancaster argues (1997: 564), within a scheme of 'citationality' the trade is only within representational conventions—'we fall into the familiar trap of seeing every practice as the blossoming forth of an Idea' (Lancaster, 1997: 564). A shortfall of this kind of Foucauldian epistemological view is that the body effectively 'disappears as a material or biological entity' (Williams & Bendelow, 1998: 35). There is a danger of discursive essentialism—an over—privileging of the 'social'—where we can never know the body in the 'raw', but only discursively. In such a scenario the mind once again becomes 'the 'true' locus of power' (Williams & Bendelow, 1998: 35). Movement training, at its best, can take the student beyond this and draw itself back from the dualism which strict social constructionism can imply. It is not necessary to reject the intellect within movement training in order to repatriate meaning within the body. We can unwork the work of culture on the body, without returning to an unreflective nature (Havers, 1997: 291). We can here return to the arguments developed in previous chapters to support the importance of the body itself in the 'knowing' of the world and the construction and operation of that which we would understand as 'mind'. As for Merleau-Ponty, so for the movement training of the actor, 'meaning (. . .) is not the product of some inner mental state. Rather, it resides in the actual concrete behavior of the sentient body-subject' (Williams & Bendelow, 1998: 53).

I have attempted to show that movement training enables the student actor to explore the complex relationship between meaning, the body and the world in a manner which simultaneously relies upon and challenges the discursive. In this sense, bodies are not simply shaped by discourses, but also (re)shape discourses and consequently the rational structures we use to understand the world:

> [O]ur understanding of the world and the way it works contains many 'pre-conceptual' and 'non-propositional' structures of experience that are rooted in our bodies—structures that can be metaphorically projected and propositionally elaborated in order to constitute a rich network of human meaning and significance. This, in turn, necessitates a fundamental rethinking of human *'experience'*, one that includes our bodily, social, emotional and linguistic as well as our intellectual being: everything, in fact, which makes us human.
>
> (Williams & Bendelow, 1998: 55)

Nonetheless attempts to explore the ontological status of the body will continue to remain problematic; linguistic prioritization of the symbolic over the 'real' inevitably defers examination of the body's status as a presocial entity—it is this problematic which is central to the difficulties in writing about movement practice. The extent and nature of any liberational effect will always depend on the social context of the movement class, on conventions and tastes of the trained body, on the learning environment; but it will also depend upon the student's openness to the possibilities offered by a phenomenological approach to the body. Our sense perception of others entangles us with the world, opening us to the experience of other bodies (Merleau-Ponty, 2000: 354): 'perception, for Merleau-Ponty, is first and foremost an embodied experience' (Williams & Bendelow, 1998: 52). Its impact is in allowing us 'a kind of crossing-over, a loss and recovery of the self' (Lancaster, 1997: 564). Merleau-Ponty's argument that,

> we are in the world through our body, and (. . .) we perceive that world with our body (. . .) by thus remaking contact with the body and with the world, we (. . .) also rediscover ourself, since, perceiving as we do with our body, the body is a natural self and, as it were, the subject of perception.
>
> (Merleau-Ponty, 2000: 206)

is echoed by the student actor, who confesses that:

> you go into such difficult places, doing movement (...) you'll suddenly approach things that you don't want to approach or you suddenly find things that just through a movement or ... you know. And undoubtedly you suddenly look at things and you go, "God, I didn't realise that about me" or "I suddenly feel differently".
> (Central School BA Acting for Stage and Screen second year student)

If movement training can open the student to this 'empathetic power of the flesh' (Lancaster, 1997: 564)—that very power which it is supposed to develop as its contribution to the acting process—then it can provide a space where the students can potentially remake their knowledge of the world sufficiently at least to interrupt the performative production of convention, 'to *wound* it with the resistance of its presence' (States, 1985: 12).

One method of opening the student to this empathy is through play. Play, through its impracticality, its lack of seriousness, its excess of effort, its wastefulness, its potential disruption of faithful reiteration, allows us to unmake and remake the world. At the heart of the play instinct is an anarchy which is enabling—'an ability to be *anything*' (Yarrow, 1986: 5). Indeed, as Bert States argues, without play, 'there *is* no delight, only the passage of information' (1985: 12). There is therefore importance in physical play, for it has value as an activity which allows us to engage in 'those carnal ways of knowing and making the world that ought to properly focus the constructionist interrogative from the start' (Lancaster, 1997: 564). Throughout my own personal experience of movement classes and of the activities I have observed in Drama Schools, and within my interviews with students, there have always been elements of delight, of play and playfulness—sometimes through improvisation, sometimes through physical interplay, sometimes through banter and jokes. For Lecoq, play ('*le jeu*') was an integral concept within the fabric of his training (Lecoq: 2000: 167), a feature I recognized within my own experiences at his school. Within all of the movement classes observed within this study there was a strong sense in which the tutors encouraged the students to engage playfully with the exercises rather than to become 'victims' to the work. Since the pioneering work of Isadora Duncan, Jacques Copeau and Suzanne Bing at the start of the Twentieth century (Evans, 2006: 66), through the introduction of games and improvisation in the teaching and texts of Michel St. Denis (1982), Keith Johnstone (1981) and Clive Barker (1977), play and playfulness in movement have increasingly become a key part of a vision for European theatre that is vital, therapeutic, liberating and challenging.

We can understand the risk, danger and ecstasy of the unruly aspects of movement training as potentially subversive and as potentially productive of new conceptions of subjectivity which affirm the flesh and its polymorphology. As with Mikhail Bakhtin's notions of the carnivalesque and the grotesque, movement training's ability to subvert is limited by its status as a licensed and permissible outlet for the body, nonetheless it offers a similar affirmation of play, of transformation and of groundedness. Furthermore, we should be suspicious of any training approaches that seek to deny playfulness, which attempt to capture the body and control too rigidly its meaning, its significance. The body cannot be treated like a photograph, cropped in time and space to the intentions of the artist—such a project is bound to fail, the most highly trained body will still erupt from such restrictions. And this is as it should be for the artist working in movement, for as Bert States suggests, surely, 'you have exhausted a thing's interest when you have explained how it works as a sign' (States, 1985: 7). Thankfully toes will always twitch and tap, and fingers will find a way to fidget. Inappropriate laughter on stage is, appropriately, referred to as 'corpsing'—the body reasserting its unruly presence. Of course such lapses are 'unprofessional', and yet every actor knows that the very possibility of 'corpsing' marks the physical immediacy within the theatre event which enables moments to be ambiguously and subversively meaningful *and* meaningless, sites of 'disclosure' as much as sites of 'reference' (States, 1985: 4). The previous chapter on movement training and the docile body examined the productive power of movement training in the construction of the body of the professional actor. This chapter has drawn out a contradictory thread concerning the extent to which movement training for actors also functions to resist passivity and develop a body that is expressive in ways not always necessarily compatible with the efficient and malleable body demanded by the industry. Unruliness, wastefulness, lack of 'neutrality' can be read unwittingly into the bodies and movements of those differentiated by gender, ethnicity, class or dis/ability, and such 'inefficiencies' are then constructed as difficult, unproductive and unprofessional within the context of professional theatre practice. But such bodies can also be importantly meaningful, culturally playful, playfully resistant and can resonate with significance for a new understanding of movement training for performance. If movement training only re-enacts the bodies of white, middle class, able-bodied young actors, then not only does it perpetuate the cultural hegemony and economic dominance of those bodies but it also denies its potential to participate in the re-invigoration of theatre practice. It is towards such challenges that drama schools and the theatre industry could now address themselves, and in some cases have already begun to do so. If they do not, actors will increasingly be produced with 'new [creative] skills' but reduced to 'chasing old [commercial] ends' (Barker, 1995: 105)—a mismatch of training and industry already identified through a recent NCDT seminar (NCDT, 2001), and which can be seen as in itself representative of larger and more profound tensions within contemporary professional theatre.

Conclusion
Movement Training for Actors: Overview and Projection

I never thought there'd be so much to it.
    (Manchester Metropolitan University second year student)

Movement training for actors has long been marginalized within the history and critical analysis of twentieth century acting. The deeply practical nature of the subject, and its association with commercial and traditional theatre practice, have led to critical attitudes which need to be re-evaluated. The early chapters of this book discussed the institutional factors which have historically operated to marginalize the movement tutor and their work. The scarcity of authoritative texts was related to the inherent difficulties in writing about the body's practices. Chapter 1 applied some of these perspectives to the history of movement training in general and in theatre in particular—examining the key texts, the historically significant practitioners, and placing the practice of movement teaching within the larger socio-cultural context of purpose, efficiency and industrial competitiveness. The concept of the 'neutral' body (Chapter 2) has become central to much contemporary occidental actor training; however its complexity as an idea, its association with particular paradigms, and the misunderstandings the concept of neutrality has generated (specifically around the notion of the 'blank sheet' or *tabula rasa*) mean that critiquing the 'neutral' body reveals the assumptions which underpin several positions which marginalize the body. The 'blank sheet' implies for instance a passive receptivity of the body, which is examined and subsequently critiqued in Chapters 3 and 4. In those last two chapters, efforts are made to reassess the importance of movement training within the training of actors. In some respects this is where its very marginality comes to the fore and the body offers, through its evasions, opacity and plasticity, a possible site from which to recognize movement training as a meeting point for many late twentieth and early twenty-first century themes (performance, care of the self, agency, the relationship between the mind, the brain and the body).

This study has aimed to examine the complex relationship between movement training and historical developments in the understanding of the moving body—revealing the role of movement both in constructing the self and in opening the body to new possibilities. It has also examined the manner in which movement training for actors combines 'care of the self' with training for work, contrasting the actor's development of an organic and instinctual physicality (see Marshall, 2001) against the need for technique and dramaturgical awareness, and the 'enjoyment' of movement against the actor's participation through movement in an embodied economy. As indicated in the Introduction, and as has been drawn out repeatedly through the following chapters, the tension between the imperative to train students for a professional career and the therapeutic effects of training which seeks to facilitate and encourage the psychophysical process from impulse to action is of profound significance for any understanding of the training of actors. Academic study of performance does not always pay due attention to the significance of socio-economical factors influencing the practice of acting and the making of theatre. The issue of vocationalism, far from compromising the study of movement, usefully draws our attention to the extent to which movements are always situated within an economy which they variously challenge, subvert, reproduce and are produced by. Movement tutors are typically honest and pragmatic about this tension. The effects of these economies cannot be swept away simply by the introduction of radical alternatives to existing movement training practice; it is necessary first to understand how *any* movement training practice functions within its complex economic context.

Mainstream theatre, and the institutions providing training for it, may be perceived as resistant to the kinds of radical change proposed by alternative practitioners; they are inevitably constrained by the financial imperative to train students for careers within the established theatre, film and television industries. But to perceive the drama schools as passive, acquiescent and subservient in relation to the dominant modes of production would be a gross oversimplification and mark a failure to recognize the patterns of subtle modification and adaptation through which actor training has developed over the last century. Drama school tutors are open and honest about their responsibilities as vocational trainers. They are equally passionate about the personal empowerment and heightened psycho-social awareness that their training offers to the students (and to others) (see Berry, Rodenburg & Linklater (1997), and Rodenburg (2000) on the effects of voice training for instance). Movement training clearly has some personal benefits for the students; the training provides awareness of movement and posture so that 'balance' and confidence is made possible on both a physical and a psychophysical level. Such an emphasis on the micro-political does invoke some limitations for the student-as-subject, restricting control over their environment to their own immediate and personal sphere. Previous chapters have argued that the individual is prioritized as the site of influence, and as a result change—critical social conceptions of gender, ethnicity, class and dis/ability, for instance—tends to be tentative and/or limited. Certainly over the last few decades it is here where vocationalism has operated restrictively; the structure of the theatre industry is such that political awareness throughout its structures has tended to become increasingly individuated and circumspect. In examining the extent to which Foucault's concept of knowledge/power is applicable, Chapter 3 has attempted to reveal the controlling mechanisms of this vocationalism.

Movement training actively positions dance and movement as culturally productive—both economically and in terms of theatrical meaning, character and performance. It is in this sense that movement becomes 'acceptable' to the theatre industry as a whole. But culturally and socially, movement, especially outside the drama school, is still associated with leisure and pleasure. For the acting student a contradiction implicit within the previous chapters resurfaces—if movement is 'work' then it is useful, but tedious and restrictive; if it is play then it is fun, but unruly, unproductive and wasteful. For Melrose this is a gendered distinction: "the phallus' (. . .) 'stands for', symbolizes, effective use of energy. Is not the professional actor at work, then, regardless of gender, in Lacanian terms theatre's 'phallus'?' (Melrose, 1994: 186). In so far as vocationalism is accepted uncritically, actor training thus implicitly prioritizes masculine concepts of efficiency. As argued in the first two chapters, the 'neutral' training process, through its emphasis on the economical and efficient use of energies, can all too easily become a gendering process, a process which produces theatre performance as part of a gendered (and ethnicized, classed and able bodied) mainstream. Chapters 2 and 4 therefore examined the extent to which actors can use their energies playfully, even 'wastefully', and through this playful excess offer resistance to powers which seek to restrict their sense of self and our sense of ourselves. The tension between the waste of energy and its effective use, as Melrose suggests (1994) is what makes a performance 'vibrate' or resonate for the spectator, as viewed within their own economies of human energy. Excess and risk are the necessary corollaries to physical efficiency; the alternative is creatively stifling. Clive Barker relates how one of Joan Littlewood's frequent injunctions to her company was 'Efficiency is death' (Barker, 2000: 124). As Jonathan Bollen (2001) argues,

> Regulatory norms are never simply reproduced because "reiterations are never simply replicas of the same". Rather, performativity is a citational process that implies degrees of "approximation" and "failure", partly because regulatory norms acquire their authority across the history of their reiterative citation, but also because regulatory norms never govern in advance the differing social contexts of their future deployment.
> (Bollen, 2001: 290–291)

The body always generates too much (or too little) and in doing so undermines any efforts at efficiently exact citation—the actor's task is to monitor that process whilst recognizing its potential.

Conclusion 179

MOVING INTO THE FUTURE

Bringing together these several conclusions, and reading these alongside the previous chapters, some important issues are raised for movement training in drama schools. The actor's energies, however 'wasteful' and unruly, once channeled into performance are employed within specific and demanding economies. The 'repertory' theatre system and the ensemble company, both dominant at the times when many of the drama schools were founded, demanded actors capable of responding to multiple roles and a range of physical challenges. Their gradual decline over the last quarter of the century, conceding ground to the television and film industries and a project-by-project approach to theatre production, has meant that flexibility and self-effacement are no longer considered quite so indispensable for the young actor. More wastefully, patterns of (un)employment in the theatre industry mean that most students will never again experience the intense rigor and the personal challenges of their training. Actors do not seem to have the same understanding of the need for continuous training as dancers do; the result can be that actors a few years out of drama school may lose the habit of keeping their bodies ready and alert. Furthermore suitable classes outside of drama school may be hard to find, especially outside of major cities. Thus it is the very economics of the theatre industry which both shapes the training and wastes what it produces—representative perhaps of the broader cultural perception of theatre as an irresponsible and wasteful art form in a society obsessed by efficiency.

This study has sought to identify the discourses, metaphors, models and ideologies that have structured and shaped the development of movement training for actors over the last century. It has done so by examining in detail the discursive formulations around movement training evident in the way groups of movement tutors and students talk about their practice. Looking ahead however, how will a world informed by the contemporary discourses, metaphors, models, ideas and images of a 'virtual', digital and screen-based era itself shape theatre and the training of actors? What role will the corporeal and embodied actor have in this new order? For one movement tutor, the questions the virtual world poses are vital for the future of movement training and theatre:

> with virtual reality (. . .) what will our bodies be able to sense? How will the next generation be able to feel a response? How big are the signals going to have to be?
>
> (Ewan, 1999b)

Movement tutors see the training they offer as part of a resistance against the de-corporealization of the body. There are concerns that within film, television and cyberspace physicalization is often minimized or even lacking. Film and television acting offers a particular model of the performing body, which is having an impact on students' conceptions of theatre training:

> There is an association in a lot of the students' minds that large scale, full commitment to physical action equals bad acting. A lot of that is to do with the primacy of film in their minds as a template for excellence.
> (Lorna Marshall in NCDT, 2001: 20)

Film, television and the internet challenge so much of the tutors' teaching: the experience of weight through movement in space; the scale and significance of publicly performed gesture; the live connection of impulse to action; the importance of the kinesthetic response. As the industry has expanded and diversified from theatre performance to include film, television, digital media, circus and variety, it has become necessary to consider the extent to which drama schools (can) cope with the increasing diversity of skills required for professional survival. The use of computer generated imagery and 'blue-screen' technology means that actors on film may be required to move in response to things that they cannot see and/or move in ways for which there is no easy preparation. Furthermore, their character's movement may have as much to do with the skills and abilities of animators and soft-ware technicians as they do with the actor's own physical abilities and understanding. Complex cultural shifts in our notions of physicality, weight, sexuality, presence and body shape may only just be beginning to impact on the performer's world of work, but their potential impact is immense. How does a performer prepare for a performance that may take place against a 'blue screen', be re-modeled and digitally transplanted onto another 'actor', and then further 'enhanced' through editing? So far, the response of movement training has been to defend the continuing value of 'pure movement' and 'neutral' body training rather than to dilute and to defocus the training through multi-skilling or niche-skilling. If such a response is resolutely modernist in principle, it does function to maintain a clear identity for movement training for actors, and to locate the practices used as part of a tradition specifically crafted for the live actor. It also functions, perhaps more importantly, to resist the implicit alienation of the 'body as representation' from the 'body as source' which is present in the digital reproduction of movement. Nonetheless, movement tutors are continually aware of the need to keep abreast of new developments, to respond to the challenges and demands of the industry, and to monitor the effects of the curriculum design choices they make.

Movement has, during the last hundred years or so, become intrinsic to what theatre actors do. Acting has become conceived of as inherently physical—it predicates an inner self and a body-as-channel through which the interior can be released and communicated. The momentum of the ideas that initially drove this change in actor training has also carried the body into further prominence in other areas of theatre practice. The development of 'physical theatre', with its roots also in the modernist experiments and avant garde performance work of the early twentieth century, has similarly marked a response to the potential of the body, and to the dominance of the large and small screen. Movement tutors are aware of this cultural shift and its impact on the students they teach and the theatrical context within which they teach:

> It's interesting, the students respond here fantastically well to physical theatre. And most of them seem to have a more dynamic response to seeing physical theatre than straight theatre, which either says something about their education or the state of straight theatre.
> (Morris, 1999)

The development of 'physical theatre' has gathered a lot of momentum over the last two decades, driven by the successes of companies such as Volcano, Frantic Assembly, DV8, Complicité and others. This growth has occurred on the back of a culture of workshop training, contact improvisation and new dance techniques, postmodern performance, and often out of university degree courses. But, through its rejection of conventional approaches to training, and through its (usually) radical political stance, physical theatre practice has in some senses begun to isolate, even to undermine, the fundamental movement training provided by the drama school tutors.

> [T]he instrument, the artist, does not develop through that work [physical theatre]. Because the emphasis is on the group, and not on the individual. I think there's a place for both. I think it's very important, the group needs a place. But I think that you've got to work on yourself always as an actor, and that's where that work—I know from having been to Lecoq—that work, unless you want to go there, doesn't push you in that way.
> (Morris, 1999)

Physical theatre is perceived by some movement tutors as a superficial approach to movement and acting. It is seen as problematic in its marginalization of dramatic intention, and as predominantly technical and visual. Such criticism marks a point of critical difference: between postmodern skepticisms towards the body, its signification and its relation to the psychological impulses of the subject (attitudes typical of many contemporary physical theatre groups), and the drama schools' modernist/humanist conception of the actor expressing through movement deep and sometimes essentialized elements of human nature. This difference is central for movement tutors, whose work is underpinned by the conviction, based on constant reflection and evaluation of their practice, that what they teach is movement training for *actors*, a system designed specifically over several decades and through long apprenticeship to respond to the needs of actors in relation to the demands of professional theatre.

Physical theatre has though had real significance for women's performance, offering space for a physicality that has helped to challenge gender stereotypes:

We like to place a lot of emphasis on women taking up space. It's wonderful to see women taking up more space; walking with larger strides on stage, for example, or running with more freedom than they think they are supposed to.

(H. Ramsden & J. Winter (1994) 'Dorothy talks', interview in *Women and Theatre: Occasional Papers*, 2: 123)

Conventional movement training should not dismiss the impact and significance of physical theatre. It may be able to learn from the successes of physical theatre and further develop its role in contesting the idea of a unitary subject, specifically in relation to the performative construction of the self as gendered. In this sense gender is one of the seats of the performative self that is central to the actor's professional–personal identity, their construction of themselves as actor-subjects. Gender performativity reveals the apparatus of production whereby constructions of the body are established; in doing so it (along with ethnicity, class and dis/ability) may reveal new possibilities of the self which enable the actor in their professional work, and may also present performance as a metaphor for production of the subject which has significance for the body politics of professional actor training (Butler, 1990: 7). By the same token, physical theatre practitioners should be careful not to dismiss conventional theatre training as lacking in political effect or intention. All this argues for a professional drama training that provides the actor not just with skills, but with a richer and more profound understanding of the implications and significance of those skills and the contexts in which they employ those skills. What Lawrence Evans refers to as 'a fundamental understanding of their role, what they are politically in the world, how vital they are to the well-being of society' (Lawrence Evans in NCDT, 2001: 24.). This investigation has aimed to look back over the last century and provide a detailed characterization of the dominant systems for movement training. The importance and relevance of this investigation is in direct relation to the need movement tutors see to empower students through their studies and to reject the possible trivialization of movement studies and actor training in a celebrity–dominated culture.

A BODY OF KNOWLEDGE—HOW SHOULD WE UNDERSTAND OUR PHYSICAL SELVES?

This book functions as a journey from an historical narrative of the body's functionality towards a theoretical engagement with the actor's body, a journey that raises some key issues in relation to our discursive engagement with our bodies. This journey forms a final, and important, frame for this investigation. It draws together our knowledges of the body, the socio-economic histories of our bodies, and their relevance to a better understanding of our movement practices. It is convenient to start with the body as anatomy. For Elizabeth Grosz, the biological body is: 'an open materiality, a set of (possibly infinite) tendencies and potentialities which may be developed, yet whose development will necessarily hinder or induce other developments and trajectories' (Grosz, 1994: 191). Anatomy thus represents a 'disposition' (limits and biologically determined patterns), 'a repository of deferred knowledge' (Hastrup, 1995: 4). But, it is culture that proposes modes of behavior. The challenge then identified is to model the relationship between anatomy and culture, in more conventional terms between body and mind. This study identifies the concept of the 'tabula rasa' as a recurrent metaphor within movement training practice; one that arises repeatedly in the context of movement training. However, 'neutral' body training, in so far as it continues to develop alongside knowledges of the specificities of the physical body, can better be compared to Grosz's own preferred model, that of etching:

> not simply then a model of an imposition of inscription on a blank slate, a page with no 'texture' and no resistance of its own (. . .) [but] a model which (. . .) take[s] into account the specificities of the materials being thus inscribed and their concrete effects in the kind of text produced.
> (Grosz, 1994: 191)

It is in this sense that 'pure movement' or 'neutral' body work in drama schools has, despite itself, its own distinctive style. This inescapable 'texture' of the body directs us back to the realization that technique needs to be constantly evaluated in relation to context.

> We cannot think our way out of our bodies. Nor can we use the idea of a natural or more real body as a vehicle to escape from discourse and culture. What we can do is locate ourselves in relation to other bodies—historically and in the present—and to the institutions and discourses that seek to define and cater to them.
> (Budd, 1997: xiv)

The language of movement training has moved historically to accommodate words which are more to do with process, flow, energies and connections, but it has not developed into the kind of technical metalanguage which the academic study of performance has generated. At the level at which training takes place, importance is given to language that can relate to and express the students' experiences and the challenges they are faced with. Movement tutors realize that the language they deal with is inevitably compromised, but that for now at least it 'serves its purpose'; pedagogically, there is also an anxiety that a metalanguage might make the lived body seem just too distant and elusive. Further research into the potential of and for such a metalanguage could be valuable, with the proviso that we need to be wary of uncritically prioritizing one language over another.

Derrida has argued that the language of research itself is not transparent but is itself a construction, one which, as Hammersley and Atkinson alert us, reflects the social character of its production and of its subject rather than *'representing* some world that is independent of it' (Hammersley & Atkinson, 1995: 14). The use of 'action' words in movement training (as discussed in Chapter 2) reflects the emphasis on process rather than result. As process, the 'neutral' body becomes dynamic rather than static, never fully constituted and perpetually negotiating between experience, perception and idea. 'Neutral' movement training functions to open the body/anatomy (sometimes uncomfortably) to a complex repeated re-constitution which, at least during the training, takes place on several levels simultaneously, whilst resisting any unthinking retreat into socially constructed patterns of behavior: 'It's just amazing how much it opens you up and broadens the way you think about things and perceive things, and the information that you get from other people as well' (Guildhall first year student).

FINALLY

> Movement constitutes an ever-present reality in which we constantly participate. We perform movement, invent it, interpret it, and reinterpret it, on conscious and unconscious levels. In these actions, we participate in and reinforce culture, and we also create it. To the degree that we can grasp the nature of our experience of movement, both the movement itself and the contexts in which it occurs we learn more about who we are and about the possibilities for knowingly shaping our lives.
>
> (Novack, 1990: 8)

The challenge for the student actor then is to understand and control their movement and its cultural, theatrical and professional significance, whilst at the same time 'losing' and 'finding' themselves in the ever-changing experience that is their own body and their consciousness of that body. This challenge is differently experienced by students according to gender (and, to different degrees, class, ethnicity and dis/ability), but, as Novack suggests, it is as central to successful acting as it is to successful living. For the twentieth century actor, movement exists on the cusp of meaning, potentially deeply implicated. It is supported by the same breath which gives power to the voice, yet institutionally still marginalized in relation to the more obviously 'meaningful' function of voice, text analysis and 'character'. In order to participate fully in the processes of cultural production, it has had to push forward its credentials, even in some cases to operate subversively, generating its own provenance and its own methodology. It is in this context that we can understand the value of the 'neutral' body to the movement tutor. The 'neutral' body training of the actor attempts several things simultaneously: to mirror the processes for the development of a free, released and uninhibited voice; to adapt the student to the economic demands of the industry; and, at the same time, to assert that it is through movement that we come to knowledge of the world. The movement training systems created for the development of an active, transformative and expressive actor have enabled the body to be explored as a site for cultural intervention, rather than just as a field of naturally determined processes (Atkinson, 1987: 54). If we are to understand how bodies have been and could be used to make meaning within a system of representation and cultural production such as theatre, then we must acknowledge the politics of these bodies on both the personal level and within the wider social context. This is a complex project, as theatre 'is inescapably concrete and material-dependent [and as] such it tends to be resistant to theory since theory of any kind (. . .) is uncomfortable with the ungoverned and heterogeneous' (Dawson, 1996: 30); but it is a project that has already begun and is still underway, and whose success is of real value to the future of theatre and performance.

Bibliography

PUBLISHED WORKS

Added, Serge (1996) 'Jacques Copeau and 'Popular Theatre' in Vichy France' in Berghaus (1996).
Adshead-Lansdale, Janet & Jones, Cooper (eds.) (1997) *Border Tensions: Dance and Discourse–Proceedings of the Fifth Study of Dance Conference*, Guildford: National Resource Centre for Dance.
Alexander, Frederick Matthias (1910) *Man's Supreme Inheritance*, London: Methuen.
Alexander, Frederick Matthias (1923) *Constructive Conscious Control of the Individual*, London: Methuen.
Alexander, Frederick Matthias (1932) *The Use of the Self: Its Conscious Direction in Relation to Diagnosis, Functioning and Control of Reaction*, London: Methuen.
Alexander, Frederick Matthias (1941) *The Universal Constant in Living*, New York: Dutton.
Alexander, Frederick Matthias (1986) *The Resurrection of the Body: The Essential Writings of F. Matthias Alexander*, (ed. Edward Maisel) Boston & London: Shambala.
Allain, Paul (1997) *Gardzienice: Polish Theatre in Transition*, Amsterdam: Harwood Academic.
Allain, Paul (2002) *The Art of Stillness: The Theatre Practice of Tadashi Suzuki*, London: Methuen.
Allan, J. McGrigot (1869) 'On the real differences in the minds of men and women' in *Transactions of the Anthropological Society of London* Vol. VII, pp. cxcv–ccviii.
Allbright, Ann Cooper (1998) 'Strategic Abilities: Negotiating the Disabled Body in Dance' in Dils & Allbright (2001) pp. 56–66.
Alter, Judith B. (1994) *Dancing and Mixed Media: Early Twentieth-Century Modern Dance Theory in Text and Photography*, New York: Peter Lang.
Anderson, Jack (1997) *Art Without Boundaries*, London: Dance Books.
Appia, Adolphe & Odier, Henri (1906) 'L'Expérience du rythme' in *Journal de Genève*, 25 September 1906 (quoted in Spector, 1990: 88).
Archer, William (1957) *Masks or Faces*, New York: Hill and Wang.
Armstrong, Frankie & Pearson, Jenny (eds.) (2000) *Well-Tuned Women: Growing Strong Through Voicework*, London: The Women's Press.
Arthurs, Jane & Grimshaw, Jean (eds.) (1999) *Women's Bodies: Discipline and Transgression*, London & New York: Cassell.
Arts Council of England (2001) *Annual Review 2001*, London: Arts Council of England.

Aston, Elaine & Savona, George (1991) *Theatre as Sign System: A Semiotics of Text and Performance*, London: Routledge.
Aston, Elaine (1999) *Feminist Theatre Practice: A Handbook*, London: Routledge.
Atkins, Robert (1994) *An Unfinished Autobiography*, (ed. George Rowell) London: Society for Theatre Research.
Atkinson, Paul (1978) 'Fitness, Feminism and Schooling' in Delamont & Duffin (1978) pp. 92–133.
Atkinson, Paul (1987) 'The Feminist Physique: Physical Education and the Medicalization of Women's Education' in Mangan & Park (1987) pp. 38–57.
Austin, Gayle (1990) 'Feminist Theories: Paying Attention to Women' in Goodman (1998) pp. 136–142.
Bablet, Denis & Bablet, Marie-Louise (1982) *Adolphe Appia: 1862–1928 actor-space–light*, (exhibition catalogue, trans. Burton Melnick) London: John Calder.
Backett-Milburn, Kathryn & Cunningham-Burley, Sarah (2001) *Exploring the Body*, Basingstoke: Palgrave.
Backett-Milburn, Kathryn & McKie, Linda (2001) *Constructing Gendered Bodies*, Basingstoke: Palgrave.
Barba, Eugenio & Savarese, Nicola (1991) *A Dictionary of Theatre Anthropology: The Secret Art of the Performer*, London & New York: Routledge.
Barba, Eugenio (2000) 'Tacit Knowledge: Heritage and Waste' in *New Theatre Quarterly*, Vol. XVI, No. 3, (NTQ 63) August 2000, pp. 263–277.
Barker, Clive (1977) *Theatre Games: A New Approach to Drama Training*, London: Eyre Methuen.
Barker, Clive (1995) 'What Training—for What Theatre?' in *New Theatre Quarterly*, Vol. XI, No. 42, pp. 99–108.
Barker, Clive (2000) 'Joan Littlewood' in Hodge (2000) pp. 113–128.
Barker, Clive & Gale, Maggie (eds.) (2001) *British Theatre between the Wars: 1918–1939*, Cambridge: Cambridge University Press.
Barker, Clive & McCaw, Dick (2001) 'Workshops for the World: The International Workshop Festival' in Watson (2001), pp. 155–169.
Barthes, Roland (1977) *Image Music Text*, (ed. & trans. Stephen Heath) London: Fontana.
Barthes, Roland (2000) *Camera Lucida*, London: Vintage.
Battye, Margarite (1954) *Stage Movement*, London: Herbert Jenkins.
Bauer, Martin W. & Gaskell, George (2000) *Qualitative Researching with Text, Image and Sound: A Practical Handbook*, London, Thousand Oaks, CA. & New Dehli: Sage.
Beacham, Richard (1985) 'Appia, Jaques-Dalcroze, and Hellerau, Part One: 'Music Made Visible' in *New Theatre Quarterly*, Vol. 1. No. 2. May 1985.
Beacham, Richard (1994) *Adolphe Appia: Artist and Visionary of the Modern Theatre*, Amsterdam: Harwood Academic Publishers.
Beard, Mary (2000) *The Invention of Jane Harrison*, Cambridge, MA. . & London: Harvard University Press.
Beddoe, Deidre (1998) *Discovering Women's History: A Practical Guide to Researching the Lives of Women since 1800*, London & New York: Longman.
Bennett, Susan (1997) *Theatre Audiences: A Theory of Production and Reception*, London & New York: Routledge.
Benson, Frank (1931) *I Want to Go on the Stage: Do! Don't! How?*, London: Ernest Benn.
Berghaus, Günter (ed.) (1989) *Theatre and Film in Exile: German Artists in Britain, 1933–1945*, Oxford & Providence, R. I.: Berg Publishers.
Berghaus, Günter (ed.) (1996) *Fascism and Theatre: Comparative Studies on the Aesthetics and Politics of Performance in Europe, 1925–1945*, Oxford &: Providence, R. I.: Berghahn Books.

Berkeley, Reginald (1927) *Machines: A Symphony of Modern Life*, London: Robert Holden & Co.
Berkoff, Steven (1977) *East*, London: John Calder.
Berry, Cicely (1973) *Voice and the Actor*, London: Harrop.
Berry, Cicely (1987) *The Actor and the Text*, London: Harrop.
Berry, Cicely (2001) *The Text in Action*, London: Virgin.
Berry, Cicely, Rodenburg, Patsy & Linklater, Kristin (1997) 'Shakespeare, Feminism, and Voice: Responses to Sarah Werner' in *New Theatre Quarterly*, NTQ 49 (February 1997) pp. 48–52.
Best, Sue (1995) 'Sexualising Space' in Grosz & Probyn (1995) pp. 181–194.
Birch, Edward, Jackson, Charles & Towse, Ruth (1998) *Fitness for Purpose Report—Dance, Drama and Stage Management Training: An Examination of Industry Needs and the Relationship with the Current Provision of Training*, London: ACE.
Blackman, Robert (ed.) (1908) *Voice Speech and Gesture: A Practical Handbook to the Elocutionary Art*, Edinburgh: John Grant.
Blair, Fredrika (1986) *Isadora: Portrait of the Artist as a Woman*, New York: McGraw Hill Book Co.
Bland, Lucy (1995) *Banishing the Beast: English Feminism and Sexual Morality 1885–1914*, Harmondsworth: Penguin.
Bloch, Susanna, Orthous, Pedro & Santibañez-H, Guy (1987) 'Effector Patterns of Basic Emotions: A Psychophysiological Method for Training Actors' in Zarrilli (1995), pp. 197–218.
Bollen, Jonathan (2001) 'Queer Kinesthesia: Performativity on the Dance Floor' in Desmond (2001) pp. 285–314.
Boston, Jane (1997) 'Voice: the Practitioners, their Practices, and their Critics' in *New Theatre Quarterly*, NTQ 51 (August 1997) pp. 248–254.
Bourke, Joanna (1996) *Dismembering the Male: Men's Bodies, Britain and the Great War*, London: Reaktion Books.
Bradby, David & McCormack, John (1978) *People's Theatre*, London: Croom Helm.
Brady, Sara (1999) *Looking for Lecoq: A Master's Legacy Lives On*, Available at URL: http:www.tcg.org/am_theatre/lecoq.htm. Accessed 13 July 2000.
Brecht, Bertolt (1961) 'On Chinese Acting' (trans. Eric Bentley) *Tulane Drama Review*, Vol. 6, No. 1 (T13, 1961) pp. 130–136, also available in Martin & Bial (2000) pp. 15–22.
Briginshaw, Valerie (2001) *Dance, Space and Subjectivity*, Basingstoke & New York: Palgrave.
Brook, Barbara (1999) *Feminist Perspectives on the Body*, London & New York: Longman.
Brook, Peter (1972) *The Empty Space*, Harmondsworth: Penguin.
Brook, Peter (1993) *There Are No Secrets: Thoughts on Acting and Theatre*, London: Methuen.
Brown, John Russell (1996) 'Performance, Theatre Training, and Research' in *New Theatre Quarterly*, Vol. XII, No. 47, August 1996.
Brown, Margaret & Somner, Betty (1969) *Movement Education: Its Evolution and a Modern Approach*, Reading, MA.: Addison-Wesley.
Brown, Shirley (1996) *Bristol Old Vic Theatre School: The First 50 Years—1946–1996*, London: Nick Hern Books.
Buckroyd, Julia (2000) *The Student Dancer: Emotional Aspects of the Teaching and Learning of Dance*, London: Dance Books.
Budd, Michael Anton (1997) *The Sculpture Machine: Physical Culture and Body Politics in the Age of Empire*, New York: New York University Press.
Bulman, James C. (ed.) (1996) *Shakespeare, Theory, and Performance*, London & New York: Routledge.

Bulwer, John (1644) *Chirologia, or, the Natural Language of the Hand*, London: Thomas Harper.
Burt, Ramsay (1995) *The Male Dancer: Bodies, Spectacle, Sexuality*, London: Routledge.
Burt, Ramsay (1998) *Alien Bodies: Representations of Modernity, 'Race' and Nation in Early Modern Dance*, London & New York: Routledge.
Burt, Ramsay (2001) 'Dissolving in Pleasure: The Threat of the Queer Male Dancing Body' in Desmond (2001) pp. 209–242.
Butkovsky-Hewitt, Anna (1978) 'Dancing with Gurdjieff in St. Petersburg and Paris' in *Gurdjieff International Review*, Spring 2002, Vol. V (1), available at http://www.gurdjieff.org/butkovsky1.htm. Accessed 24 June 2002.
Butler, Judith (1989) 'Foucault and the Paradox of Bodily Inscriptions' in Welton (1999).
Butler, Judith (1990a) *Gender Trouble: Feminism and the Subversion of Identity*, London & New York: Routledge.
Butler, Judith (1990b) 'Performative Acts and Gender Constitution: An Essay in Phenomenology and Feminist Theory' in Case (1990) pp. 270–282.
Butler, Judith (1993) *Bodies That Matter: On the Discursive Limits of 'Sex'*, London & New York: Routledge.
Butler, Judith (1997) *The Psychic Life of Power: Theories in Subjection*, Stanford, Ca.: Stanford University Press.
Butler, Judith (2002) 'Bodies and Power, Revisited' in *Radical Philosophy: A Journal of Socialist and Feminist Philosophy*, No. 114, July/August 2002, pp. 13–19.
Cain, Maureen (1993) 'Foucault, Feminism and Feeling: What Foucault Can and Cannot Contribute to Feminist Epistemology' in Ramazanoğlu, (1993) pp. 73–96.
Cairns, Adrian (1996) *The Making of the Professional Actor: A History, an Analysis and a Prediction*, London: Peter Owen.
Callery, Dymphna (2001) *Through the Body: A Practical Guide to Physical Theatre*, London: Nick Hern Books.
Carey, Jonathan & Kwinter, Sanford (1992) *Zone 6: Incorporations*, New York: Zone.
Carnegie Trust (1985) *Arts and Disabled People: Report of a Committee of Inquiry under the Chairmanship of Sir Richard Attenborough*, London: Bedford Square Press.
Carnegie Trust (1988) *After Attenborough: Arts and Disabled People—Carnegie Council Review*, London: Bedford Square Press.
Carnicke, Sharon (1998) *Stanislavski in Focus*, Amsterdam: Harwood Academic Publishers.
Carter, Alexandra (1999) 'Feminist Strategies for the Study of Dance' in Goodman (1998) pp. 247–250.
Carter, Huntly (1925) *The New Spirit in the European Theatre 1914–1924: A Comparative Study of the Changes Effected by the War and Revolution*, London: Ernest Benn.
Case, Sue-Ellen (1988) 'Towards a New Poetics' in Goodman (1998) pp. 143–148.
Case, Sue-Ellen (ed.) (1990) *Performing Feminisms: Feminist Critical Theory and Theatre*, Baltimore and London: John Hopkins University Press.
Chadwick, Edwin (1860) *National Association for the Promotion of Social Science, Transactions 1860*, London: John W. Parker.
Chamberlain, Franc & Frost, Anthony (eds.) (2002) *Jacques Lecoq and the British Theatre*, London: Routledge.
Clarke, Mary (1962) *Dancers of Mercury: The Story of the Ballet Rambert*, London: A & C Black.

Cohen, Richard (2002) *By the Sword: Gladiators, Musketeers, Samurai Warriors, Swashbucklers and Olympians*, London & New York: Macmillan.
Cole, Toby & Chinoy, Helen K. (eds.) (1970) *Actors on Acting: The Theories, Techniques, and Practices of the World's Great Actors, Told in Their Own Words*, New York: Crown.
Copeau, Jacques (1970) 'Notes on the Actor' (trans. Harold Salemson) in Cole & Chinoy (1970) pp. 216–225.
Copeau, Jacques (1990) *Copeau: Texts on the Theatre*, (eds. & trans. John Rudlin & Norman Paul) London & New York: Routledge.
Coton, A. V. [Haddakin, Edward] (1946) *The New Ballet: Kurt Jooss and his Work*, London: Dennis Dobson.
Cousin, Glynis (2000) 'Focus Group Research' available at: http://dh1a-2.coventry.ac.uk/taskforce/Documents/fogrweb.html. Accessed 3 March 2000.
Craig, Edward Gordon (1911 [1957]) *On the Art of the Theatre*, London: Heinemann.
Craig, Edward Gordon (1977) *Gordon Craig on Movement and Dance*, (edited by Arnold Rood) London: Dance Books.
Craig, Edward Gordon (1983) *Craig on Theatre*, (edited by J. Michael Walton) London: Methuen.
Crow, Aileen. (1980) 'The Alexander Technique as a Basic Approach to Theatrical Training' in Rubin (1980) pp. 1–12.
Csikszentmihalyi, Mihaly (2002) *Flow*, London: Rider.
Cunningham-Burley, Sarah & Backett-Milburn, Kathryn (2001) *Exploring the Body*, Basingstoke: Palgrave.
Cutler, Anna (1998) 'Abstract Body Language: Documenting Women's Bodies in Theatre' in *New Theatre Quarterly*, vol. XIV, no. 2 (NTQ 54), May 1998 (pp. 111–118).
Daly, Ann (1995) *Done Into Dance: Isadora Duncan in America*, Bloomington & Indianapolis: Indiana University Press.
Damasio, Antonio (2000) *The Feeling of What Happens: Body, Emotion and the Making of Consciousness*, London: Vintage.
Danaher, Geoff, Schirato, Tony & Webb, Jen (2000) *Understanding Foucault*, London, Thousand Oaks & New Delhi: Sage.
Darwin, Charles (1872) *The Expression of the Emotions in Man and Animals*, London: John Murray.
Dasgupta, Gautum (1993) 'Commedia Delsarte' in *Performing Arts Journal*, No. 45, Vol. XV, No. 3 (September 1993) pp. 95–102.
Davis, Kathy (1997) *Embodied Practices: Feminist Perspectives on the Body*, London, Thousand Oaks & New Dehli: Sage.
Davis, Tracy C. (1991) *Actresses as Working Women: Their Social Identity in Victorian Culture*, London: Routledge.
Dawson, Andrew 'Why Feldenkrais is Important in Theatre and Acting' available at http://www.feldenkrais.co.uk/articles/Andrew-Dawson.htm. Accessed 3 January 2002.
Dawson, Anthony (1996) 'Performance and Participation: Desdemona, Foucault, and the Actor's Body' in Bulman (1996) pp. 29–45.
Decroux, Etienne (1985) 'Words on Mime' (trans. Mark Piper) in *Mime Journal: Words on Mime*, Claremont, Ca.: Pamona College.
Delamont, Sara & Duffin, Lorna (eds.) (1978) *The Nineteenth Century Woman: Her Cultural and Physical World*, London: Croom Helen.
Demeny, Georges (1905) *Mécanisme et Éducation des Mouvements*, Paris: Félix Alcan
Dempster, Elizabeth (1988) 'Women writing the body: let's watch a little how she dances' in Sheridan (1988) pp. 35–54.

Dennis, Anne (1995) *The Articulate Body: The Physical Training of the Actor*, New York: Drama Book Publishers.
Denscombe, Martyn (1995) 'Explorations in Group Interviews: An Evaluation of a Reflexive and Partisan Approach' in *British Educational Research Journal*, Vol. 21, No. 2. 1995, pp. 131–148.
Desmond, Jane (ed.) (2001) *Dancing Desires: Choreographing Sexualities on and off the Stage*, Madison: University of Wisconsin Press.
Diderot, Denis (1957 [1773]) *The Paradox of the Actor* (trans. Walter Herries Pollock) New York: Hill and Wang.
Dils, Ann & Allbright, Ann Cooper (2001) *Moving History/Dancing Cultures: A Dance History Reader*, Middletown, Co.: Wesleyan University Press.
Dingwall, Robert (1997) 'Accounts, Interviews and Observations' in Miller & Dingwall (1997) pp. 51–65.
Doat, Jan (1944) *L'Expression Corporelle du Comédien*, Paris: Librarie Théatrale.
Dorcy, Jean (1961) *The Mime*, (trans. Robert Speller, Jr. & Pierre de Fontnouvelle) New York: Robert Speller & Sons.
Dox, Donnalee (1997) 'Thinking Through Veils: Questions of Culture, Criticism and the Body' in *Theatre Research International*, Vol. 22, No. 2 pp. 150–161.
Drain, Richard (1995) *Twentieth Century Theatre: A Sourcebook*, London & New York: Routledge.
Duncan, Dorée, Pratl, Carol & Splatt, Cynthia (eds.) (1993) *Life Into Art: Isadora Duncan and Her World*, London & New York: W. W. Norton & Co.
Durivage, Francis A. (1871) 'Delsarte' in *The Atlantic Monthly*, Vol. 27, Issue 163, May 1871, pp. 613–621.
Dutton, Kenneth (1995) *The Perfectible Body: The Western Ideal of Physical Development*, London: Cassell.
Eldridge, Sears A. & Huston, Hollis W. (1995) 'Actor Training in the Neutral Mask' in Zarrilli (1995) pp. 121–128.
Eldridge, Sears (1996) *Mask Improvisation for Actor Training and Performance: The Compelling Image*, Evanston, Ill.: Northwestern University Press.
'Eloquent Bodies' in *The Economist*, Vol. 352, No. 8136, 11 September 1999.
Emil-Behnke, Kate (1930) *Speech and Movement on the Stage*, Oxford: Oxford University Press.
Erickson, Jon (1995) *The Fate of the Object: From Modern Object to Postmodern Sign in Performance, Art, and Poetry*, Ann Arbor: University of Michigan Press.
Evans, Mark (2001) 'Looking Good?: Perceptions of the Body in the Dance/Theatre of Volcano and Frantic Assembly' in *Dance Theatre: An International Investigation*, (2001) Proceedings of the first MoMentUm conference, September 9–12, 1999, pp. 135–146.
Evans, Mark (2006) *Jacques Copeau*, London: Routledge.
Ewing, William A. (ed.) (2000) *The Century of The Body: 100 Photoworks 1900–2000*, London: Thames & Hudson.
Eynat-Confino, Irene (1987) *Beyond the Mask: Gordon Craig, Movement, and the Actor*, Carbondale & Edwardsville: Southern Illinois University Press.
Featherstone, Mike, Hepworth, Mike & Turner, Bryan (eds.) (1991) *The Body: Social Process and Cultural Theory*, London, Newbury Park & New Dehli: Sage.
Feldenkrais, Moshe (1977) *Awareness Through Movement: Health Exercises for Personal Growth*, Harmondsworth: Penguin.
Feldenkrais, Moshe (1992) *The Potent Self: A Guide to Spontaneity*, San Francisco: Harper & Row.
Felner, Mira (1985) *Apostles of Silence: The Modern French Mimes*, Cranberg, NJ, London & Mississauga, Ont.: Associated University Press.
Fettes, Christopher (2002) 'Yat Malmgren: Obituary' in *Guardian*, 13 June 2002, 22.

Fiedler, Jeannine & Feierabend, Peter (eds.) (1999) *Bauhaus*, Cologne: Könemann Verlagsgesellschaft.
Fishman, Morris (1961) *The Actor in Training*, London: Herbert Jenkins.
Fletcher, Sheila (1984) *Women First: The Female Tradition in English Physical Education 1880-1980*, London & Dover, NH.: The Athlone Press.
Fletcher, Sheila (1987) 'The Making and Breaking of a Female Tradition: Women's Physical Education in England 1880-1980' in Mangan & Park (1987) pp. 145-160.
Fo, Dario(1991) *The Tricks of the Trade*, (trans. Joe Farrell; ed. Stuart Hood) London: Methuen.
Foregger, Nikolai (1975) 'Experiments in the Art of the Dance' in *The Drama Review*, Vol. 19, No. 1 (T-65) March 1975, pp. 74-77.
Foster, John(1977) *The Influences of Rudolf Laban*, London: Lepus Books.
Foster, Susan Leigh (ed.) (1995) *Choreographing History*, Bloomington & Indianapolis: Indiana University Press.
Foster, Susan Leigh (ed.) (1996) *Corporealities: Dancing Knowledge, Culture and Power*, London & New York: Routledge.
Foucault, Michel (1973) *The Birth of the Clinic: An Archaeology of Medical Perception*, London: Tavistock.
Foucault, Michel (1984) *The Foucault Reader: An Introduction to Foucault's Thought*, (edited by Paul Rabinow) London: Penguin.
Foucault, Michel (1990) *History of Sexuality: Volume 1, An Introduction*, London: Penguin.
Frank, Arthur. W. (1991) 'For a Sociology of the Body: An Analytical Review' in Featherstone, Hepworth, & Turner (1991) pp. 36-102.
Franklin, Paul (2001) 'The Terpsichorean Tramp: Unmanly Movement in the Early Films of Charlie Chaplin' in Desmond (2001) pp. 35-72.
Franko, Mark (2002) *The Work of Dance: Labor, Movement and Identity in the 1930s*, Middletown, Co.: Wesleyan University Press
Friedler, Sharon & Glazer, Susan (eds.) (1997) *Dancing Female: Lives and Issues of Women in Contemporary Dance*, Amsterdam: Harwood Academic Publishers.
Frost, Anthony & Yarrow, Ralph (1990) *Improvisation in Drama*, Basingstoke: Macmillan.
Garb, Tamar (1998) *Bodies of Modernity: Figure and Flesh in Fin-de-Siècle France*, London: Thames & Hudson.
Gaskell, George (2000) 'Individual and Group Interviewing' in Bauer & Gaskell (2000) pp. 38-56.
Giedion, Siegfried (1948) *Mechanization Takes Command: A Contribution to Anonymous History*, New York: Oxford University Press.
Gilbert, Jeremy & Pearson, Ewan (1999) *Discographies: Dance Music, Culture and the Politics of Sound*, London & New York: Routledge.
Gilbreth, Frank (1911) *Motion Study: A Method for Increasing the Efficiency of the Workman*, New York: D. Van Nostrand.
Ginner, Ruby (1933) *The Revived Greek Dance: Its Art and Technique*, London: Methuen & Co.
Goffman, Erving (1971) *Relations in Public: The Micro-Politics of Social Order*, London: Allen Lane.
Golding, Sue (ed.) (1997) *Eight Technologies of Otherness*, London & New York: Routledge.
Goodman, Lizbeth with de Gay, Jane (eds.) (1998) *The Routledge Reader in Gender and Performance*, London & New York: Routledge.
Goodridge, Janet (1999) *Rhythm and Timing of Movement in Performance: Dance, Drama and Ceremony*, London & Philadelphia: Jessica Kingsley.

Gordon, Mel (1975a) 'Foregger and the Dance of the Machines' in *The Drama Review*, Vol. 19, No. 1 (T-65), March 1975, pp. 68–73.
Gordon, Mel (1975b) 'German Expressionist Acting' in *The Drama Review*, vol. 19, no. 3 (T-67), September 1975, pp. 34–50.
Gottlieb, Vera & Chambers, Colin (eds.) (1999) *Theatre in a Cool Climate*, Oxford: Amber Lane Press.
Gould, Stephen (1981) *The Mismeasure of Man*, New York: W. W. Norton.
Grimshaw, Jean (1999) 'Working Out with Merleau-Ponty' in Arthurs & Grimshaw (1999), pp. 91–116.
Grosz, Elizabeth (1994) *Volatile Bodies: Toward a Corporeal Feminism*, Bloomington & Indianapolis: Indiana University Press.
Grosz, Elizabeth (1995) *Space, Time and Perversion*, London: Routledge.
Grosz, Elizabeth & Probyn, Elspeth (eds.) (1995) *Sexy Bodies: The Strange Carnalities of Feminism*, London & New York: Routledge.
Grotowski, Jerzy (1968) *Towards a Poor Theatre*, (ed. Eugenio Barba) London: Methuen and Co.
Hall, Edward T. (1969) *The Hidden Dimension*, New York: Doubleday & Co.
Hall, Stuart & Gieben, Bram (eds.) (1992) *Formations of Modernity*, London: Polity Press.
Hammersley, Martyn & Atkinson, Paul (1995) *Ethnography: Principles and Practice*, (2nd ed.) London: Routledge.
Hanna, Judith Lynne (1988) *Dance, Sex and Gender: Signs of Identity, Dominance, Defiance, and Desire*, Chicago & London: University of Chicago Press.
Hargreaves, Jennifer (1987) 'Victorian Familism and the Formative Years of Female Sport' in Mangan & Park (1987) pp.130–144.
Hargreaves, Jennifer (1994) *Sporting Females: Critical Issues in the History and Sociology of Women's Sport*, London & New York: Routledge.
Harrop, John (1992) *Acting*, London & New York: Routledge.
Hastrup, Kirsten (1995) 'Incorporated Knowledge' in *Incorporated Knowledge: Mime Journal, 1995* (ed. Thomas Leabhart) Claremont, CA: Pomona College Theatre Department, pp. 2–9.
Haver, William (1997) 'Queer Research; or, How to Practise Invention to the Brink of Intelligibility' in Golding (1997) pp. 277–292.
Hayman, Ronald (1973) 'The Actor Prepares—for What?' in *Theatre Quarterly*, vol. III, no. 11, July–September 1973, pp. 49–57.
Hayman, Ronald (1977) *Artaud and After*, Oxford, London & New York: Oxford University Press.
Hébert, Georges (1949) *L'Éducation Physique du L'Entrainement Complet par la Méthode Naturelle,*. Paris: Librarie Vuibert.
HEFCE (1999) *The Hosier Report: Funding of Specialist Performing Arts Institutions*, London: HEFCE.
Heilpern, John (1977) *The Conference of the Birds: The Story of Peter Brook in Africa*, London: Faber & Faber.
Hennessey, Rosemary (2000) *Profit and Pleasure: Sexual Identities in Late Capitalism*, London & New York: Routledge.
Herrigel, Eugen (1985) *Zen in the Art of Archery*, London: Penguin.
Hiley, Jim (1988) 'Moving Heaven and Earth' in *Observer*, 20 March 1988.
Hilton, Julian (1987) *Performance*, Basingstoke: Macmillan.
Hobbs, William (1995) *Fight Direction For Stage and Screen*, London: A & C Black.
Hodge, Alison (ed.) (2000) *Twentieth Century Actor Training*, London & New York: Routledge.
Holloway, Wendy (1989) *Subjectivity and Method in Psychology: Gender, Meaning and Science*, London: Sage.

Holt, Richard (1990) *Sport and the British: A Modern History*, Oxford: Oxford University Press.
Howarth, Jessmin (2002) 'Remember Inner Work' in *Gurdjieff International Review*, Spring 2002, Vol. V (1), available at: http://www.gurdjieff.org/howarth1.htm. Accessed 24 June 2002.
Howe, Dianne (1996) *Individuality and Expression: The Aesthetics of the New German Dance, 1908–1936*, New York: Peter Lang.
Hulbert, Henry H. (1921) *Eurhythm: Thought in Action—The Principles and Practice of Vocal and Physical Therapy*, London: Novello & Co.
Huxley, Michael, Leach, Martin & Stevens, Jayne. (1995) 'Breaking Down the Barrier of Habit: An Interdisciplinary Perspective on the Ideas of F. M. Alexander and the Theory and Practice of Dance' in Adshead-Lansdale & Jones (1997) pp. 155–180.
Huxley, Michael & Witts, Noel (eds.) (1996) *The Twentieth Century Performance Reader*, London: Routledge.
Innes, Christopher (1993) *Avant Garde Theatre: 1892—1992*, London & New York: Routledge.
Ives, Alice E. (1893) 'The Delsarte Girl' in *The Century*, Vol. 46, Issue 2 (June, 1893).
James, Martin (2002) 'Out of Control' in *The Sunday Times*, 'Culture' supplement, Sunday 15 September, p. 59.
Jaques-Dalcroze, Emile (1906) *Méthode Jaques-Dalcroze: Pour le Développement de l'instinct Rythmique du Sens Auditif et du Sentiment Tonal, en 5 Parties*, Neuchatel: Sandoz, Jobin & Cie.
Jaques-Dalcroze, Emile (1921) *Rhythm, Music and Education*, Bucks: Dalcroze Society.
Jenkins, Ron (2001) 'A Prophet of Gesture who got Theater Moving' in *The New York Times*, 18 March 2001.
Johnstone, Keith (1981) *Impro: Improvisation and the Theatre*, London: Methuen.
Jousse, Marcel (1974) *Anthropologie du Geste*, Paris: Gallimard.
Juhan, Deanne (2003) *Job's Body: A Handbook for Bodywork*, Barrytown, NY.: Station Hill Press.
Kahn, Naseem (1990) *A Way Through the Mimefield: The Mime Training Report*, London: ACGB.
Karina, Lilian & Kant, Marion (2003) *Hitler's Dancers: German Modern Dance and the Third Reich*, New York: Berghahn Books.
Keats, Daphne (2000) *Interviewing: A Practical Guide for Students and Professionals*, Buckingham & Philadelphia, PA.: Open University Press.
Keefe, John (1993a) *Training for Tomorrow: Report on the National Conference on Mime and Physical Theatre Training*, London: Mime Action Group.
Keefe, John (1993b) *A Critical Practice: Report on the Seminar focusing on the Training and Development Needs of Mime and Physical Theatre Practitioners*, London: Mime Action Group.
Khatchadourian, Haig (1978) 'Movement and Action in the Performing Arts' in *The Journal of Aesthetics and Art Criticism*, Vol. XXXVII, No. 1, Fall 1978.
Kirby, Vicki (1997) *Telling Flesh: The Substance of the Corporeal*, London: Routledge.
Knowles, Richard Paul (1996) 'Shakespeare, Voice and Ideology: Interrogating the Natural Voice' in Bulman (1996) pp. 92–112.
Kumiega, Jennifer (1985) *The Theatre of Grotowski*, London: Methuen.
Kupers, Petra (2003) *Disability and Contemporary Performance: Bodies on Edge*, London: Routledge.
Kusler, Barbara Leigh (1979) 'Jacques Copeau's School for Actors: Commemorating the Centennial of the Birth of Jacques Copeau' in *Mime Journal: Numbers Nine and Ten*, Claremont, Ca.: Pamona College.

Bibliography

Laban, Rudolf (1948) *Modern Educational Dance*, London: Macdonald & Evans. [1975 edition].
Laban, Rudolf (1950) [reprinted 1988] *The Mastery of Movement on the Stage*, London: Macdonald & Evans.
Laban, Rudolf (1954) 'The Work of the Art of Movement Studio' in *Journal of Physical Education*, vol. XLVI, no. 137 (March 1954), pp. 23–30.
Laban, Rudolf (1966) *Choreutics*, London: MacDonald & Evans.
Laban, Rudolf & Lawrence, Frederick C. (1947) *Effort*, London: MacDonald & Evans.
Lamb, Warren (1965) *Posture and Gesture*, London: Duckworth.
Lancaster, Roger (1997) 'Guto's Performance: Notes on the Transvestism of Everyday Life' in Lancaster & di Leonardo (1997) pp. 559–574.
Lancaster, Roger & di Leonardo, Micaela (1997) *The Gender/Sexuality Reader: Culture, History, Political Economy*, London: Routledge.
Lang, S. E. (ed.) (1929) *Education and Leisure: Addresses at the Fourth Triennial Conference on Education held at Victoria and Vancouver Canada, April 1929*, London & Toronto: Dent & Sons Ltd.
Leabhart, Thomas (1989) *Modern and Postmodern Mime*, Basingstoke: Macmillan.
Leabhart, Thomas (1996) 'L'Homme de Sport: Sport, Statuary and the Recovery of the Pre-Cartesian Body in Etienne Decroux's Corporeal Mime' in *Mime Journal: Theatre and Sport*, Vol. 21. Claremont, Ca.: Pamona College, pp. 31–66.
Leach, Robert (1989) *Vsevolod Meyerhold*, Cambridge: Cambridge University Press.
Leach, Robert (2006) *Theatre Workshop: Joan Littlewood and the Making of Modern British Theatre*, Exeter: Exeter University Press.
Lecoq, Jacques (1981) 'Mime, Movement, Theatre' in Rolfe (1981) pp. 151–153.
Lecoq, Jacques (ed.) (1987) *Le Théâtre du Geste: Mimes et Acteurs*, Paris: Bordas.
Lecoq, Jacques (2000) *The Moving Body: Teaching Creative Theatre*, (trans. David Bradby) London: Methuen.
Lecoq, Jacques (ed.) (2006) *Theatre of Movement and Gesture*, (trans. David Bradby) London: Routledge.
Leder, Drew (1990) *The Absent Body*, Chicago: Chicago University Press.
Leicht, Urs (ed.) (1985) *Jooss: Dokumentation von Anna und Hermann Markard*, Cologne: Ballett-Bühnen-Verlag Rolfe Garske.
Lenskyj, Helen (1987) 'Physical Activity for Canadian Women, 1890–1930: Media Views' in Mangan & Park (1987) pp. 208–231.
Lepecki, André (2006) *Exhausting Dance: Performance and the Politics of Movement*, London: Routledge.
Levine, Donald (1991) 'Martial Arts as a Resource for Liberal Education: The Case of Aikido' in Featherstone, Hepworth & Turner (1991) pp. 209–224.
Linklater, Kristin K. (1976) *Freeing the Natural Voice*, New York: Drama Book Publishers.
Linklater, Kristin (1992) *Freeing Shakespeare's Voice: The Actor's Guide to Talking the Text*, New York: Theatre Communications Group.
Linklater, Kristin (2000) 'Overtones, Undertones and the Fundamental Pitch of the Female Voice' in Armstrong & Pearce (2000), pp. 26–41.
Littlewood, Joan (1994) *Joan's Book: Joan Littlewood's Peculiar History As She Tells It*, London: Methuen.
Locke, John (1975 [1690]) *An Essay Concerning Human Understanding*, (ed. A. D. Woozley) London: Collins/Fontana.
Logie, Lea (1995a) 'Theatrical Movement and the Mind-Body Question' in *Theatre Research International*, Vol. 20, No. 3 pp. 255–265.
Logie, Lea (1995b) 'Developing a Physical Vocabulary for the Contemporary Actor' in *New Theatre Quarterly*, Vol. XI, No. 43, August 1995 pp. 230–240.

Lust, Annette (2000) *From the Greek Mimes to Marcel Marceau and beyond: Mimes, Actors, Pierrots, and Clowns—A Chronicle of the Many Visages of Mime in the Theatre*, Lanham, Md. & London: Scarecrow Press.
Mac An Ghaill, Máirtín (1996) *Understanding Masculinities: Social Relations and Cultural Arenas*, Buckingham & Philadelphia: Open University Press.
McCarren, Felicity (2003) *Dancing Machines: Choreographies of the Age of Mechanical Reproduction*, Stanford, Ca.: Stanford University Press.
McConnell, Carolyn (1997) 'The Body Never Lies' in Friedler & Glazer (1997) pp. 215–226.
McCrone, Kathleen E. (1987) 'Play up! Play up! And Play the Game! Sport at the Late Victorian Girls' Public Schools' in Mangan & Park (1987).
McEvenue, Kelly (2001) *The Alexander Technique for Actors*, London: Methuen.
McGaw, Dick (2001) 'Lifelong Listening: An Appreciation of the Fifty-year career of Teacher and Choreographer Geraldine Stephenson' in *Dance Theatre Journal*, Vol. 17, No. 1, 2001.
McIntosh, Peter C. (1968) *Physical Education in England Since 1800*, London: G. Bell & Sons.
McKenzie, Jon (2001) *Perform or Else: From Discipline to Performance*, London & New York: Routledge.
McNeill, William (1995) *Keeping Together in Time: Dance and Drill in Human History*, Cambridge, MA. & London: Harvard University Press.
McRobbie, Angela (1994) *Postmodernism and Popular Culture*, London & New York: Routledge.
Mamet, David (1998) *True and False: Heresy and Common Sense for the Actor*, London: Faber & Faber.
Mangan, James A. & Park, Roberta J. (eds.) (1987) *From 'Fair Sex' to Feminism: Sport and the Socialization of Women in the Industrial and Post-Industrial Eras*, London & Totowa, NJ.: Frank Cass & Co.
Marchant, Graham (2001) 'The Funding of Drama Student Training in Britain' in *New Theatre Quarterly*, Volume XVII Part 1 (NTQ 65) February 2001 pp. 31–44.
Marcuse, Herbert (1969 [1955]) *Eros and Civilization: A Philosophical Inquiry into Freud*, Boston: Beacon Press.
Marey, Étienne J. (1873) *La Machine Animale: Locomotion Terrestre et Aérienne*, Paris: Librairie Gemer Baillière.
Marshall, Gail (1998) *Actresses on the Victorian Stage: Feminine Performance and the Galatea Myth*, Cambridge: Cambridge University Press.
Marshall, Lorna (2001) *The Body Speaks: Performance and Expression*, London: Methuen.
Martin, Carol & Bial, Henry (eds.) (2000) *Brecht Sourcebook*, London & New York: Routledge.
Martin, Emily (1997) 'The End of the Body?' in Lancaster & di Leonardo (1997) pp. 543–558.
Martin, Jacqueline (1991) *Voice in Modern Theatre*, London & New York: Routledge.
Martin, John (2004) *Intercultural Performance Handbook*, London: Routledge.
Matthews, Eric (1996) *Twentieth Century French Philosophy*, Oxford & New York: Oxford University Press.
Maudsley, Henry (1874) 'Sex in Mind and in Education' in *Fortnightly Review* (1874), Vol. 15, pp. 466–483.
Mauss, Marcel (1934) 'Techniques of the Body' in Carey & Kwinter (1992) pp. 454–477.
Mawer, Irene (1925) *The Dance of Words*, London: J. M. Dent & Sons Ltd.
Mawer, Irene (1932) *The Art of Mime: Its History and Technique in Education and the Theatre*, London: Methuen & Co.

Mayhew, Henry (1968) *London Labour and the London Poor—Volume 3. The London Street-Folk (concluded)*, New York: Dover Publications.
Melrose, Susan (1994) *A Semiotics of the Dramatic Text*, Basingstoke: Macmillan.
Melrose, Susan (1998) 'My Body, Your Body, Her-His Body: Is/Does Somebody (Live) Here?' in *New Theatre Quarterly*, vol. XIV, no. 2 (NTQ 54), May 1998, pp. 119–125.
Melrose, Susan (1999) 'Introduction to Part Four: 'What do women want (in theatre)?" in Goodman (1998) pp. 131–135.
Merleau-Ponty, Maurice (2000) *Phenomenology of Perception*, (trans. Colin Smith) London & New York: Routledge.
Meyer, Moe (1994) 'Reclaiming the Discourse of Camp' in Goodman (1998) pp. 255–258.
Meyer-Dinkgraffe, Daniel (2001) *Approaches to Acting: Past and Present*, London: Continuum.
Meyerhold, Vsevolod (1969) *Meyerhold on Theatre*, (trans. & ed. Edward Braun) London: Eyre Methuen.
Miller, Gale & Dingwall, Robert (1997) *Context and Method in Qualitative Research*, London, Thousand Oaks, CA. & New Dehli: Sage.
Mingalon, Jean-Louis (1999) 'An Interview with Marie-Hélène Dasté' in *Mime Journal: Transmissions*, Claremont, Ca.: Pamona College, pp. 11–27.
Mitter, Shomit (1992) *Systems of Rehearsal: Stanislavski, Brecht, Grotowski and Brook*, London: Routledge.
Morris, Margaret (1969) *My Life in Movement*, London: Owen.
Morrison, Hugh (1998) *Acting Skills*, London: A & C Black.
Mosse, George (1996) *The Image of Man: The Creation of Modern Masculinity*, Oxford: Oxford University Press.
Moynihan, D. S. with Odom, Leigh. G. (1984) 'Oskar Schlemmer's Bauhaus Dances: Debra McCall's Reconstructions' in *The Drama Review*, vol. 28, no. 3 (T-103), Fall 1984, pp. 46–50.
Mueller, Ludwig (1929) 'The German Youth Movement' in Lang (1929).
Mulvey, Laura (1975) 'Visual Pleasure and Narrative Cinema', *Screen*, 16/3 (Autumn), pp. 6–18.
Murray, Simon (2003) *Jacques Lecoq*, London: Routledge.
Murray, Simon & Keefe, John (2007) *Physical Theatres: A Critical Introduction*, London: Routledge.
Muths, Johan Guts (1800) *Gymnastics for Youths*, London: J. Johnson.
Nathan, Thomas (1997) 'Dalcroze Eurhythmics and the Theatre' http://www.msu.edu/user/thomasna/dalthea1.html accessed 29/09/00.
National Council for Drama Training [NCDT] (1999) *Criteria and Procedures for Accreditation of Courses 1999/2000*, London: NCDT.
National Council for Drama Training [NCDT] (2001) *Movement Training for Actors: Olivier Foundation Seminar*, London: NCDT.
National Council for Drama Training [NCDT] (2002) 'Education and Training Information Sheet 5: Acting—why should I train?' http://www.ncdt.co.uk/Acting.html.
National Council for Drama Training [NCDT] (2004) 'How Much Does Training Cost?' http://www.ncdt.co.uk/cost.asp.
National Council for Drama Training [NCDT] (2008) *Accreditation Guide*, London: NCDT.
Ness, Sally Ann (1996) 'Dancing in the Field: Notes from Memory' in Foster (1996) pp. 129–154.
Newlove, Jean (1993) *Laban for Actors and Dancers: Putting Laban's Movement Theory into Practice—A Step-by-Step Guide*, London: Nick Hern Books.

Novack, Cynthia (1990) *Sharing the Dance: Contact Improvisation and American Culture*, Madison: University of Wisconsin Press.
O'Connor, Barry (2001) 'Mapping Training/Mapping Performance: Current Trends in Australian Actor Training' in Watson (2001), pp. 47–60.
O'Connor, Gary (1982) *Ralph Richardson: An Actor's Life*, London: Hodder & Stoughton.
Oida, Yoshi with Marshall, Lorna (1992) *An Actor Adrift*, London: Methuen.
Oida, Yoshi & Marshall, Lorna (1997) *The Invisible Actor*, London: Methuen Drama.
Olivier, Laurence (1983) *Confessions of an Actor*, London: Hodder & Stoughton.
Onions, Charles T. (ed.) (1973) *The Shorter Oxford English Dictionary: on Historical Principles*, Oxford: Clarendon Press [OED].
Orbach, Jack (ed.) (1982) *Neuropsychology after Lashley: Fifty Years since the Publication of 'Brain Mechanisms and Intelligence'*, Hillsdale, NJ. & London: Lawrence Erlbaum Associates.
Park, Glen (2000) *The Art of Changing: Exploring the Alexander Technique and its Relationship to the Human Energy Body*, Bath & London: Ashgrove Publishing.
Parker, Andrew & Sedgwick, Kosofsky Eve (eds.) (1995) *Performativity and Performance*, London & New York: Routledge.
Parviainen, Jaana (1998) *Bodies Moving and Moved: A Phenomenological Analysis of the Dancing Subject and the Cognitive and Ethical Values of Dance Art*, Tampere, Finland: Tampere University Press.
Paterson, Kate (2001) 'Disability Studies and Phenomenology: Finding a Space for both the Carnal and the Political' in Backett-Milburn & Cunningham-Burley (2001) pp. 81–97.
Pavis, Patrice (1993) *Languages of the Stage: Essays in the Semiology of the Theatre*, Baltimore & London: John Hopkins University Press.
Pavis, Patrice (1998) *Dictionary of the Theatre: Terms, Concepts and Analysis*, (trans. Christine Shantz) Toronto & Buffalo: University of Toronto Press.
Peacock, Alan & Rizzo Ilde (eds.) (1994) *Cultural Economics and Cultural Policies*, Dordrecht: Kluwer Academic Publishers .
Phelan, Peggy (1995) 'Thirteen Ways of Looking at Choreographing Writing' in Foster (1995) pp. 200–210.
Phelan, Peggy (1997) *Mourning Sex: Performing Public Memories*, London & New York: Routledge.
Pines, Jim (ed.) (1992) *Black and White in Colour: Black People in British Television since 1936*, London: British Film Institute.
Pisk, Litz (1975) *The Actor and His Body*, London: Harrap.
Polhemus, Ted (1998) 'The Performance of Pain' in *Performance Research: 'On Ritual'*, Vol. 3 No. 3 (Winter, 1998) pp. 97–103.
Potter, Charlie Lee (1984) *Sportswear in Vogue Since 1910*, London: Thames & Hudson.
Potter, Nicole (ed.) (2002) *Movement for Actors*, New York: Allworth Press.
Powney, Janet & Watts, Mike (1987) *Interviewing in Educational Research*, London: Routledge & Kegan Paul.
Pradier, Jean Marie (1990) 'Towards a Biological Theory of the Body in Performance' in *New Theatre Quarterly*, Vol. VI, No. 2, 1990, pp. 86–98.
Preston-Dunlop, Valerie (1998) *Rudolf Laban: An Extraordinary Life*, London: Dance Books.
Price, Janet & Shildrick, Magrit (eds.) (1999) *Feminist Theory and the Body*, Edinburgh: Edinburgh University Press.
Ramazanoğlu, Caroline (1993) *Up Against Foucault: Explorations of Some Tensions between Foucault and Feminism*, London & New York: Routledge.

Rea, Kenneth (1981) 'Drama Training in Britain, Part I' in *Theatre Quarterly*, Vol. X, No. 39, Spring-Summer 1981, pp. 47–58.
Rea, Kenneth (1981) 'Drama Training in Britain, Part II' in *Theatre Quarterly*, Vol. X, No. 40, Autumn-Winter 1981, pp. 61–73.
Rée, Jonathan (1999) *I See a Voice: Language, Deafness and the Senses—A Philosophical History*, London: Harper Collins.
Rene, Natalia (1963) 'Isadora Duncan and Constantin Stanislavski' in *Dance Magazine*, 1963, Vol. 37, part 7, pp. 40–43.
Richards, Thomas (1995) *At Work with Grotowski on Physical Actions*, London: Routledge.
Risum, Jane (1996) 'The Sporting Acrobat: Meyerhold's Biomechanics' in *Mime Journal: Theatre and Sport*, Claremont, Ca.: Pamona College.
Rivington, Robert T. (1983) *Punting: Its History and Techniques*, Oxford: R. T. Rivington.
Roach, Joseph (1993) *The Player's Passion: Studies in the Science of Acting*, Ann Arbor: University of Michigan Press.
Robinson, Jacqueline (1997) *Modern Dance in France: An Adventure 1920–1970*, Amsterdam: Harwood Academic.
Rodenburg, Patsy (1992) *The Right to Speak: Working with the Voice*, London: Methuen.
Rodenburg, Patsy (1993) *The Need for Words: Voice and the Text*, London: Methuen.
Rodenburg, Patsy (1996) *The Actor Speaks: Voice and the Performer*, London: Methuen.
Rodenburg, Patsy (2000) 'Powerspeak: Women and Their Voices in the Workplace' in Armstrong & Pearson (2000) pp. 96–109.
Rodenburg, Patsy (2002) *Speaking Shakespeare*, London: Methuen.
Rogers, Clark (1969) 'Appia's Theory of Acting: Eurhythmics for the Stage' in E. T. Kirby (ed.) (1969) *Total Theatre: A Critical Anthology*, New York: Dutton & Co., 20–28.
Rolfe, Bari (ed.) (1981) *Mimes on Miming: Writings on the Art of Mime*, London: Millington.
Roose-Evans, James (1989) *Experimental Theatre: From Stanislavsky to Peter Brook*, London: Routledge.
Ross, Janice (2000) *Moving Lessons: Margaret H'Doubler and the Begiining of Dance in American Education*, London: University of Wisconsin Press.
Roth, Gabrielle (2002) 'New Dimensions Interview' Available at URL: http://www.newdimensions.org/article/roth.html. Accessed 17 March 2002.
Rubin, Harriet (2000) 'Boooorrriinng!!!: That's exactly what Philippe Gaulier teaches leaders not to be.' *FC Issue 35, p.228*. Available at URL: http://www.fastcompany.com/online/35/gaulier.html. Accessed on 13 July 2000.
Rubin, Lucille S. (ed.) (1980) *Movement for the Actor*, New York: Drama Book Specialists.
Rudlin, John (1986) *Jacques Copeau*, Cambridge: Cambridge University Press.
Rudlin, John (2000) 'Jacques Copeau: The Quest for Sincerity' in Hodge (2000) pp. 55–78.
Ruffini, Franco F. (1995) 'Mime, The Actor, Action: The Way of Boxing' in *Mime Journal: Incorporated Knowledge*, Vol. 20. Claremont, Ca.: Pamona College, pp. 54–69.
Ruyter, Nancy Lee Chalfa (1996a) 'Antique Longings: Genevieve Stebbins and American Delsartean Performance' in Foster (1996) pp. 70–88.
Ruyter, Nancy Lee Chalfa (1996b) 'The Delsarte Heritage' in *Dance Research*, Vol. X1V, No. 1, Summer 1996, pp. 62–74.

St. Denis, Michel (1982) *Training for the Theatre: Premises and Promises*, (ed. Suria St. Denis) London: Heinemann.
Samuel, Raphael, MacColl, Ewan & Cosgrove, Stuart (1985) *Theatres of the Left 1880–1935: Workers' Theatre Movements in Britain and America*, London: Routledge and Kegan Paul.
Sanderson, Michael (1984) *From Irving to Olivier: A Social History of the Acting Profession in England 1880–1983*, London: Athlone Press.
Sandler, Julie (1997) 'Standing in Awe, Sitting in Judgement' in Friedler & Glazer (1997) pp. 197–206.
Sarlós, Robert & McDermott, Douglas (1995) 'The Impact of Working Conditions upon Acting Style' in *Theatre Research International*, Vol. 20, No. 3, pp. 231–236.
Schechner, Richard (2002) *Performance Studies: An Introduction*, London & New York: Routledge.
Schlemmer, Oskar (1971) *Man: Teaching Notes from the Bauhaus*, (ed. H. Kuchling, trans. J. Seligman) London: Lund Humphries.
Schmidt, F. A. & Miles, Eustace H. (1901) *The Training of the Body: For Games, Athletics, Gymnastics, and Other Forms of Exercise and for Health, Growth, and Development*, London: Swan Sonneshein & Co.
Searle, Geoffrey R. (1990) *The Quest for National Efficiency: A Study in British Politics and Political Thought, 1899–1914*, London: Ashfield Press.
Segal, Lynne (1994) 'Body Matters: Cultural Inscription' in Price & Shildrick (1999) pp. 105–110.
Segel, Harold. B. (1998) *Body Ascendant: Modernism and the Physical Imperative*, Baltimore & London: John Hopkins University Press.
Sellers-Young, Barbara (1999) 'Technique and the Embodied Actor' in *Theatre Research International*, Vol. 24, No. 1 (Spring, 1999) pp. 89–96.
Senelick, Laurence (1997) 'Early Photographic Attempts to Record Performance Sequence' in *Theatre Research International*, Vol. 22 No. 3.
Shapiro, Sherry (ed.) (1998) *Dance, Power and Difference: Critical and Feminist Perspectives on Dance Education*, Champaign, Il.: Human Kinetics.
Shawn, Ted (1974) *Every Little Movement: A Book About François Delsarte*, New York: Dance Horizons.
Sheridan, Susan (ed.) (1988) *Grafts: Feminist Cultural Criticism*, London: Verso.
Shusterman, Richard (2000) *Performing Live: Aesthetic Alternatives for the Ends of Art*, Ithaca, NY: Cornell University Press.
Siegel, Paul (2001) 'A Right to Boogie Queerly: The First Amendment on the Dance Floor' in Desmond (2001) pp. 267–283.
Smedley, Constance (1924) *The Greenleaf Theatre Elements: I. Action*, London: Duckworth & Co.
Smith, Anthony Charles H. (1973) *Orghast at Persepolis: An International Experiment in Theatre directed by Peter Brook*, New York: Viking Press.
Smith, Clyde (1998) 'On Authoritarianism in the Dance Classroom' in Shapiro (1998) pp. 123–146.
Smith, Joan (2001) 'Wedlocked' in *The Guardian*, Weekend magazine, 12 May 2001, pp. 46–52.
Smith, W. David (1974) *Stretching Their Bodies: The History of Physical Education*, London: David & Charles.
Smith-Rosenberg, Caroll & Rosenberg, Charles (1987) 'The Female Animal: Medical and Biological Views of Women and Their Role in Nineteenth-Century America' in Mangan & Park (1987) pp. 13–37.
Souriau, Paul (1983) *The Aesthetics of Movement*, (trans. & ed. Manon Souriau, foreword Francis Sparshott) Amherst: University of Massachusetts Press.

Southern, Richard (1970) *The Victorian Theatre: A Pictorial Survey*, Newton Abbot: David & Charles.
Spector, Irwin (1990) *Rhythm and Life: The Work of Emile Jaques-Dalcroze*, Stuyvesant, NY: Pendragon Press.
Spencer, Herbert (1859) *Education: Intellectual, Moral and Physical*, London: Williams & Norgate.
Spencer, Herbert (1901) *Essays: Scientific, Political and Speculative*, London: Williams & Norgate.
Stanislavski, Constantin (1979) *Building a Character*, (trans. Elizabeth Reynolds Hapgood) London: Eyre Methuen.
Stanislavski, Constantin (1980) *An Actor Prepares*, (trans. Elizabeth Reynolds Hapgood) London: Eyre Methuen.
States, Bert. O. (1985) *Great Reckonings in Little Rooms: On the Phenomenology of Theater*, Berkeley, Los Angeles & London: University of California Press.
Stephenson, Geraldine (1959) 'Laban's Influence on Dramatic Movement' in *New Era*, (May, 1959).
Stewart, Nigel (2001) 'The Punctum of Performance' in *Dance Theatre: An International Investigation* (2001) Proceedings of the first MoMentUm conference, September 9–12, 1999, pp. 69–80.
Straus, Erwin (1966) 'The upright posture' in *Phenomenological Psychology* (New York: Basic Books) pp. 137–165.
Šumič-Riha, Jeliça (1997) 'The Diasporic Dance of Body-Enjoyment: Slain Flesh/Metamorphosing Body' in Golding (1997) pp. 225–235.
Summers, Leigh (2001) *Bound to Please: A History of the Victorian Corset*, Oxford: Berg.
Taylor, Brandon & van der Will, Wilfried (1990) *The Nazification of Art: Art, Design, Music, Architecture and Film in the Third Reich*, Winchester: The Winchester Press.
Taylor, Frederick Winslow (1911) *The Principles of Scientific Management*, London: Harper and Row.
Taylor, Frederick Winslow (1964) *Scientific Management: Comprising Shop Management, The Principles of Scientific Management, Testimony Before the Special House Committee*, London: Harper & Row.
Taylor, George (1989) *Players and Performances in the Victorian Theatre*, Manchester & New York: Manchester University Press.
Taylor, George (1999) 'François Delsarte: A Codification of Nineteenth-Century Acting' in *Theatre Research International*, Vol. 24. No. 1 pp. 71–81.
Terry, Ellen (1908) *The Story of My Life*, London: Hutchinson & Co.
Throsby, David (1994) 'A Work-Preference Model of Artistic Behaviour' in Peacock & Rizzo (1994) pp. 69–80.
Todd, Mabel E. (1968) *The Thinking Body: A Study of the Balancing Forces of Dynamic Man*, New York: Dance Horizons.
Toepper, Karl (1997) *Empire of Ecstasy: Nudity and Movement in German Body Culture 1910–1935*, Berkeley, Los Angeles & London: University of California Press.
Tomlinson, Richard (1982) *Disability, Theatre and Education*, London: Souvenir Press.
Trussler, Simon (1994) *The Cambridge Illustrated History of the British Theatre*, Cambridge: Cambridge University Press.
Tuckman, B. (1965) 'Developmental Sequences in Small Groups' in *Psychological Bulletin*, 63, pp. 384–399.
Tufnell, Miranda & Crickmay, Chris (1990) *Body Space Image: Notes towards improvisation and performance*, London: Dance Books

Tufnell, Miranda & Crickmay, Chris (2004) *The Widening Field: Journeys in body and imagination*, Alton: Dance Books.
Turner, Bryan (1991) 'Recent Developments in the Theory of the Body' in Featherstone, Hepworth & Turner (1991) pp. 1–35.
Turner, Victor (1988) *The Anthropology of Performance*, New York: PAJ.
van der Will, Wilfried (1990) 'The body and the body politic as symptom and metaphor in the transition of German Culture to National Socialism' in Taylor & van der Will (1990) pp. 14–52.
Verma, Jatinder (1999) 'Sorry, No Saris!' in Gottlieb & Chambers (1999), pp. 179–190.
Vertinsky, Patricia (1994) *The Eternally Wounded Woman: Women, Doctors and Exercise in the Late Nineteenth Century*, Urbana & Chicago: University of Illinois Press.
Wardle, Irving (1978) *The Theatres of George Devine*, London: Jonathan Cape.
Watson, Ian (1993) *Towards a Third Theatre: Eugenio Barba and the Odin Teatret*, London: Routledge.
Watson, Ian (ed.) (2001) *Performer Training: Developments Across Cultures*, Amsterdam: Harwood Academic Publishers.
Watt, David & Welton, Rick (1991) *Training: Discussion Document*, London: Arts Council of Great Britain & The National Arts and Media Strategy Unit.
Welton, Donn (ed.) (1998) *Body and Flesh: A Philosophical Reader*, Oxford: Blackwell.
Welton, Donn (ed.) (1999) *The Body: Classic and Contemporary Readings*, Oxford: Blackwell.
Werner, Sarah (1996) 'Performing Shakespeare: Voice Training and the Feminist Actor' in *New Theatre Quarterly*, NTQ 47 (August 1996) pp. 249–258.
Williams, Simon & Bendelow, Gillian (1998) *The Lived Body: Sociological Themes, Embodied Issues*, London & New York: Routledge.
Willson, Francis (1997) *In Just Order Move: The Progress of the Laban Centre for Movement and Dance 1946—1996*, London: Athlone Press.
Wilshire, Bruce (1982) *Role Playing and Identity: The Limits of Theatre as Metaphor*, Bloomington: Indiana University Press.
Winearls, Jane (1968) *Modern Dance: The Jooss-Leeder Method*, London: A. C. Black.
Winearls, Jane (1990) *Choreography: The Art of the Body—An Anatomy of Expression*, London: Dance Books.
Wolff, Janet (1995) 'Dance Criticism: Feminism, Theory and Choreography' in Goodman (1998) pp. 241–246.
Wolford, Lisa & Schechner, Richard (eds.) (1997) *The Grotowski Sourcebook*, London: Routledge.
Worpole, Ken (2001) *Here Comes The Sun: Architecture and Public Space in Twentieth-Century European Culture*, London: Reaktion.
Wright, John (2002) 'The Masks of Jacques Lecoq' in Chamberlain & Yarrow (2002), pp. 71–84.
Yarrow, Ralph (1986) '"Neutral" Consciousness in the Experience of Theatre' in *Mosaic*, Vol. XIX, No. 3, pp. 1–14.
Young, Iris (1990a) *Throwing Like a Girl*, Bloomington, Indiana: Indiana University Press.
Young, Iris (1990b) 'Throwing Like a Girl' in Welton (1998) pp. 259–273.
Young, Iris (1998) '"Throwing Like a Girl": Twenty Years Later' in Welton (1998) pp. 286–290.
Zarrilli, Phillip (1995) *Acting (Re)Considered: Theories and Practices*, London & New York: Routledge.

Zarrilli, Phillip (2000) *Kathakali Dance-drama: Where Gods and Demons Come to Play*, London & New York: Routledge.
[Zeami] Motokiyo, Zeami (1984) *On the Art of the Nō Drama: The Major Treatises of Zeami*, (trans. J. Thomas Rimmer & Yamazaki Masakazu) Princeton, N.J.: Princeton University Press.

VIDEO

Les Deux Voyages de Jacques Lecoq (1999), (Video, VHS) Directed by Jean-Noël Roy, Jean-Gabriel Carasso, & Jean-Claude Lallias, Paris: ANRAT.
The Liberation of the Body: Following in the Tracks of E. Jaques-Dalcroze and his Students (2001), (Video, VHS) Directed by Norbert Göller, Dresden: Balance Film GmbH.
The Work of Yat Malmgren (1997), (Video, VHS) Directed by Jan Sargent, London: Moyla.

UNPUBLISHED TEXTS AND CORRESPONDENCE

Evans, Mark (1983) personal notes from classes as a student at L'École Jacques Lecoq, Paris (1982–1983).
Evans, Mark (2003) *Movement Training for the English Actor in the Twentieth Century: Body Learning and Conceptual Structures*, PhD Thesis, Coventry University.
Kusler, Barbara Leigh (1974) *Jacques Copeau's Theatre School: L'École du Vieux Colombier, 1920–1929*, PhD Thesis, University of Wisconsin.
Mirodan, Vladimir (1997) *The Way of Transformation (the Laban-Malmgren system of dramatic character analysis)*, PhD Thesis, University of London.
Rogers, Clark (1966) *The Influence of Dalcroze Eurhythmics in the Contemporary Theatre*, PhD Thesis, Louisiana State University.
Tarr, Jen (2002) 'Beasts, Babes, Savages and Greeks: 'Natural Bodies' in Contemporary Dance and Movement Re-education', conference paper at *New Scholars Day 2002 (Society for Dance Research)*, Coventry University (20 April 2002).
Verma, Jatinder (vaio@tara-arts.com)(16 July 2002) *Re: Movement and Acting*, e-mail to Mark Evans (m.evans@coventry.ac.uk).

INTERVIEW MATERIAL (UNPUBLISHED)

Interviews with Movement Tutors

Allnutt, Wendy (Head of Movement at Guildhall School of Music and Drama) *Interview with Mark Evans*, at Guildhall School of Music and Drama, 4 June 1999.
Arnold, Patricia [Trish] (retired movement tutor—LAMDA, Guildhall School of Music and Drama [GSMD]) *Interview with Mark Evans*, at private residence, 18 November 1999.
Dowling, Niamh (Head of Movement and Head of School of Theatre at Manchester Metropolitan University [MMU]), *Interview with Mark Evans*, at MMU, 1 March 2000.

Ewan, Vanessa (Senior Tutor Movement at Central School of Speech and Drama) (1999a), *Interview with Mark Evans*, at Central School of Speech and Drama, 2 February 1999.

Ewan, Vanessa (1999b), *Interview with Mark Evans*, at Central School of Speech and Drama, 11 November 1999.

Morris, Shona (former Head of Movement at Rose Bruford College, currently Senior Lecturer in Acting at Drama Centre, London) *Interview with Mark Evans*, at Rose Bruford College, 7 October 1999.

Interviews with Student Groups

Central School of Speech and Drama, ten Year 1 Central School BA Acting for Stage and Screen Students, *Interview with Mark Evans*, at Central School, 17 November 1999.

Central School of Speech and Drama, nine Year 2 Central School BA Acting for Stage and Screen Students, *Interview with Mark Evans*, at Central School, 31 January 2001.

Guildhall School of Music and Drama, ten Year 1 BA (Hons)/Associate Diploma Acting Students, *Interview with Mark Evans*, at Guildhall School of Music and Drama, 5 June 2000.

Guildhall School of Music and Drama, ten Year 2 BA (Hons)/Associate Diploma Acting Students, *Interview with Mark Evans*, at Guildhall School of Music and Drama, 13 June 2001.

Manchester Metropolitan University, seven Year 1 BA (Hons) Acting Students, *Interview with Mark Evans*, at MMU, 1 March 2000.

Manchester Metropolitan University, seven Year 2 BA (Hons) Acting Students, *Interview with Mark Evans*, at MMU, 30 May 2001.

Rose Bruford College, eight Year 1 BA (Hons) Acting Students, *Interview with Mark Evans*, at Rose Bruford College, 1 February 2001.

Rose Bruford College, six Year 2 BA (Hons) Acting Students, *Interview with Mark Evans*, at Rose Bruford College, 1 February 2001.

Index

7:84 Theatre Company, 116

A
absent body, 118
active consciousness, 102, 150
actor training (nineteenth century), 37–39
Alexander, F. M., 4, 8, 11, 34–35, 91, 93
Alexander Technique, 84, 172; for actors, 58–59; animals and, 92; children and, 92; gymnastics and, 74; physiology and, 111; the 'primitive' body and, 77–78; therapy and, 106; use of weight and, 147
Alexander, Gerda, 59
Allbright, Ann Cooper, 104, 106
Allnutt, Wendy, 97, 100; on rhythm, 93; on pure movement, 94; on Litz Pisk, 97, 127; on neutral body, 100; on dance, 127
Ancient Greece: the classical body, 33, 44–45, 75–76
Appia, Adolphe, 51–52, 53
Arnold, Patricia: on Delsarte, 43; St. Denis and, 55; Jooss-Leeder Method and, 57; Lecoq and, 60
Artaud, Antonin, 12, 25, 76, 145, 149
Arts Council England, 2, 64
Asian theatre, 113
Atkins, Robert, 42, 43
Atkinson, Madge, 46–47, 49
ausdrucktanz, 72

B
Bakhtin, Mikhail, 174
Ballet, 86, 105, 115, 116, 147, 166, 168
Barba, Eugenio, 3, 13, 76, 82, 83, 98. *See also* Odin Teatret
Barker, Clive: on actor training and movement, 37, 122, 123, 133, 140, 175; on consciousness, 146; on games, 148, 174; on Laban's influence, 56; Littlewood and, 178, texts on movement, 116; releasing in movement, 150
Barrault, Jean-Louis, 62
Barthes, Roland, 6, 96; jouissance and, 151–152, 164–165, 166, 167, 171; plaisir and, 164, 169, 171; punctum and, 164–165; studium and, 164–165, 166; 'grain' and, 164
Beaton, Norman, 112–113
Beijing Opera, 76, 113
Bellugue, Paul, 60
Benson, Sir Frank, 40, 73, 76
Bergson, Henri, 158
Bhangra, 113
Bing, Suzanne, 82, 92, 174
Blatchley, John, 58
Bollen, Jonathan, 178
Brecht, Bertolt, 58, 76, 116
Britzman, Deborah, 110
Brook, Peter, 11, 50, 58, 122, 145, 162
Buckroyd, Julia, 169
Budd, Michael, 1, 183
Bulmershe College of Higher Education, 105
Butler, Judith, 6, 7, 120, 168, 172; neutral body, 70, 9; the resistant body, 162–163, 167, 169–170; body politics, 182

C
Calisthenics, 73, 115

Cambridge Ritualists, 45
Carpenter, Bill, 57
Case, Sue Ellen, 110
CAST, 116
Central School of Speech and Drama, 8, 40, 43, 44, 58, 72, 127, 131
Centre for Performance Research, 67
Cheeseman, Peter, 116, 168
Circus, 4, 72, 115, 180
Cixous, Hélène, 13
Clarke, Mary, 127
class; social, 103; neutral body and, 114–117
Coghill, George, 92–93
Les Comediens de Grenoble, 61
Commedia dell'Arte, 14, 60
Complicité, Théâtre de, 181
contact improvisation, 166, 181
Copeau, Jacques: actor training, 53, 82, 133, 145; animals and movement, 92; children and movement, 91; Dalcroze and, 52; Duncan and, 46; École Vieux Colombier and, 54; games, 174; gesture, 22; Lecoq and, 60; Les Copiaux and, 61; neutral mask, 78–80, 81; St. Denis and, 54, 80; Souriau and, 23
Craig, Edward Gordon, 49–50, 53, 80
Crickmay, Chris, 13
crit, 128–129
Csikszentmihalyi, Mihaly, 89, 150

D

Dalcroze, Emile Jaques, 76, 82, 132; costume for lessons, 127; Delsarte and, 22, 23; Duncan and, 46, 47; eurhythmics, 27–29, 44; Ginner and, 48; gymnastics, 25; Laban and, 32; movement and children, 91; theatre and, 50–53
Daly, Ann, 46, 75, 76, 77, 83
Damasio, Antonio, 90
Darwin, Charles, 18, 77, 78
Dasté, Jean, 60
Dawson, Andrew, 1, 23, 185
de Beauvoir, Simone, 108
Decroux, Etienne, 19, 25, 61, 62, 82, 127
Delsarte, François, 76, 82, 132; actor training, 28; Craig and, 50; Dalcroze and, 28, 53; the development of dance, 25; drama schools, 42–43; Duncan and, 46; eurhythmics and, 44; gesture and emotion, 20–23; Greek Dance and, 45, 47; 55, Laban and, 32; Ling and, 58; movement analysis, 95
Demeny, Georges, 19–20, 45, 51, 95, 96
Derrida, Jacques, 143, 184
Devine, George, 54, 58
Diderot, Denis, 36, 126, 130
disability, 103; neutral body and, 104–106
Disability Discrimination Act, 105
discipline, 135–136
Dorcy, Jean, 60, 79
Dowling, Niamh, 9, 59; Alexander technique, 59; movement and imagination, 89, 93; movement and masculinity, 109; Roth and, 156; teaching process, 12; voice and movement, 9
Dox, Donalee, 162
Drama Centre, 58
Descartes, Réne,16
Drama School: and patriarchal structures 7, and UK Higher Education 64
du Maurier, Gerald, 115
Duncan, Isadora, 53, 166, 174; Delsarte and Greek Dance, 23, 45–46, 48–49, 75–76, 77; Litz Pisk and, 58; natural dance and, 83; Copeau and, 91; Craig and, 47, 50
DV8 Physical Theatre, 181

E

Education par le jeu dramatique (EPJD), 60
efficiency: actor training, 66–67; aesthetics of, 14–16; capitalism and, 26–27; nationalism and physical efficiency, 29–32; Souriau and physical efficiency, 23–26
Eldredge, Sears, 10, 79, 81, 88, 94, 97, 98, 102, 107, 119, 122
Empire Road, 112
Enlightenment, The, 16, 17, 19, 76, 145
ethnicity, 26, 68, 103, 175, 178, 182, 184; neutral body and, 112–114
eurhythmics. *See* Dalcroze
Evans, Lawrence, 182
Ewan, Vanessa, 2, 124, 135, 142, 154, 155; actions, 89; animal studies, 92; body as instrument, 131;

disability and movement training, 105; inner and outer self, 130; Laban, 56; movement and virtual reality, 179; movement class uniform, 127; role of the tutor, 134; systems of training, 132; weight, 147

F

Feldenkrais, Moshe, 12, 59, 60, 74, 111
fencing, 5, 40, 41, 42, 43, 115, 116
Fligg, Annie, 55, 73, 127
flow, 89, 149, 183. *See* Csikszentmihalyi
Fo, Dario, 61–62
Foco Novo Theatre Company, 116
Fogerty, Elsie, 40, 43, 44
Foucault, Michel, 6; desire, 162; docile body, 120, 123; knowledge, 136, 178; neutral body, 70
Franklin, Paul, 111
Frantic Assembly, 181
Freud, Sigmund, 24, 160; post-Freud, 101
Froebel, Friedrich, 74

G

Garba, 113
Garber, Marjorie, 111
Gardzienice, 3, 67
Gaulier, Philippe, 133
gender, 15, 18, 34, 68, 73, 119, 152, 175, 177, 178, 184; Butler and, 163, 169–170, 182; dance and, 168; neutral body and, 71, 72, 103, 106–112; physical theatre and, 181–182; sexual pleasure and, 159–160
Gibson, Jane, 60, 80
Gilbreth, Frank, 27, 62
Ginner, Ruby, 32, 46–49, 57, 76, 91
Graeae Theatre Company, 104, 105
Granville Barker, Henry, 52
Greek Dance, 45, 46–47, 57
Grimshaw, Jean, 110
Grosz, Elizabeth: and the volatile body, 6, 143–144, 163, 165, 170, 172, 183
Grotowski, Jerzy, 3, 87, 145, 155, 156, 162
Guildhall School of Music and Drama, 8, 40, 57, 113
Gielgud, John, 58
Gurdjieff, George, 75, 133

gymnastics, 2, 21, 16–18, 59, 74–75; Hébert and natural gymnastics, 54, 60, 61; movement training and, 22, 25, 32, 33

H

Harrop, John, 66, 136, 146, 156, 162, 163
Havers, William, 110, 173
Hawtrey, Charles, 115
Hébert, Georges, 24, 54, 60, 61, 82. *See also* gymnastics
Hepburn, Katherine, 43
Hereward College, Coventry, 105
Hulbert, Dr Henry, 43–44

I

instrumentalism, 130–132
International Workshop Festival, 3, 67, 113
Irving, Sir Henry, 35

J

Jackley, Nat, 36
Jackson, Trevor, 135
James, Martin, 115
James, William, 33, 53
Jeßner, Leopold, 52
Johnstone, Keith, 174
Jooss, Kurt, 55, 57
Jousse, Marcel, 60
Juhan, Deane, 83

K

Kant, Emmanuel, 10
Kathakali, 113
Kean, Edmund, 39
Keefe, John, 3, 9, 52
keep-fit movement, 29–30
Kemp, Joan, 57
Kirby, Vicky, 97–98

L

Laban, Rudolf, 4, 8, 11, 20, 22, 23, 25, 30–33, 52, 80, 82, 132, 133; Alexander and, 34–35, 59; Art of Movement Studio, 57–58; body memory, 90; Drama Schools, 55–58; Duncan and, 46; efforts, 62; expressive movement, 111; flow, 89; Greek culture and, 75–76; holistic approach to movement, 34; Jungian psychology 57; kinesphere, 95; Margaret

Morris and, 47–48; movement as therapy, 106; weight, 147
Lamb, Warren, 89
Lancaster, Roger, 172, 173, 174
Lashley, Karl, 83
Lawrence, Frederick, 33, 56, 62
Lecoq, Jacques, 1, 4, 8, 10, 11, 12, 19, 20, 22, 26, 82, 132; disponibilité, 87, 98, 151; efficiency, 60–63; effort rose, 95; Hébert and, 54; Laboratoire d'Étude du Mouvement, 96; movement uniform, 19, 127; neutral body, 103; neutral mask , 80; physical theatre and, 181; play, 174; primacy of movement, 23; Shona Morris and, 133; Souriau and, 23, 24
Leder, Drew, 118
Leeder, Sigurd, 55, 57, 147
Lefton, Sue, 60, 80
Lester, Adrian, 104
Ling, Per Henrik, 16, 17, 29, 30, 33, 58
Littlewood, Joan: eurhythmics, 52; RADA training, 55, 73, 127; Theatre Workshop 55, 115–116; *Oh What a Lovely War* 115
Locke, John, 91, 95
Logie, Lea, 82, 84, 157
London Academy of Music and Dramatic Art (LAMDA), 40, 55, 57
London International Festival of Theatre (LIFT), 3, 114
Lunt, Alfred, 143

M

MacColl, Ewan, 115, 116
machine, 3, 14, 19, 26, 47, 49; body as, 19, 21, 34, 104, 145
McRobbie, Angela, 109, 165
Malmgren, Yat, 8, 55, 56, 57, 58, 89
Manchester Metropolitan University (MMU), 8, 9, 59, 114, 156
Marceau, Marcel, 62
Marcuse, Herbert, 160
Marey, Étienne Jules, 18–19, 20, 23; Ancient Greek culture, 45; movement analysis, 60, 95, 96; rhythm, 51
Marque, Albert, 79
Marshall, Lorna, 10, 13, 63, 80, 82–83, 91, 92, 110, 177, 180
martial arts, 4, 113, 115, 134, 135, 155
masks, 50, 126, 169; neutral mask 78–81, 88, 90, 96, 103, 156

Mauss, Marcel, 6, 14
Mawer, Irene, 10, 47, 49, 50, 76
mechanization, 15, 26, 49. *See also* machine
Melrose, Susan, 13, 120, 143, 178
Merleau-Ponty, Maurice, 107, 108, 164, 173
Meyerhold, Vsevelod, 52, 82, 116, 145
Mime Action Group, 9
mind/body dualism, 56, 57, 86, 102, 125, 139, 170, 172; inner and outer self, 130
Mirodan, Vladimir, 58
Mobius strip, 126
modern dance, 8, 22, 25, 32, 57, 115
Montaigne ,76
Moscow Arts Theatre, 4, 52, 82
movement for film, 179–180
movement tutors, 67, 75, 101, 123, 129, 134, 176, 184: career structures, 8–9
Morris, Margaret, 32, 47
Morris, Shona: body and meaning, 99, 101, 102; body as instrument, 130; body knowledge, 83, 88, 94, 137; emotion and the body, 157; female movement teachers, 7; Lecoq, 60, 80, 133, 181; movement training, 4, 9, 117–118, 119, 124, 126, 134, 140; movement training and sex, 160; movement training and writing, 8; neutral body, 69, 70, 85, 98; uniform for movement training, 126, 127; vulnerability, 121
Mulvey, Laura: 'male gaze', 109
Murray, Simon, 3, 52
Music Hall, 36, 72, 115, 116
Muybridge, Eadweard, 19, 23, 96

N

National Council for Drama Training (NCDT), 2, 4, 5, 64–65, 123, 135, 175
National Theatre, 104
Naturalism, 15, 21, 22, 86, 95
neutral body; 6, 69–71, 184; actor training and, 176; anatomy and, 81–83, 183; the animal and, 92–94; body knowledge and, 83–86; the child and, 90–92; materiality of, 154; meaning and, 155; movement training and, 108, 110–111, 118,

149, 159, 164, 167, 171, 183, 184; the natural body and, 48, 69–78, 82; phenomenology and, 107–108, 163; the pre-inscripted body, 144; pure movement, 94–96, 165, 180; consciousness and, 150. *See also* disability, gender, ethnicity, and class
Newlove, Jean, 10, 13, 56
Nietzsche, Friedrich, 75, 77
Novack, Cynthia, 184

O

Odin Teatret, 67
Oida, Yoshi, 2, 113–114
Olivier, Laurence, 143
Olympics (1936), 31

P

Pagneux, Monika, 12, 59, 60
Paris Conservatoire, 20, 42, 43
Paterson, Kate,118
Pavis, Patrice, 100, 138, 145
pedagogy; 42, 125, 128, 132; dance pedagogy, 135; Lecoq School pedagogy, 60, 61; movement class and, 120, 134; process and, 70; queer pedagogy, 110
Peking Opera. *See* Beijing Opera
Penny Gaff clowns, 37
Pestalozzi, Johan, 74
photography, 19, 23, 26
physical culture, 18, 25, 26, 31, 73
physical theatre, 3, 9, 168, 180, 181–182
Pisk, Litz, 10, 13, 56, 58, 92, 97, 127
Plato, 11
play, 74, 84, 85, 92, 148, 175, 178
posture, 33, 34, 88, 92, 93, 117, 122, 138, 150, 151, 154, 168, 177; bad posture, 114; meaning and, 100
Pradier, Jean Marie, 84–90, 93, 98, 158, 160
punting, 62–63

R

Rea, Kenneth, 40, 113
Rivington, R. T., 62
Roach, Joseph, 1, 11, 12, 14, 19, 36, 126, 145
Rodenburg, Patsy, 108, 140, 177
Rodin, Auguste, 77
Roth, Gabrielle, 155–156
Rousseau, Jean-Jacques, 74, 76, 91

Royal Academy of Dramatic Art (RADA), 40, 43, 44, 55, 57, 58, 63, 72, 73, 115, 127
rhythm, 21, 23, 89, 93–94, 113, 135, 168; Dalcroze and, 28, 51; Laban and, 33; Hulbert and, 44; Greek Dance, 47, 48; Lecoq and, 61; Roth's Five Rhythms, 155–156; Souriau and, 158
Rudlin, John, 60, 78, 79

S

St. Denis, Michel, 54–55, 58, 78, 80, 92, 133, 174; London Theatre Studio, 54, 80, 92 ; neutral mask, 92; Old Vic Theatre School, 54, 58, 80, 92
Sanderson, Michael, 39, 40, 42, 43, 70, 72, 114–115
Schlemmer, Oskar, 95
scrutiny, 15, 27, 81, 125–126, 128–130, 135, 136, 169
Second World War, 27, 33, 55, 57, 58, 64, 78, 80, 114
Shaban, Nabil, 104
Shaw, Fiona, 104
Shawn, Ted, 20–23
Siegel, Paul, 104
Silly Billies, 37
Soriau, Paul, 23–26, 29, 45, 51, 56, 60, 96, 158
Sparshott, Francis, 15, 22, 24, 25
Spong, Aimie, 47
stage combat. *See* fencing
Stanislavski, Constantin, 46, 50, 52, 53, 55, 56, 59, 76, 82, 86, 94, 145, 146
States, Bert, 174, 175
Stebbins, Genevieve, 45
Stephenson, Geraldine, 56
Straus, Erwin, 106, 107
street performers; 36, 38, 4. *See also* Penny Gaff clowns, Silly Billies
Sufism, 133
Šumič-Riha, Jeliça, 161, 162
Suzuki, Tadashi, 3
Sweigard, Lulu, 88

T

Tarr, Jen, 73
Taylor, Frederick Winslow, 18, 27, 34, 62
Terry, Ellen, 41
Theatre of Action, 115
Tufnell, Miranda, 13

U

uniform, 126–128, 138, 168
Unity Theatre, 115

V

Variety, 36, 38, 39, 72, 115, 180
Verma, Jatinder, 113, 114, 117
voice, 9–10, 40, 44, 59, 99, 123; Alexander and, 34; received pronunciation, 115; voice training, 22, 43, 101, 119, 121, 123, 147, 177; voice tutors, 140, 177
Volcano Theatre Company, 181

W

Wall, Max, 36
Werner, Sarah, 99
Wigman, Mary, 60
Winearls, Jane, 57
Wolff, Janet, 166–167, 170
Wolkonsky, Prince Sergei, 52
Worker's Theatre Movement, 115

Y

Yarrow, Ralph, 85, 87, 148–149, 150, 151, 174
yoga, 4, 76, 113
Young, Iris, 106–108, 110–112, 118, 131, 155, 169

Z

Zarrilli, Phillip, 2, 113
Zola, Emile, 39

Lightning Source UK Ltd.
Milton Keynes UK
UKOW052152240912

199565UK00013B/91/P